PROPORTIONATE SENTENCING

Proportionate Sentencing

Exploring the Principles

Andrew von Hirsch
and
Andrew Ashworth

OXFORD
UNIVERSITY PRESS

OXFORD
UNIVERSITY PRESS

Great Clarendon Street, Oxford OX2 6DP

Oxford University Press is a department of the University of Oxford.
It furthers the University's objective of excellence in research, scholarship,
and education by publishing worldwide in

Oxford New York

Auckland Cape Town Dar es Salaam Hong Kong Karachi
Kuala Lumpur Madrid Melbourne Mexico City Nairobi
New Delhi Shanghai Taipei Toronto

With offices in

Argentina Austria Brazil Chile Czech Republic France Greece
Guatemala Hungary Italy Japan Poland Portugal Singapore
South Korea Switzerland Thailand Turkey Ukraine Vietnam

Oxford is a registered trade mark of Oxford University Press
in the UK and in certain other countries

Published in the United States
by Oxford University Press Inc., New York

First published 2005

British Library Cataloguing in Publication Data
Data available

Library of Congress Cataloging in Publication Data
Data available

Typeset by Newgen Imaging Systems (P) Ltd., Chennai, India
Printed in Great Britain
on acid-free paper by
Biddles Ltd., King's Lynn

ISBN 0–19–927260–3

1 3 5 7 9 10 8 6 4 2

Preface

In view of the continuing penological interest of the idea of proportionate sentencing, we have set out in this volume to develop and refine that conception in the context of several contemporary debates about punishment, to explore some problematic areas, and (in Chapter 9) to offer a restatement of the main criteria for proportionality. Two of the chapters were based on previously published essays: Chapter 3 develops further the article published as A. von Hirsch, 'Proportionate Sentences for Juveniles' (2001) *Punishment and Society*, and Chapter 8 is based on 'Specifying Aims and Limits for Restorative Justice: a "Making Amends" Model?' in A. von Hirsch, J. Roberts, A.E. Bottoms, K. Roach and M. Schiff (eds), *Restorative Justice and Criminal Justice: Competing or Reconcilable Paradigms?* (2003). We acknowledge the contribution of Clifford Shearing, who was the third co-author (with the two of us) of Chapter 8. Appendix 3 is a revised version of A. von Hirsch and N. Jareborg, 'Gauging Criminal Harm: a Living-Standard Analysis' (1991) 11 *Oxford Journal of Legal Studies* 1–38, and we are grateful to Professor Jareborg for his support of and advice on this project.

We are indebted to several friends and colleagues who read drafts of our work and offered comments. Andrew Simester gave generously of his time and offered valuable suggestions on the structure of our main arguments. Don Scheid provided particularly full comments on various draft chapters, and Julian Roberts, Antony Duff, Douglas Husak, and Michael Tonry also offered extensive suggestions. We are grateful to the following colleagues and friends for helping us to reflect on specific issues we discuss: Petter Asp, Meena Bhamra, Anthony Bottoms, Derek Joliffe, Tapio Lappi-Seppälä, and John Tasioulas. We have benefited throughout from excellent secretarial assistance at the Centre for Penal Theory and Penal Ethics in the Institute of Criminology, Cambridge, first from Helen Griffiths and latterly from Ann Phillips, and we are most grateful to them. Thanks also to Ben Juratowitch for his work on the Bibliography.

Andrew von Hirsch
Andrew Ashworth
October 2004

Contents

Table of Cases

Germany

United Kingdom

United States

Table of Legislation

1

Introduction: The Scope of this Book

The idea of the proportionate or 'deserved' sentence has had considerable influence during the last two and a half decades. In the United States, some states having (by American standards) comparatively liberal political traditions have relied on this conception in fashioning guidelines for sentencing.[1] In Europe, two jurisdictions – Finland in 1976, and Sweden in 1988[2] – have adopted and continue to maintain legal norms for sentencing that emphasize notions of proportionality. Canada has recently adopted a general statement of sentencing principles that gives proportionality a central role;[3] and has approved a juvenile-justice law with comparable emphasis on proportionality.[4] The New Zealand sentencing statute, adopted in 2002, does likewise for adult offenders.[5] South Africa's Law Commission has recently proposed a scheme of desert-oriented sentencing guidelines.[6] England in 1991 adopted statutory guiding principles emphasizing proportionality. It modified that statutory scheme in 2003, but in a manner that permits issuance of sentencing guidelines[a] that take proportionality considerations substantially into account.[7] There is also evidence that proportionalism has altered thinking about punishment more widely.[8] It remains, in any event, influential among academics writing on sentencing theory and policy.[9]

In previous decades beginning in the mid-1970s, the proportionalist sentencing model – sometimes referred to as the 'just deserts' model – has been discussed in a number of works by one or other of present authors. These previous works addressed the criteria for proportionality of sentence: they dealt with such issues as the penalty structure, the assessment of the

[a] This legislation creates, for the first time, a scheme of comprehensive sentencing guidelines for England and Wales. Its guidance will probably be set forth in words, rather than the numerical tables utilized in many US guideline systems.

In early 2004, the US Supreme Court handed down a decision calling into question sentencing courts' authority to increase sentence above the guidelines' recommended sentencing ranges, on account of aggravating circumstances. The impact of this decision on American sentencing guidelines is still uncertain, and further clarification from the court is expected, *Blakely v. Washington* (2004) 124 S.Ct 2531. However, this decision applies only to US jurisdictions, and concerns a particular technique of sentencing guidance. Thus the sentencing guidelines issued for England and Wales would not be directly affected, nor would be European statutory guiding principles for sentencing, such as Sweden's or Finland's. The issue is not, in any event, an issue for proportionality theory itself.

seriousness of crimes, the role of previous convictions, and the scaling of non-custodial sentences. What remained to be explored, however, were the 'borderlands' of desert theory: how the desert model might apply to certain kinds of important special cases, and how it relates to other conceptions of sentencing with which it seems to have some elements in common. It is these latter questions that the present volume chiefly explores.

1.1 The Topics of this Volume

The contents of the present volume have been shaped by our thinking about sentencing theory for the past decade, since the publication in 1993 of Andrew von Hirsch's monograph, *Censure and Sanctions*. In the topics they address, the ensuing chapters may be grouped as follows:

The first of the chapters, Chapter 2, addresses why the institution of punishment should exist at all. While we have written about this important question earlier,[10] we believe that further analysis is needed – particularly, about the authoritative character of penal censure and the state's role in punishment.

The next six chapters, constituting the main part of the book, deal with the 'borderlands' of desert theory. They address the following questions:

- Chapter 3 examines extending the desert rationale to juvenile offenders. Particularly, it puts forward reasons why that rationale justifies overall reductions in the severity of young offenders' punishments, compared with those for adults.
- Chapter 4 takes a critical look at a model proposed by Anthony Bottoms and Roger Brownsword for imposing extended sentences for especially dangerous offenders. The analysis thus explores some of the possible reasons for derogating from proportionality requirements in certain kinds of particularly troublesome cases.
- Chapter 5 considers whether the sentences for socially deprived offenders should be reduced. We have touched on this issue in earlier writings, but return to it here, because we have not been satisfied with our earlier efforts.
- The next chapter, Chapter 6, shifts to political matters. It examines the claim, made by a number of critics of desert theory, that proportionalist conceptions of sentencing have legitimated a toughening of sentencing policy. We explain why this 'desert-severity' thesis lacks evidentiary support and is unsustainable.
- In Chapter 7, we consider another influential desert-based justification: the penance theory of R.A. Duff. That chapter addresses especially his recent arguments, set forth in a 2001 volume.

- Chapter 8 deals with restorative justice, identifying some of the difficulties with the theoretical foundations of current restorative approaches, and examining a possible 'making amends' model that is designed to remedy some of these deficiencies.

The final chapter, Chapter 9, addresses the criteria for proportionate sentences. These criteria have been discussed in earlier writings of ours, but those discussions appeared in a number of different volumes and articles.[11] Given the continuing interest in proportionality of sentence, we felt that it would be helpful to have these criteria summarized and systematized, and also brought up to date.

The volume also contains three Appendices.

- Appendix 1 deals with a topic that is novel for us, and which generally has received scant attention: 'equity' factors in sentencing. Courts often reduce sentences, on compassionate grounds, in cases such as those involving old or ill defendants, those whose crimes occurred long ago, and those who have made significant efforts to alleviate the offence's consequences after the event. The question we address (in tentative and exploratory fashion) is the extent to which it is possible to account for this practice in a manner that is consistent with some of the ideas underlying a desert rationale.
- Appendix 2 examines 'Limiting Retributivism' – a sentencing philosophy that was first developed in the 1970s and early '80s by Norval Morris, and which is relied upon in the American Law Institute's draft revised Model Penal Code. This perspective treats desert as providing only certain limits on the permissible sentence. Its proponents here recently put forward some additional suggestions about how such a philosophy might be conceptualized and implemented. We will examine these suggestions in the light of desert theory (see also 9.8).
- Appendix 3 sets forth the 'living-standard' conception of criminal harms – an analysis that bears upon rating the seriousness of crimes (see 9.5). This appeared originally in a 1991 article by Andrew von Hirsch and Nils Jareborg. As it needs updating, and more ready availability, we have included a revised version here.

1.2 Why has the Desert Model been Influential?

In the first two-thirds of the 20th century, the idea of proportionate sentencing was largely invisible: sentencing policy was supposed to be shaped principally by crime-prevention concerns of rehabilitation, deterrence and incapacitation.[12] When the 'desert model' emerged in the mid-1970s, it swiftly gained much influence.[13] That influence continues today: jurisdictions that developed desert-oriented schemes two or three decades ago, such as Sweden and Finland, maintain them today. Other jurisdictions, such as Canada, New Zealand and South Africa, have more recently introduced proportionalist elements into their sentencing systems, or are seriously contemplating doing so.[14] What features of the proportionalist sentencing model contributed to this influence?

1.2.1 The appeal to fairness

Preventively-oriented sentencing theories,[15] even when they purport to be humane, address instrumental concerns: how a sentencing strategy can better protect *us*, the citizenry, from the depredations of *them*, the criminals. An instrumental perspective of this kind threatens unjust results, unless carefully hedged by ethical constraints: if the aim is prevention, why not intervene drastically whenever that might 'work'? During the heyday of rehabilitation, this threat seemed muted – for the rehabilitative sentence was supposed to promote the offender's interests as well as our own. But as faith declined in the identity of the offender's interests with those of the larger society, the potential oppressiveness of primarily crime-preventive sentencing strategies became more apparent. Such problems of justice were illustrated, in the debates that took place during the emergence of the desert theory in the 1970s, by the well-documented abuses of the indeterminate sentence;[b] and they continue to be apparent in more recent schemes aimed at enhancing sentences' preventive effect by (for example) imposing sharply increased penalties on recidivist offenders.[16]

Proportionalist sentencing is designed to avoid unjust results – through giving conceptions of justice a central role in sentencing policy.[c] The desert rationale rests on the idea that the penal sanction should fairly reflect the degree of reprehensibleness (that is, the harmfulness and culpability) of the actor's conduct. This comports with common-sense notions of justice, that how severely a person is punished should depend on the degree of blameworthiness of his conduct. The perspective also helps to resolve the tension over whether penal policy should favour societal interests or the interests of offenders. In desert theory, the societal interest is expressed in the recognition that typical crimes (eg, those of force and fraud) are *wrongs*, for which public censure through criminal sanction is due. The

[b] The indeterminate sentence involved sentencing the convicted offender for indefinite periods, until it was believed that he was 'cured' of his criminal inclinations. It often led to lengthy periods of confinement of persons convicted of less serious crimes.

[c] During the emergence of desert theory in the 1970s, there was also a shift in liberal opinion generally toward giving more emphasis to concerns about fairness in social policy. Influential in this regard was John Rawls' widely-cited 1971 book, *A Theory of Justice*.

offender's interests are protected through his right not to be subjected to a sanction that is more onerous than the degree of blameworthiness his conduct would warrant.

Traditional retributive conceptions of punishment have held little attraction among modern penologists, because they seemed to constitute a reversion to pre-Enlightenment notions – a return to talionic conceptions of an eye-for-an-eye. Desert theory, however, offers an altered conception of deservedness, resting on the idea of *proportion*, rather than harm-for-harm equivalence. This has permitted reformers to espouse graded schemes of punishment whilst nevertheless supporting moderate penalty levels (see more fully, Chapters 2 and 6, and 9.4).

1.2.2 Practical guidance

Proportionalism has had the further attraction of providing a degree of practical guidance for sentencing decisions: it suggests a way of scaling penalties. Traditional crime-preventive approaches to sentencing have had great difficulty in furnishing such guidance. In Sweden, for example, the former (pre-1989) statutory provisions of sentencing called upon the court to fashion a disposition serving to promote the defendant's rehabilitation, while taking into account the need to foster general public compliance with law.[17] These provisions were criticized by reformers as providing scant assistance to sentencers, in deciding on what kind and amount of sentence would be appropriate.[18] Likewise, the new English sentencing statute enacted in 2003, which calls upon judges to give enhanced emphasis to such crime-preventative aims, is likely to face comparable difficulties – unless the Sentencing Guidelines Council decides to issue guidelines with substantial proportionality constraints.[19]

To bring these problems of insufficient guidance into perspective, consider two of the traditional preventive aims: deterrence and rehabilitation. If one asks how sentences might be scaled according to their supposed deterrent impact, the answer is indeterminate, because not enough is known about the comparative marginal deterrent effects of different levels of sentence severity.[d] With rehabilitation, matters are only somewhat better. To the extent that treatment programmes work at all, they appear to succeed for carefully selected subgroups of offenders; no 'cure' is known for routine cases of car theft, burglary, robbery and

[d] Three recent surveys and analyses of empirical studies of deterrence conclude that variations of sentence severity have little or no discernible effects on crime rates: see Nagin 1998; von Hirsch, Bottoms, Burney, *et al.* 1999; and Doob and Webster 2003. The same conclusion generally holds for incapacitative strategies. It has long been possible to make rough-and-ready predictions about which offenders may be statistically more likely to commit crimes. However, there is little empirical evidence that incapacitation strategies would have significant net effects on crime rates: see Nagin 1998.

the like.[e] There is also considerable difficulty translating rehabilitative concerns – which address modalities of treatment – into the kind of decisions sentencers must take, about the type and duration of the sanction.

A proportionalist sentencing theory provides better guidance on scaling issues: sentences are to be ranked in severity to reflect the comparative seriousness of crimes. Granted, there are unresolved questions: the theory for assessing crimes' comparative seriousness needs further development, and there has been some continuing debate among desert theorists regarding the role of previous convictions in determining sentence.[20] Nevertheless, grading is not an unmanageable task. The sentencing commission of Minnesota, for example, was able to grade crimes in seriousness, without great difficulty or dissention; and to construct presumptive sentence ranges on that basis.[21]

Guidance for sentencers does not necessarily require numerical guidelines; it can be accomplished instead through statutory guiding principles, as Finland and Sweden have done. Formerly, the courts in those countries tried to develop a sentencing tariff on the basis of a non-very-well delineated rationale, in which deterrence and rehabilitation were supposed to play important roles. The adoption of desert-oriented statutory principles, in 1976 and 1989 respectively, furnished a more workable criterion, according to which the gravity of the criminal act should primarily be determinative.[22] It became easier to assess whether one crime is typically more serious than another than to fix the penalties for those crimes on the basis of their supposed preventive effects.

Proportionalism can also be useful as an aid to implementing other practical sentencing aims. Consider a matter that has drawn much interest in the last two decades: intermediate, non-custodial penalties. For such sanctions to function successfully as substitutes for imprisonment, they must be carefully targeted – so that the more onerous non-custodial sanctions may be used only for middle-level crimes, not lesser ones; and so that incarceration is used only sparingly as the penalty for those who breach the terms of their community sentences. A proportionalist sentencing rationale yields this kind of result, because a system of penalties graded according to crime-seriousness would not permit the more severe non-custodial sanctions to be used for lesser offences; and because mere

[e] A recent Home Office report has made ambitious claims concerning the effects of rehabilitative programmes on recidivism, citing a possible 5–16% reduction in recidivism rates: see Home Office 2001b, 9. However, recent evidence is considerably more equivocal concerning the extent of treatment programmes' impact. An example of such difficulties is suggested by an ambitious recent Home Office study on the effects of two kinds of cognitive skills programmes, 'Reasoning and Rehabilitation' and 'Enhanced Thinking Skills', on a large sample of prisoners. It was found that there was no statistically significant impact on recidivism rates, over a one-year and two-year period; see Home Office Research Finding No. 226 (2003). There is continuing research today on a variety of treatment programmes, and others might prove more successful. Considerable caution is indicated, however, regarding claims that rehabilitative efforts can have substantial net effects on recidivism or on crime rates.

breaches of programme conditions would not be serious enough to deserve substantial stints of confinement.[23]

1.3 Multiple Aims?

Proportionalism sets priorities among sentencing aims. A desert model assumes that it is more important to have proportionately ordered sanctions than to seek other objectives – say, incapacitating offenders who are deemed higher risks. This understandably evokes discomfort: why cannot one seek proportionality *and* pursue other desired ends, whether they be treatment, incapacitation or something else?

In the 1970s in the United States, notions of proportionality came to prominence at the same time as growing scepticism about the feasibility of effective treatment. However, the exclusion of treatment considerations is not presupposed by the desert model. Treatments may be offered to imprisoned offenders *within* the duration of their proportionate sentence; and when two non-custodial sanctions of approximately equivalent severity are available (say, a financial penalty of so many days' earnings and intensive probation of a specified duration), desert constraints are not offended when one is chosen over the other on rehabilitative grounds.[24] What proportionalism excludes is imposing sentences of markedly differing severity on those convicted of comparably serious criminal conduct, in the hope of achieving rehabilitative goals.

However, a desert model remains somewhat constraining: ulterior factors may be relied upon only where those do not substantially alter the ranking of penalties. Giving substantial extra prison time to persons deemed higher risks would breach the model's limits, for example. Why not, then, relax the model's constraints to allow greater scope to other, seemingly reasonable aspirations?

A possibility would be to relax desert constraints to a limited extent. Proportionality would ordinarily determine comparative punishment levels, but substantial upward deviations might possibly be permitted in extraordinary cases, to restrain especially dangerous individuals (a scheme which we will consider in Chapter 4). Alternatively, deviations from the deserved sanction might ordinarily be permitted, but these would be restricted in extent: say, to deviations of no more than 10 or 15 per cent (see 9.8; Appendix 2). These approaches still make desert the primary determinant of the ordering of penalties, but leave some extra scope for ulterior aims. Such schemes, however, impose their own constraints. Especially dangerous offenders might possibly be given extra prison time, but not the ordinary potential recidivist. Some additional leeway may be granted in choosing a non-custodial penalty suited to an offender's apparent treatment needs, but not a great deal.

Could still more scope be given to non-desert considerations? If, in ordinary cases, the seriousness of the current crime continues to be the chief determinant of the severity of the penalty, the system remains desert-dominated. This has the attractions mentioned above: it helps to promote fairer outcomes, and provides a degree of useful guidance to decision-makers. Our limited knowledge of how to achieve preventive effects will also be no great obstacle: we do know something about effective treatments in *some* situations, and when we do that may (to the requisite limited degree) affect the disposition. If ulterior aims are given still greater scope, however, that tends to create a system dominated by those aims. Desert would then serve only as a (much less important) outer limit. This reintroduces the difficulties mentioned earlier: the risk of inequitable outcomes, and the problem of insufficient practical guidance.

The writings of some of the proponents of 'mixed' models reflect these tensions. Norval Morris, Michael Tonry and others have advocated a mixed model, which they term 'limiting retributivism'.[25] According to this view, desert would set certain bounds to the severity of punishment, within which the sentence would be fixed on other (notably, crime-preventive) grounds. The American Law Institute is now considering recommending that this model be used by sentencing commissions in developing sentencing guidelines.[26]

How constraining should the desert bounds be, under this mixed model? The question is of critical importance, because it determines whether the emphasis in deciding penalties should be on desert factors relating to crime-seriousness, or on ulterior goals such as incapacitation or rehabilitation. Providing an answer, however, would require an explanation of what kind of conception of desert is being relied upon, in treating proportionality only as a limiting principle. The advocates of limiting retributivism have not explored such issues in much depth.

Morris, in his initial formulation, treated these desert limits as being based on community sentiment: sentences are not to exceed *what is seen by current popular mores* as excessive.[f] This, however, would provide only very limited constraints on penalties: desert would merely provide certain outer limits, and crime-control aims such as deterrent and incapacitation could chiefly decide the penalties.

Lately, beginning in the mid-1990s, Michael Tonry and Richard Frase have moved away from the community-mores conception of desert limits; they suggest, instead, that their model's limits should be derived from the censuring implications of punishment (although they do not explain the manner of this derivation).[27] This could permit more narrowly drawn bounds sufficiently on the severity of punishments (which Tonry and Frase

[f] Morris 1974, 74–76; John Monahan (1982) also opts for such a consensus approach to setting desert limits, and suggests a procedure for determining the consensus that is designed to give less weight to 'outlying' views.

have endorsed in some writings),[28] and thus allow crime-seriousness to become the principal determinant of the sanction. However, such a censure-based approach would seem to place normative concerns closely akin to those of the desert model at centre stage. On this view, limiting retributivism's limits would probably have to be rationalized by drawing on basic conceptions of the desert rationale (for fuller analysis, see Appendix 2).

1.4 Prospects for Proportionalist Sentencing Policies

What then are the prospects for the proportionate sentence? Will the features of proportionalist sentencing spoken of here – the appeal to fairness, and the practical guidance offered to sentencers – make this approach of continuing interest to those who think about and who fashion sentencing policy? Or will proportionalist sentencing gradually become eclipsed, as a once-fashionable but no longer influential idea? Proportionalism's attraction, in our judgement, depends on the degree of influence of certain more basic normative assumptions – and those are worth pointing to.

The proportionalist approach to sentencing is a version of what one of us has termed the 'sentencing reform project' in criminal justice.[29] Such an approach, which has been influential since the mid-1970s, involves the following postulates. First, a principled approach to sentencing: sentencing reform, it is assumed, should be guided by a coherent set of aims. A principled approach does not necessarily require that there be a single, exclusive penal purpose; several aims may properly be pursued, so long as there are explicit norms concerning their interrelationship.[30]

Second, there should be an emphasis on sparing use of punishment. This principle, properly understood, reflects a notion of informed self-restraint: it recognizes the pain and deprivation that punishments (especially severe ones) inevitably inflict on offenders.[g]

Third, there should be an emphasis on fairness: the sentence should visit an equitable sanction on the offender. There may be continuing debate about the criteria of fairness – for example, about how great a restraining role proportionality should have. Notwithstanding these divergences of view, however, fairness is to be treated as a fundamental, not just a

[g] This principle of sparing use is based on certain normative grounds. Convicted defendants are assumed to have continued human status and continuing membership in the legal and moral community; and as such, are entitled to concern for their welfare and dignity. Punishment, involving as it does the censure of the offender and the purposeful infliction of deprivations on him, is viewed as painful and potentially humiliating; and imprisonment particularly so. Such impositions must be inflicted with a sense of restraint.

marginal, desideratum. This concern with the justice of sentence depends on the assumption of convicted offenders having continued membership of the moral and legal community.

The attractiveness of a proportionalist approach to sentencing will depend, in important part, on the extent to which these three more general assumptions have credibility among judges and policymakers. To the extent the assumptions are influential, an approach to sentencing reform that emphasizes proportionality will, in our judgement, continue to be attractive – because of its appeal to conceptions of fairness and because of the greater degree of guidance it offers. To the extent these assumptions are rejected, however, the desert perspective will become less influential. Where a penal-populist political ethos is strong, for example, a proportionalist approach is unlikely to prevail – because that ethos is fundamentally at odds with aims of parsimony and equity in sentencing. If the desideratum becomes that of using sentences to express resentment against crime and criminals, it is not surprising that more liberal and rationalist sentencing approaches have worsened chances for survival (see Chapter 6 below).

Will a proportionality-oriented approach to sentencing continue to be influential then? It depends on what policymakers' more fundamental priorities are. In settings where there continues to be an interest in developing and maintaining sentencing standards that help guide sentencing decisions, and which can provide reasonably fair and predictable outcomes, a desert rationale will probably continue to be attractive for the reasons we have just sketched. In places where political priorities have shifted to demonstrating ferocity about crime, such a rationale will no longer seem appealing to policymakers – but, then, neither will other sentencing rationales making comparable assumptions about the need for guidance and fairer outcomes.

It is our view, in sum, that the proportionalist sentencing model has the attractions of offering a fairer and more workable way of scaling penalties; and that it is likely to retain a substantial degree of influence. These are both reasons warranting a fuller exploration of the ideas underlying this model. This book is devoted to such an exploration.

Notes

1. The most notable of these is Minnesota's sentencing scheme, see von Hirsch 1995.
2. For a description and analysis, see Lappi-Seppälä 2001 on Finland, and Jareborg 1995 on Sweden.
3. See Roberts and von Hirsch 1999.
4. Canada's Youth Criminal Justice Act 2002, which provides that 'the sentence must be proportionate to the seriousness of the offence and the degree of responsibility of the young person for that offence'. For analysis, see Doob and Sprott 2004.

5. Roberts 2003.
6. South African Law Commission (2000).
7. von Hirsch and Roberts 2004.
8. See, eg, Canadian Sentencing Commission 1986; Council of Europe 1992.
9. See, eg, Duff 2001; Ashworth 2000; Jareborg 1995; Schünemann 1987; Hörnle 1999.
10. See, eg, von Hirsch 1993, Ch. 2.
11. See, eg, von Hirsch 1976; von Hirsch 1981; von Hirsch 1985; Ashworth 2000.
12. For a sketch of these developments, see von Hirsch 1983.
13. Ibid.
14. See notes 1–7 above.
15. For readings, see von Hirsch and Ashworth 1998, Chs. 1, 2 and 3.
16. See 6.3.2 below.
17. These were the aims prescribed in Ch. 7, s. 1 of the Swedish Criminal Code before 1989.
18. See, eg, Brottsförebyggande Rådet 1977; Heckscher, *et al.* 1980.
19. For a critique and analysis of these provisions of Criminal Justice Act 2003, see von Hirsch and Roberts 2004.
20. Compare von Hirsch 1998 with Fletcher 1978, 460–66; see also 9.6 below.
21. Ibid.
22. Jareborg 1995.
23. See 9.7.1 of this volume; von Hirsch 1993, Ch. 7.
24. See 9.7.2; von Hirsch 1993, Ch. 7.
25. Morris 1982, ch. 5; Tonry and Morris 1990, Ch. 4.
26. See Appendix 2, below.
27. Tonry 1994; and Frase 2004.
28. Tonry 1998.
29. von Hirsch 2001.
30. On this point, see Council of Europe 2001.

2

The Justification for Punishment's Existence: Censure and Prevention

2.1 Introduction

Before addressing the rationale for criminal sentencing, the main theme of our book, it is important to consider first why the institution of the criminal sanction should exist at all. This concerns the so-called *general justification for punishment*: not how penalties should be allocated among convicted offenders, but the more fundamental question of why persons found to have committed proscribed conduct should be dealt with through state-imposed criminal penalties, rather than by some other possible means.[a]

Why, then, should the institution of the criminal sanction exist? Is it to prevent crime or to punish offenders as they deserve? Much traditional discussion has focused on one or the other of these aims exclusively. Instrumental penal theories have concerned themselves with crime prevention, and such consequentialist aims are sometimes said to be the only appropriate ones for a modern state to pursue.[b] In contrast, traditional retributive justifications disregard consequences and focus exclusively on notions of the deservedness of punishment. These theories tend to be highly abstract and universalist in character – and depend on such notions as that wrongdoing in itself justifies the imposition of suffering on the wrongdoer.

In this chapter, we argue that a workable theory of why the criminal sanction should exist needs to rest primarily on normative, non-consequentialist claims, but needs also to be concerned in part with

[a] The general justification for punishment is distinct also from questions of *criminalization*. The latter concerns the permissible scope of the criminal law: whether, for example, only conduct that is harmful or potentially harmful may be criminally proscribed; or whether, for example, offensive behaviour may also be so (see, eg, Simester and von Hirsch 2002). The general justification of punishment concerns the logically prior question of whether *any* behaviour should be dealt with via state-imposed criminal sanctions.

[b] The rationale for the existence of the criminal sanction is distinct also from the principles of substantive criminal liability. Some modern Anglo-American, as well as German, penal theories have adopted an instrumental (namely, crime-preventive) justification for the existence of the criminal sanction, but have nevertheless espoused principles of criminal liability (concerning, eg, the culpability constraints of substantive criminal law) that have deontological elements; see the views of Hart and Roxin, discussed below.

consequences. In particular, such an account must contain a deontological element, related to how the offender should be addressed as an agent capable of moral deliberation; yet must nevertheless consider preventive effects to some degree – so that, in principle, the system of criminal law and sanctions could be abolished, were it no longer deemed essential to prevent crime. A proposed justification for the criminal sanction that emphasizes the idea of penal censure, but gives a limited complementary role to prevention, is developed here. We shall also briefly suggest here – and elaborate in a later chapter (Chapter 9) – why such a combined account of the criminal sanction's existence may properly be linked with a theory of sentencing which relies primarily on desert-based concerns relating to the seriousness of the offence.

2.2 Traditional Retributive Justifications and their Problems

A variety of purely retributive conceptions of punishment exist in the literature, although they have relatively few adherents today. One is what the Germans call '*Vergeltung*': that the doing of a wrong generates a moral obligation to visit suffering on the wrongdoer,[1] or that the wrongdoer should be 'paid back' for his wrong. Another is the unfair-advantage theory: that the actor who victimizes another while benefiting from law-abiding persons' self-restraint gains an 'unjust advantage' over such other persons, and that the criminal sanction's function is to impose an offsetting disadvantage.[2] Still another concerns the reaffirmation of the legal order: a crime, on this view, constitutes a challenge to the very principle of a legal order, and a penal response constitutes that principle's reaffirmation.[3] These accounts share a number of well-known difficulties; such objections may briefly be summarized as follows.

One drawback of these retributive accounts is their opacity: no readily comprehensible reasons are offered about *why* punishment is deserved. In some versions of traditional retributivism, no explanation is provided at all, and appeal is made to intuition.[4] In other versions, the explanation seems largely metaphorical. Punishment 'requites' or 'pays back' the wrong, but it is not made clear how or why it does so; or punishment 'undoes' the unfair advantage obtained by the wrongdoer, but the modalities of this undoing remain unexplained.[5]

Another difficulty is that while such theories call for *something* to be done to the offender, they fail to explain why that something should take the form of punishment. Why, for example, should reaffirming the legal order involve *punishing* the offender (with that response's characteristic censuring connotations) rather than imposing some other, more neutral form of disadvantage or sanction?[6]

These theories' lack of an adequate account of the *state's* involvement in punishment is a further problem. The state, in a liberal society, should not have a generalized mission of upholding the moral order, but rather such more circumscribed functions as the prevention of harm and the fostering and maintenance of the means for citizens to have a good existence. These, however, appear (at least in considerable part) to be consequentialist concerns, and the point of traditional retributivism has been to exclude such concerns from the justification for punishment. What function, then, is the criminal sanction performing that is a proper one for the state in a free society?

A final drawback is the universalizing claims of traditional retributivism. If, for example, punishment serves to repair the affront to the legal order, it would seem to be required in any society that has a legal order. Suppose, however, that a society were to become so peaceable that predatory conduct was comparatively infrequent. The criminal sanction – with the suffering it visits and with its potential for abuse – then might possibly no longer be needed to keep such conduct at tolerable levels. Would such a society still be obliged to retain the criminal sanction in order to deal with the occasional hurtful act? Later in this chapter, we suggest that the answer should be negative, but such an answer requires at least some consideration of consequences. If consequences had to be disregarded, however, the answer would have to be a necessary and universal affirmative. A theory that puts such questions beyond debate for all times and places seems a strange one.

2.3 Purely Instrumental Justifications and their Problems

Let us consider next various instrumental (particularly, crime-preventive) justifications for punishment's existence that have been put forward in English-language (and also German) writings on penal theory. These include the Benthamite deterrence-based justification, and its modern (and more differentiated) version developed by HLA Hart; and the German theory of *Integrationsprävention*. Such theories rely, directly or indirectly, on crime prevention as the sole warrant for the institution of the penal sanction; and therein lie their difficulties.

2.3.1 Negative general prevention: The Benthamite model

The utilitarian conception of punishment, derived from Jeremy Bentham, relies straightforwardly on 'negative' general prevention – that is, general deterrence – as the basis for punishment. The institution of the criminal sanction is established in order to prevent potential offenders from offending. The quantum of punishment is to be determined by weighing its aggregate crime-preventive benefits against the human and financial costs of punishing.[7]

The difficulties of this model have long been familiar. A major objection is that it provides little place for ethical limitations on whom or how much to punish.[8] Vicarious penal liability, criminal liability without regard to the actor's fault, and disproportionate punishments might all be permissible to the extent of their net social utility. The other, equally familiar, objection is that punishment under this theory fails to address the actor as a moral agent; he is to be made to suffer merely in order to intimidate others from disobeying the law.[9]

HLA Hart has attempted to formulate an answer to the first objection, regarding the absence of limits. Relying on crime prevention as the reason for the existence of the criminal sanction still leaves room, he argues, for imposing non-utilitarian limits on the distribution of penalties so long as the latter may independently be justified.[10]

Hart proposes such an independent justification for an important limit in substantive criminal law: the restriction of criminal liability to conduct involving the actor's fault. His argument rests on notions of choice. In a free society, citizens should have a fair opportunity to avoid impositions of the criminal law, by choosing to remain law abiding. This they can only have if criminal liability requires fault, because otherwise a purely accidental breach could trigger criminal liability.[11] The German penal theorist Claus Roxin advances comparable arguments for the fault requirements in the substantive criminal law.[12]

A different kind of argument for limits would be needed, however, when one moves from substantive law to sentencing policy and considers the latter's most important fairness constraint, the principle of proportionality: that punishments should be proportionate in severity with the seriousness of crimes.[13] Hart accepts the principle 'of a proportion within a system of penalties between those imposed for different offences where these have a distinct place in the commonsense scale of gravity'.[14] He is, however, equivocal about the relationship between this principle and what he regards as the 'General Justifying Aim' of punishment, crime prevention. He recognizes that such a 'principle of justice' may 'qualify the pursuit of the General Justifying Aim'. However, he offers a reason for maintaining proportionality (the 'risk of either confusing common morality or flouting it and bringing the law into contempt') that appears to be largely instrumental, and to have little to do with normative concerns about fairness or liberty.[15]

2.3.2 Positive general prevention

German penal theorists have in recent decades tended to prefer a different kind of preventive theory: that of 'positive' general prevention. This view, in one of its influential versions (that of *Integrationsprävention*), stresses the role of punishment as a reinforcer of citizens' internal norms against injurious conduct. The criminal sanction, it is said, through its censuring features constitutes a concrete expression of social disapproval of such behaviour, and thereby helps reaffirm, reinforce or stabilize the moral norms among citizens that restrain criminal behaviour.[16]

This norm-reinforcing function is said to provide support for the culpability requirements of the substantive criminal law, and for proportionality requirements in sentencing law. A penalty structure, it is asserted, will be perceived as more just if it requires fault for criminal liability and observes proportionality constraints in sentencing; and being so perceived, will better reinforce citizens' self-restraint and respect for law. Liability without fault, or disproportionate sanctions, it is said, would breed disrespect for law and hence a weakening of the moral influence of the penalty structure.[17]

This argument ultimately remains one of crime prevention. It involves the assertion that if one punishes fairly and proportionately, this will better reinforce the citizenry's moral scruples against offending, which in turn will enable the criminal law to carry out its crime-preventive role better. One question that comes to mind is: how does one know? While it is plausible to suppose that punishment has at least a modicum of crime-preventive impact,[c] there is only limited evidence concerning the extent to which this operates through reinforcing law-abiding attitudes, rather than directly through deterrence.[18] Given such empirical uncertainties, the norm-reinforcement account could provide only uncertain support for the existence of the criminal sanction.

Even were better evidence of the criminal sanction's positive general-preventive effects available, the link from those effects to the criminal law's ethical limits would remain weak. The theory points to the supposed 'dissonance' in citizens' perceptions of the legal order that criminal liability without fault or disproportionate sanctions would evoke, and the weakening of their inhibitions against criminal behaviour that might result. But as Wolfgang Frisch has pointed out,[19] there is little reason to believe that citizens are much concerned about culpability principles in the substantive criminal law or about proportionality in sentencing; or, even if they were concerned, that they take sufficient notice of the specifics of criminal-law doctrines to have their moral inhibitions against offending affected.

There is also a more fundamental objection to positive general prevention as the primary basis for the criminal sanction – namely, such an

[c] While there is little evidence that crime rates respond significantly to changes in sentence severity, there appears to be some basis for believing the existence of a penal system as a whole would have some overall preventative effect, compared to having no penal responses to crime at all; see, eg, von Hirsch, Bottoms *et al.* 1999, 5.

account's failure to treat the offender as a moral subject. *Integrationsprävention* is being invoked because citizens supposedly would be made more compliant through sanctions containing moral appeals than through bare threats. The censure in punishment – while purporting to speak in desert terms and to engage with the offender's capacity to evaluate the rightness or wrongness of his actions – is thus actually given a purely instrumental justification, concerned with influencing others' behaviour of others in future. The offender is thus not taken seriously as a moral agent, since the theory makes no claims that the censure imposed on the offender is morally warranted.[20]

2.4 The Censuring Element in Punishment

Punishment involves imposing a *deprivation* ('hard treatment') on someone, in a manner that conveys *censure*. A satisfactory account of the criminal sanction needs to address both these elements. Let us begin with censure, the element that plays a crucial, justificatory role.[d]

2.4.1 The role of censure

That punishment connotes blame or reprobation is evident enough. But why *should* there be a blaming response to the core conduct with which the criminal law deals? Without an answer to that question, legal punishment might arguably be replaced by some other institution that had no censuring implications – a response akin to a tax meant to discourage certain behaviour.

A central reason for such a blaming response concerns penal censure's role as moral communication to the act's perpetrator. The punishment conveys to the actor a certain critical normative message concerning his conduct: for example, that he has culpably harmed or risked harming someone, and is disapproved of for having done so. This message treats him as a moral agent – that is, an agent capable of moral deliberation.[e] He is being confronted with disapproval in virtue of the wrongfulness of his conduct, and not solely in order to produce preventive or other societal benefits that such censure might achieve.

[d] A 1993 volume by one of the authors, *Censure and Sanctions*, attempted to provide such an account: von Hirsch 1993. We will draw on it in the discussion which follows, but examine several of the relevant theses (eg, those concerning the authoritative character of punishment and the state's role) in greater depth.

[e] See von Hirsch 1993, ch. 2. A person is treated as moral agent if the reasons he is offered for specified choices are of a moral character, and if he is assumed capable of comprehending and acting on such reasons. Normal human beings (other than those suffering from certain mental disabilities) possess this capacity, it is assumed – whether they decide actually to make good choices or not.

When the offender is thus censured, a moral response on his part would be deemed appropriate – for example, an expression of concern, an acknowledgement of wrongdoing, or an effort at better self-restraint. A reaction of indifference would, if the censure is warranted, be an inappropriate response. The censure, however, serves only to give the actor the *opportunity* to make such a response. The approach thus differs from a penance theory, according to which the sanction should be fashioned to elicit certain specified sentiments in the actor, of shame, repentance, or the like.[f] On the view we advance here, there is no need to tailor the censuring response to the actor's supposed degree of receptivity.

Our account explains why predatory conduct should not be dealt with through neutral sanctions that convey no disapproval. Such sanctions – even if they were no less effective in discouraging the behaviour – would fail to accord the person the status of an agent capable of moral understanding. A neutral sanction would treat offenders or potential offenders much as beasts might be treated in a circus, as beings that have to be restrained, intimidated, or conditioned into compliance. A condemnatory sanction treats the actor as a *person* who is capable of such understanding.[g]

Penal censure also has the role of addressing third parties – namely, members of the public. Unlike blame in everyday contexts, the criminal sanction announces in advance that specified categories of conduct are punishable. Because the prescribed sanctions are of a kind that express disapprobation, this conveys the message that the conduct is deemed reprehensible. This is not necessarily a matter of teaching people that the conduct is wrong, for those addressed (or many of them) may well understand that already. Rather, the censure embodied in the prescribed sanction serves as an *appeal* to people's sense of the conduct's wrongfulness, as a reason for desisting.

Such a censure-oriented view assumes that criminal conduct is, in some sense, wrongful and hence warrants blame. Modern criminal prohibitions have wide scope, however, and include conduct that seems in no way

[f] Such a penance theory has been put forward by R.A. Duff. On his view, the hard treatment in punishment is justified as the means for bringing the criminal to repent his wrongdoing – and also to provide a vehicle through which he may 'work through' and express his penitent understanding; see Duff 1986, ch. 9; Duff 2001, chs. 3 and 4. For a critique of this penance perspective (particularly as regards its suitability as a function of the liberal state), see ch. 7 below.

[g] Certain kinds of state-imposed directives deal with citizens in non-moral terms, offering only prudential reasons for refraining from given courses of conduct. This is true, for example, of rules in tort law that impose on those who engage in certain kinds of potentially injurious conduct an obligation of compensating others if injuries take place. Criminal prohibitions, however, constitute outright proscriptions of behaviour, and supply sanctions – sometimes, of a very substantial character – for non-compliance. With the person's choice thus restricted, it becomes particularly important that the prohibitory scheme operates in a fashion that treats the actor as an agent capable of moral deliberation. For further discussion of non-punitive sanctions, see 2.6.2.

reprehensible. A censure-oriented conception, however, need not defend all such prohibitions. It suffices for the theory if the core conduct which the criminal law centrally addresses can legitimately be characterized as blameworthy – because, for example, it involves culpably harming someone (theft or violence), creating unwarranted risks of injury (drink-driving), or flouting important communal obligations (tax evasion).[h] Indeed, treating the criminal law as essentially involving censure provides a 'critical edge': it furnishes a reason to decriminalize conduct that cannot reasonably be accounted for as involving wrongdoing of some kind.[21]

2.4.2 The authoritative character of penal censure

If penal censure thus constitutes a moral communication with the agent, that communication is *authoritative* in character.[i] What constitutes unacceptable conduct; which procedures are utilized to determine guilt; and what excuses or claims in mitigation are admissible, are all determined authoritatively (by the formal criminal law), rather than through a free interchange of reasons between the censuring agency and the actor. As such, this form of response to criminal conduct falls outside the Jürgen Habermas' model, so influential in German legal theory, of *herrschaftsfreier Diskurs* (domination-free discourse).[22]

Penal censure's authoritative character is something shared by a variety of social institutions that address boundaries between acceptable and unacceptable forms of behaviour. When a university establishes a scheme of sanctions against academic misconduct, for example, it makes an authoritative determination of what kinds of behaviour are deemed unacceptable; these are not matters chiefly to be settled through free discussion in individual cases between the university authorities and the person charged. This degree of authoritativeness is essential, if there are to be stable and predictable norms of conduct concerning the behaviour involved.

Authoritativeness, however, does not in itself negate penal censure's character as moral communication. Where reasons can be supplied why the conduct is wrongful; where reasonable scope is permitted for claims in excuse or mitigation; and where the penal communication to the actor is

[h] In addition, certain kinds of conduct that constitutes *offensive* behaviour might appropriately be criminalized. For the scope and limitations of an Offence Principle, see Simester and von Hirsch 2002; von Hirsch and Simester 2005.

[i] Ordinary language distinguishes *blaming*, which involves expressions of disapproval in everyday discourse, from *censuring*, which involves authoritative expressions of disapproval. When someone carelessly steps on my toe, my disapproving response is one of visiting blame. When he plagiarizes my latest article and is subjected to a university disciplinary proceeding, the disciplinary board may issue a formal judgment of disapproval which is termed censure. The authoritative character of the judgments of disapprobation expressed through punishment makes them expressions of censure.

designed to convey disapproval in a form that invites him to consider the propriety of his conduct, this still treats the person as one whose actions are capable of being guided by moral reasons.[23]

2.4.3 Censure and *Integrationsprävention*

The normative message expressed in penal statutes is not reducible, as some German advocates of *Integrationsprävention* assert,[24] to an inducement to law-abidingness that is utilized because the citizenry may be more responsive to moral appeals than to bare threats. Rather, the censure expressed through punishment is legitimated through its being an ethically appropriate way of addressing the perpetrator, seen as an agent capable of moral deliberation. The message of disapproval of the proscribed behaviour, expressed in penal statutes to members of the general public, likewise derives its legitimacy from that message's being an ethically appropriate way of addressing such persons, viewed as moral agents. Any positive-general-preventive effect that such messages have would be secondary to such normative reasons.[25]

Censure's normative message is also not reducible to disapproval directed at the offender for having infringed a legal rule;[26] it is directed, instead, at the substance of the wrongdoing involved in the conduct. The censure due for a criminal assault, for example, should relate to the wrongfulness of having thus culpably injured someone, and not just to the fact of having engaged in a prohibited act.

2.4.4 Censure and the criminal law's fairness constraints

Giving censure this central role provides better support for the fairness constraints of the criminal law. Requiring culpability in the criminal law's General Part, and requiring the severity of punishments to reflect the degree of blameworthiness of the conduct in sentencing law, can now be derived directly from the blaming features of the criminal sanction. Consider the basic culpability requirements of the substantive criminal law: that the conduct must be committed with the requisite criminal intent or (for certain kinds of conduct) with recklessness or gross carelessness. This need no longer rest on hard-to-confirm empirical claims that such requirements will help reinforce law-abiding moral attitudes in the average citizen. The argument consists, instead, in a simpler and more direct chain of reasoning: that punishment not only does but *should* involve blame; and that blame is not appropriate where the actor acts without fault.[j] The same kind of reasoning holds for doctrines of excuse in the

[j] By 'acting without fault' we include acting without the requisite criminal intent or (where applicable) criminal negligence. Why is punishment inappropriate when the actor thus acts without fault? Because punishing someone involves conveying disapproval of the person for his

substantive law – for example, excusing necessity. The rationale for the latter excuse lies not in the lack of preventive impact of punishing in such situations but, rather, in fact that the offender should not reasonably be held to blame for his injurious act, when compliance would have led to devastating consequences to himself.[27]

Similar, censure-based arguments supply a justification for the principle of proportionality in sentencing. The severity of the sanction implies the degree of censure imposed on the offender for his conduct, so that a (comparatively) more onerous punishment connotes more blame (see, more fully, 2.5.4 below, and 9.2). It is because of this link between severity of the sanction and the implied censure (and not because of possible effects on citizens' law-abiding attitudes) that penalties should be arrayed according to the seriousness of the offences involved.

2.5 The 'Hard Treatment' Element in Punishment and its Justification

Punishment conveys censure, but it does not consist solely of it. The censure in punishment is expressed through the imposition of a deprivation ('hard treatment') on the offender. It thus becomes necessary to consider how this other constitutive element, the hard treatment, may be justified. Accounting for this other element requires, in our view, the invocation of preventive considerations – which means it will also be necessary to address how such preventive concerns relate to the criminal sanction's censuring role of which we have just spoken.

2.5.1 Can the justification for the deprivation be derived from censure?

A possible strategy of argument would be to try to derive the element of deprivation in punishment from the censure itself. Thus John Kleinig argues that censure (at least in certain social contexts) cannot be expressed adequately in purely verbal or symbolic terms; that hard treatment is needed to show that the disapprobation is meant seriously.[28] For example,

act (as we just have argued) and that is appropriate only when the act speaks badly of the person doing it. Where the harm done is purely accidental – that is, done without intent or negligence – this does not speak badly of the person who does it. But why should this be the case? (A conceivable morality might, after all, view with disapproval those who do harm accidentally, as persons who 'bring ill fortune' – see Williams 1993 on early Greek morality.) The reason for withholding blame with respect to accidental conduct relates to the person's ex ante guiding reasons for desistance. In a purely accidental injury there are no unreasonable risks of which he should have been aware and taken into consideration when embarking on the conduct; and in the absence of such reasons, he does not appear to have behaved reprehensibly. Hence, he should not be visited with penal censure.

an academic department does not show sufficient disapproval of a serious lapse by a colleague through a mere verbal admonition; to convey the requisite disapproval, a curtailment of privileges is called for. Similarly, the state should not respond to predatory behaviour through a verbal or symbolic expression of disapproval; making the censure credible calls for the imposition of some actual deprivation on the offender.

Within modern Western societies, this account has considerable plausibility. It would be difficult to imagine a purely verbal or symbolic response to harmful and culpable acts that could meaningfully convey the requisite disapproval: ours are not societies where there exist authority figures who could provide credible responses of a purely symbolic kind.

Nevertheless there is a lacuna in this argument. Even if the communication of censure itself treats those addressed as moral agents to whom respect is due, so should the *manner* in which that censure is expressed. To take an everyday example: imagine that *A* commits a wrong, and *B* wishes to admonish him for his wrongdoing. Suppose that *A* seems inclined to ignore a mere verbal admonition, so that *B* – in order to claim *A*'s attention and dramatize his admonition – expresses his disapproval by shouting at *A* or striking him. Even if admonishing *A* does constitute respectful treatment, one might well object that the *manner* of the admonition is far from respectful. And it is not a sufficient answer to assert that shouting or striking makes the admonition more 'credible'; for even if it did so, the means of its expression also stand in need of justification, and additional 'credibility' is not a sufficient moral explanation.

When used to try to justify the existence of the criminal sanction, Kleinig's account also overlooks this institution's manifest function as a disincentive to criminal behaviour. When the state adopts a criminal prohibition of certain conduct, it conveys a legal threat: that the conduct is prohibited, and violations will result in imposition of certain sanctions. This threat plainly appears to be designed to discourage members of the public from engaging in the conduct.

Speaking of 'disincentives' brings us back to punishment's crime-preventive role. Purely deterrent penal theories are wanting, we have seen, because they fail to address the actor or potential actors as moral agents.[29] This, however, leaves open the possibility of situating penal disincentives within a censuring framework.

2.5.2 The hard treatment as a preventive element located within a censuring framework

It is preferable, we think, to recognize that the hard-treatment element in punishment, the deprivation imposed on the punished offender, has also a preventive function: it supplies a prudential reason for desistance from offending, but one that is tied to the normative reason conveyed by penal censure.[30] The criminal law, through the censure embodied in its prescribed sanctions, conveys that the conduct is wrong, and a moral agent is thus furnished with reason for desistance. Given human fallibility, however, he may be tempted nevertheless. The explanation why, in punishment, hard treatment (instead of purely symbolic means) is used as the vehicle for censuring is that this provides him with a further reason, a prudential one, for resisting the temptation. (Indeed, an agent who has accepted the sanction's message that he ought not to offend, and who recognizes his susceptibility to temptation, could well favour the adoption of a censuring response that also supplies such a prudential disincentive, as an aid to carrying out what he himself recognizes as the proper course of conduct.)

A certain conception of human nature, and of reasons for action, underlies this account. Persons, it is assumed, are neither like angels for whom purely normative appeals would suffice, nor like brutes which could be influenced only by threats. Human beings, instead, are moral but fallible creatures – capable of being motivated by normative appeals, but sometimes strongly inclined to offend nevertheless. Human choice, Anthony Bottoms has recently suggested,[31] should thus be seen as a 'complex interactive process' involving both a distinctively human capacity for moral reasoning, and strong instincts and inclinations – for example, of greed, aggression, and the like. On this view of human nature, we require a response that both takes humans' capacity for moral judgement seriously and yet provides them with disincentives that can help them to control certain inclinations.[k] Persons' character as moral agents makes them capable of taking into account the censuring message conveyed through the sanction, that the conduct is reprehensible. Given human fallibility, however, the temptation to offend becomes easier to resist if the censure is expressed in a manner that also operates as a prudential disincentive against the conduct. But providing such a disincentive does not render the sanction purely coercive: it does not make fear of unpleasant consequences the *only* basis for compliance. It is possible, given this account of human nature, to have a response that supplies both moral and prudential reasons for desistance (see further 2.5.3 below).

Prevention, on this account, cannot stand alone. If the sanction conveys blame, its mode of expression may take the form that embodies also a

[k] Human nature is variable, however, with some persons more susceptible to temptation than others. Social and legal institutions also are variable in the extent to which they make allowances for 'human fallibility' – consider, for example, the rather demanding standards for recruitment to certain (eg high judicial) offices. Why, then, should the criminal law make any greater allowances for fallibility? The reason is that the law's application cannot be restricted to any specially selected group. Since the criminal law serves to protect citizens from the predatory behaviour of others, it must apply to everyone – including those who are more readily tempted.

prudential disincentive. But if it imposes hard treatment only, it remains purely coercive (in the sense of failing to treat the person as an agent). Granted, a morally committed person might find that even a neutral, non-condemnatory sanction makes it easier to resist temptation, and thus to comply with moral obligations he himself recognizes. The sanction itself would not be respectful of his agency, however, if it were couched as a naked threat. Whatever the actor's reasons for compliance, the sanctioner would be treating him as a creature to be intimidated or controlled, not as someone for whom normative reasons for acting matter.

The structure of this proposed justification for punishing is one in which the censuring function retains a central role. A condemnatory response to culpably injurious conduct might conceivably be expressed either in a purely (or primarily) symbolic mode, or else through the visitation of hard treatment. The criminal sanction is a response of the latter kind. It is preferred to the purely symbolic response because of its supplementary role as a disincentive. The preventive function operates, however, only *within* the framework of a censuring institution.

The censure and the hard treatment are thus intertwined in the way punishment is structured. A penal measure provides that a specified type of conduct is punishable by certain onerous consequences. Those consequences both constitute the hard treatment and express the censure and its degree. This intertwining of punishment's blaming and hard-treatment features is important for the rationale of the principle of proportionality of sentence, as we will see below.

This two-pronged justification would permit the abolition of the institution of punishment, were it not needed for preventive purposes. Imagine a hypothetical society in which social and economic conditions had improved so much that predatory conduct became much more infrequent than it is today. The criminal sanction – with its armament of courts, correctional agencies and sanctions – might, conceivably, no longer be required in order to keep such conduct within tolerable levels. Would such a society, in that event, still be obliged to preserve this institution to deal with the occasional predatory act? Not necessarily. While it still might be deemed desirable to retain some form of official censure to convey the requisite disapproval of such acts, there would be a considerably weaker case for so ambitious, intrusive, and burdensome an institution as the criminal sanction.

2.5.3 Moral agency and the threat of adverse consequences

The rationale that we have outlined here for the hard-treatment element of the penal sanction is in part a preventive one, relying on the notion of a disincentive against conduct. A justification for punishment which relies purely on deterrence would fail to treat a person as a moral agent, as we have seen earlier in this chapter. Might our limited introduction of an element of prevention, even within a censuring framework, suffer from the same objection?

The answer depends on how narrowly one conceives of moral agency. On a narrow view (sometimes attributed to Kant[l]) an agent makes a moral choice only if the reasons for action he is offered and takes into account are *purely* moral reasons. Introduction of any prudential considerations (whether in the form of incentives or disincentives) would divest the appeal to the actor of its essential moral character, and thus be unacceptable. This stringent perspective, however, is unhelpful when considering how the criminal law might properly deal with the actual, fallible human beings that constitute the citizenry.

An alternative, more modest view of moral agency is the one relied upon in our account of the role of hard treatment in punishment. A demand by the state treats the actor as an agent capable of moral deliberation, in our view, if it offers the actor normative reasons for acting, even if these are not exclusive reasons. A purely deterrence-based scheme would not meet this standard; the actor is informed that he had better comply or suffer the consequences, but is not being provided with any moral claim that he *ought* to comply. On our suggested account, however, the actor is given such grounds: through the censure embodied in the sanction, the actor is conveyed the message, issued by an authoritative source, that the conduct is reprehensible and should therefore be eschewed. Granted, this is not the *only* type of reason being put forward: the censuring response is expressed through hard treatment, which serves also as a disincentive against the temptation to commit the conduct notwithstanding its asserted wrongfulness. But if one accepts the conception of humans that has been propounded here – as fallible agents capable of acting on moral reasons but possibly requiring some practical disincentives to aid them in resisting such temptation – this still takes the capacity for moral agency seriously.

This last-mentioned point is important for our proposed rationale, for it responds to an objection sometimes voiced: that our theory must fail as a moral account of the criminal sanction, since it offers a partly instrumental account for punishment's hard-treatment element.[m] Our point is that an account of punishment need not be wholly deontological in character, in order to take offenders' capacity for moral agency seriously. A sanction that provides a disincentive as well as expressing disapprobation may, if

[l] Kant's views are actually more differentiated, for he distinguishes between reasons for acting that have personal moral worth for the actor, and reasons which the law may legitimately invoke in its public standards.

[m] Don Scheid (1997) thus makes this objection: that while our rationale might show that censure is a morally warranted response to wrongdoing, it does not establish why the hard treatment is morally justifiable.

appropriately constituted, still deal with those it addresses as persons capable of moral deliberation.[n]

2.5.4 Effect of introducing the hard-treatment element on the fairness limits of the criminal law

A major drawback of purely prevention-based accounts of punishment, as we have seen, is that they tend not to give adequate support to fault-based fairness limitations on criminal liability or on the quantum of sentence. Criminal liability without fault or disproportionate sentences could become permissible, to the extent these would promote the system's preventive aims. An important attraction of a censure-based account is that it provides direct principled support for those limits.

Now, however, we are proposing a 'mixed' account, containing a preventive as well as a censuring element. Might not this introduction of a preventive element permit fault constraints to be overridden, to the extent that would promote prevention more effectively?

Were the two justifying elements, censure and prevention, to operate separately on different features of the criminal law, this would be a problem. Suppose, for example, that one were to assert that the conviction represented censure of the offender, and the penalty subsequently imposed served primarily a preventive function. Then, the sanction's severity might be determined on preventive grounds. Such a model, however, would be unacceptable under the rationale proposed here: because if the penalty were to operate purely preventively, instead of expressing censure for the offender's conduct, then this separate non-condemnatory response would clearly fall outside our proposed justification for punishment. One would no longer be speaking of a censure-expressing response that, for preventive reasons, conveys its disapproval through material deprivation rather than purely symbolic means. Instead, the deprivation imposed on the offender would be solely preventive: it would be of the 'beast control' kind that would not address the actor as a moral agent.

What is crucial about the 'mixed' rationale suggested here is the intertwining of punishment's reprobative and hard-treatment features. It is the penal deprivation, not just the defendant's conviction, that expresses the censure as well as serving as the prudential disincentive. Imposing a penal deprivation on the offender visits him with blame that is justifiable only if

[n] Notice that we are speaking here of why prevention might in principle be a legitimate supporting reason for punishment's existence. What needs still to be considered is the general onerousness of the penalty scale. If overall penalty levels rise to sufficiently high levels, the normative reasons for desistance supplied by penal censure could become 'drowned out' by the magnitude of the deterrent threat, and thus become of little practical significance. If minimal prudence would virtually compel compliance, what difference could the sanction's normative message make? This militates, as we discuss in a subsequent chapter (see 9.4), in favour of keeping the system's general degree of punitiveness at moderate levels.

he is at fault – which is why the fault requirements of the substantive criminal law should be observed. Varying the amount of penal deprivation alters the relative degree of censure conveyed, and is warranted only when the sanction's severity comports with the degree of blameworthiness (ie the seriousness) of the criminal conduct – which is why the requirements of proportionality of sentence ought to be observed.

The arguments just stated make use of a well-known distinction drawn by HLA Hart, to which we have referred earlier in this chapter. This is the distinction between the general justification for the criminal sanction (namely, why the entire penal system should exist at all) and the principles governing the allocation of penalties (including the sentencing question, of how much offenders should be punished compared to one another). Our proposed dual-purpose account, relying on prevention as well as censure, should govern only at the general-justification level, of why the whole system should exist. The allocation of penalties at the sentencing level should be governed primarily by considerations of penal censure (rather than any such dual-purpose rationale), for the reasons we have just outlined. We shall return to this issue later in this volume, when we address desert-based criteria for sentencing in more detail (see Chapter 9).

2.6 Penal Censure and the Role of the State

A deficiency of traditional retributive theories of punishment, we noted at the outset, has been their failure adequately to address the state's role in punishing. We need to examine why establishing and operating the institution of the criminal sanction is a proper role for the state.

Dealing with this issue calls for a change in focus of argument. In the two preceding sections, we were in large part considering the institution of punishment from the perspective of those punished or threatened with punishment: why offenders and potential offenders may properly thus be treated. Now, our argument shifts to the role of the state. Even if it can be explained why the institution of punishment would deal with those punished in a morally acceptable fashion, it does not necessarily follow that creating and operating a system of criminal sanctions is a role the state may undertake. We need to provide arguments (ones which our earlier writings did not fully explore) why the state's proper functions include those of issuing prohibitory norms against specified kinds of harmful conduct, and of doing so in a 'moralizing' fashion (that is, in a fashion that visits censure). It is the latter question that interests us here, particularly. A modern state is not assumed to have any generalized role of visiting approbation or disapprobation on citizens for their conduct. Why, then, may it properly impose censure, within the context of the criminal sanction?

2.6.1 The monopoly-of-coercion argument

A familiar argument in favour of entrusting the state with the authority to punish is that only the state should have such coercive powers over its citizens. Punishment is a particularly powerful form of coercion. To grant this power to private parties would invite retaliation on the part of those suffering such sanctions. It would also open the way to serious injustice, given the partiality of those who would inflict such privately-imposed sanctions.

This argument, however, does not suffice. It provides an explanation of why it would be unwise (and unfair) to entrust penalizing responses primarily to private citizens or parties. But it does not develop with any clarity what positive reasons there might be for the state's involvement in a system of criminal sanctions. We need to explore these latter reasons.

2.6.2 The state's role in harm prevention

Could the preventive aspect of our previously outlined justification for punishment (see 2.5.2) make the state's involvement easier to account for? John Gardner provides a mode of argument that suggests how it might.[o]

The argument begins with the relatively straightforward proposition that helping to prevent persons from mistreating others is an important and legitimate function of the state. The underlying idea is that the state has, as one of its defining roles, that of encouraging peaceable living among citizens, and of safeguarding the basic means by which citizens can live good lives. An important way of helping to prevent such injurious behaviour, as we have seen earlier in this chapter (2.5.2), is through the issuance of prohibitory norms, with sanctions attached as a disincentive to the behaviour. Hence, we have a reason why the state's proper functions include that of issuing such prohibitions.[p]

But why should these state-imposed prohibitions involve censure? This is because it is also an important duty of the state to carry out its major

[o] Gardner develops this argument, in connection with his discussion of the criminal law's function of controlling private reprisals. This latter aim is also a consequentialist one: of establishing a system of state prohibitions of criminal conduct, so that persons injured by such conduct and their supporters do not retaliate themselves. If such a system of prohibitions is established, he argues, it needs to operate in a manner that recognizes the punished person's status as a moral agent; that, in turn, calls for responses that reflect the degree of blameworthiness of the conduct. See Gardner 1998a, 35.

[p] It would also be necessary to consider whether and to what extent the prevention of harm to others be accomplished through non-censuring state responses. Modern states have a number of such legal techniques at their disposal, including licensing, regulatory schemes and, of course, the law of torts. Tort law is partly a loss-shifting device and partly a form of corrective justice, designed to permit injured persons to receive compensation for damage inflicted; it may also authorize injunctions to restrain further harmful acts. However, there are important differences between criminal and tort law which indicate that the state could not satisfactorily provide protection for citizens by relying only on a tort system. One reason is that the initiation of tort

functions – especially those involving coercion – in a manner that treats those who are subjected to such measures with a proper degree of respect. A censuring sanction treats offenders and potential offenders in such a fashion, in a way that a purely 'neutral' prohibitory response would not: it addresses such persons as agents, capable of moral deliberation (see 2.4 above). Imposing censure is appropriate, of course, only if the conduct is wrongful. But conduct which culpably does or risks injury to others is wrongful, as we have argued earlier; and thus may be treated as such by the state.

This version of the argument does not yet assert, however, that blaming is in itself an important state mission: it is harm and its prevention that do the main explanatory work. The blaming aspect emerges out of a constraint upon the sanction's prohibitory features: namely, that these should operate in a fashion that is respectful to those punished or threatened with punishment. What further reason, then, might there be why imposing penal censure should in itself be a legitimate function for the state?

2.6.3 Penal censure and recognition of wrongdoing

An important further reason concerns the need for a response that recognizes typical criminal acts' character as wrongs. An accidentally inflicted injury and a criminal injury may produce similar physical and material consequences. In view of the latter conduct's culpable character, however, it *wrongs* the person affected in a way that a purely accidental injury does not. If *A* runs over *B* in his car (or narrowly misses him) because his newly purchased tyre explodes, that is gravely harmful or potentially harmful to *B*, but involves no reprehensible disregard of *B's* legitimate interests. But if *A* intentionally runs or tries to run *B* over, or hits or nearly hits him by virtue of his grossly negligent driving of the vehicle, that does constitute a disregard for the latter's legitimate and vital interests.[q]

Through its character as a censuring response, punishment provides recognition of the conduct's wrongfulness. Penal censure conveys that the

proceedings depends on the person ostensibly injured: if no injured party brings an action, the tortfeasor will not be held to account. The criminal law, by contrast, is supported by state agencies such as police and prosecutors whose function is to identify wrongdoers and bring them to account. Another difference is that where the conduct merely risks harm but none results, there are unlikely to be sufficient grounds for an action in tort; but the criminal law typically includes a law of attempts and creates other offences aimed at those who culpably create risks of harm. A third and in our view the most important reason, relating to recognizing the *wrongfulness* of the conduct, is developed in 2.6.3 and 2.6.4.

[q] This feature of wrongdoing may itself also be an element in the conduct's degree of injuriousness. Getting a black eye by walking accidentally into a glass door seems a rather minor injury; receiving the same injury in an assault is considerably worse because of the additional element of humiliation involved. That additional humiliation stems from the conduct's wrongful character – namely, the disrespect conveyed through the fact that the injury is an intentional one (see App. 3, part 7).

person has not just been injured or exposed to risk of injury, but *mistreated* through someone's culpable act. It would thus not suffice just to acknowledge the injury or provide compensation (as may be appropriate when people have been injured by pure mishap). Penal censure, by directing disapprobation to the person responsible, provides acknowledgement that the injury or risk of injury has taken place through another's fault; and that he is being confronted with disapproval having thus behaved.[r]

The importance of acknowledgement of wrongdoing, then, provides reason for a censuring response. Were a 'neutral' prohibitory sanction to be the sole response to the kinds of behaviour now typically proscribed by the criminal law, this would not only fail to treat the actors as moral agents, but also fail those injured or placed at risk – because the response would not provide them with acknowledgement of the wrongdoing involved. The state would be seeking to discourage the conduct, but in a manner that did not testify to the recognition of its wrongful character.

Nevertheless, we need to pursue further the question of the state's involvement in censure. Were the state's response a 'neutral' prohibitory one, this would still maintain the state's monopoly of coercion, of which we spoke earlier. What further purpose would be served, then, in having the *state* provide recognition of the conduct's wrongful character through a censuring response, rather than leaving such judgements of disapproval to informal sources – to friends, neighbours, and local communities? The answer to this question, we believe, concerns the need for a public valuation of conduct.

2.6.4 Criminal sanctions and public valuation of conduct

If there is to be a censuring response, on whose behalf should it be made? Were the disapproving response to the conduct left to victims and others immediately affected, this would treat the matter as one of primary concern to them. But notwithstanding that many offences cause injury or create risks of injury primarily to those directly affected (or sometimes also, their immediate circle), the judgement of wrongfulness should be made on behalf of the wider community – because it relates to basic norms of decent interaction among citizens. State involvement in penal censure thus is capable of providing a *public valuation* of the conduct. The state's judgements of penal censure purport to speak not just on behalf of victims or their sympathizers, but on behalf of the wider community of citizens.[s]

This public valuation stems in part from the *authoritativeness* of judgements of penal censure, of which we have spoken earlier (see 2.4.2).

[r] This point was made by Joel Feinberg (1970), in his essay, 'The Expressive Function of Punishment'; see also, von Hirsch 1993, 10.

[s] In arguing for such a public valuation, we are not claiming that this would have greater effect in inducing citizens to desist from injurious behaviour – which may or may not be the

The censure should not just reflect some wider consensus; the censuring agency should be in a position to speak on the larger community's behalf, when judging the conduct and its perpetrator adversely. With state involvement, it may also be possible to have more considered and consistent judgements concerning how reprehensible the conduct is, and what severity of punishment should express the appropriate degree of disapprobation.

Even if the foregoing reasons would help explain why the state might legitimately be involved in a censuring response, why is it uniquely suited to do so? Why might the state not delegate that response down to some other body or group, subject to appropriate restrictions? (Restorative justice is one possible delegation: where victim and offender, and their respective supporters, are authorized to negotiate the disposition.) We shall not attempt to provide a general answer to that question here, for it may depend on how, and to whom, for what purposes, and with what restrictions the delegation is made. Any such delegation should, however, be judged in part by the desiderata of consistency, reflectedness and authoritativeness just discussed. We examine restorative justice later in this volume (Chapter 8) – and indicate why we have some doubts.

How willing and able, however, would the state be to make considered and impartial censuring judgements on behalf of the wider community of citizens? The answer depends in part on one's view of the legitimacy of state authority – so that it is not surprising that some of the most vigorous recent critics of desert theory have been those holding a sceptical view of state power.[32] It depends also on what kind of state we are speaking of: for example, how committed it is to dealing with its citizens with a modicum of justice. It is thus also not surprising that in places where substantial segments of the community feel that the state does not legitimately represent their interests, there is a heightened interest in alternative approaches to dealing with crime.[33]

2.7 Concluding Remarks

Efforts to provide a satisfactory account for the institution of punishment have sometimes been impeded by assumptions that such justifications need either to be wholly instrumental and preventative, or else to be wholly deontological in character. Neither of these 'pure' accounts can be satisfactory. Solely preventive accounts, as we have seen, fail to treat

case. Since punishing necessarily involves evaluations of conduct, however, it needs to be established whose norms should apply – those of the immediately affected parties, or those representing a wider community. Our view is that the judgements concerning wrongfulness in the criminal law should be made on behalf of the wider community, since they relate to the basic norms of decent interaction among citizens; and that, under normal circumstances, this can preferably be achieved through state involvement in penal censure. For a further discussion of punishment as public valuation, see Duff 2001, 56–66.

the actor respectfully, as an agent capable of moral deliberation; and fail also to give adequate support to the fault-based limits of the substantive law and the proportionality requirements of sentencing law. Traditional, exclusively retributive accounts tend to have obscure explanations of the deprivation ('hard treatment') element in punishment, and fail to give an adequate explanation for the state's involvement. Conceivably, greater ingenuity could permit these difficulties to be overcome, but a way to do so scarcely seems apparent.

The institution of the criminal sanction, on its face, seems to be supported by both preventive and deontological reasons. Its censuring element – of visiting the offender with formal disapprobation for his conduct – involves a moral appeal that cannot properly be reduced to a mere disincentive. However, the criminal sanction has other features – particularly in the manner in which it threatens certain unpleasant consequences – that seem clearly to have something to do with inducing people to desist. The most plausible direction of analysis, therefore, is toward a principled account that includes both deontological features and those concerned with consequences.

This chapter provides an analysis of penal censure that treats this response as primarily (though not exclusively) deontological: as an appeal directed to actors deemed capable of moral deliberation. It is this censuring feature which supports the fault-based fairness limits of substantive and sentencing law, including the principle of proportionality of sentence. Hard treatment (deprivation) is also an integral aspect of the criminal sanction. It is both the means through which the censure is expressed, and serves as a prudential disincentive against offending that operates within a censuring framework. The reason for having such a disincentive – rather than having solely symbolic censure as the response – is to some degree preventive: it is designed to assist human beings (as moral agents but fallible ones) to resist temptations to offend. Recognizing this limited preventive role for hard treatment still permits the maintenance of fairness constraints on punishment, such as the requirements of criminal fault and sentence proportionality. And the introduction of this preventive element, we have argued, does not undermine the character of the response as an appeal to the actor's moral agency.[t]

[t] In a recent commentary on desert theory, Anthony Bottoms raises the question of the relative primacy that should be given to the two constitutive elements of punishment, censure and prevention. He characterizes the *Censure and Sanctions* account as one giving primacy to censure; but argues that the two elements should be given equal weight; Bottoms 1998, 87–91. The discussion in the present chapter suggests, however, that the question of primacy should depend on the issue being addressed. When speaking of the justification of punishment's impositions on those punished, emphasis should be given to treating persons as moral agents – which suggests (as we have seen in 2.4 and 2.5) a primacy for the censuring element. When speaking, however, of the reasons for the *state's* involvement in punishment, consequences may matter more – because the state's primary concerns relate to the consequences of its measures for its citizenry.

In discussing such issues, in short, we need to be mindful of the interaction of moral and instrumental concerns. Institutions of punishment call for moral and not mere instrumental justifications; but that those arguments need to be addressed to punishment seen as a social institution, involving the exercise of state power, that must have some pragmatic goals concerning the welfare of citizens.

While this chapter concludes that valid reasons can be advanced in favour of having a system of criminal sanctions, we should remain mindful that this institution has great drawbacks. Punishment, by its very nature, takes away important rights that people ordinarily are entitled to have. The more onerous sanctions, particularly imprisonment, also involve depriving people of critical social and economic opportunities, and condemning them to live regimented lives with other persons not of their choosing. Giving a state the power to punish creates strong temptations for misuse: to extend the reach of criminal prohibitions unduly; to utilize unfair procedures for determining guilt and unjust measures for the quanta of punishments; and to confine many offenders in grim (and often dangerous) institutions of confinement. The authority to punish must thus strongly be hedged with safeguards: including an insistence on sparing use of onerous sanctions, and adoption of fairness constraints regarding the comparative severities of sanctions. Much of the remainder of this book will be devoted to exploring such constraints.

Notes

1. For an English-language version of this view, see Moore 1987.
2. See, eg, Finnis 1980, 263–64.
3. See Frisch 1998, 139 et seq.
4. See, eg, Moore 1987, 179 et seq.
5. For a critique of the 'unfair advantage' theory, see Duff 1986, ch. 9; von Hirsch 1993, 7–8.
6. Hörnle and von Hirsch 1998, 86 et seq.
7. Bentham 1982, ch. 14.
8. Hart 1968, ch. 1.
9. For further discussion of these two objections, see von Hirsch and Ashworth 1998, 44–51.
10. Hart 1968, chs. 1, 7. While Hart thus offers deontological reasons for the culpability requirements of the criminal law, his general justification for punishment – that is, the reasons he supplies why the institution of punishment should exist – is consequentialist, and relies on crime prevention. That is why we classify his views among 'purely instrumental justifications'.
11. Hart 1968, ch. 7.
12. Roxin 1997, 740–745.
13. Duff and von Hirsch 1997, 103 et seq.
14. Hart 1968, 25.

15. Hart 1968, 24–25.
16. Roxin 1997, 50–51; Baurmann 1998.
17. Roxin 1979, 279 et seq.
18. Schumann 1998.
19. Frisch 1998, 125 et seq.
20. See Hörnle and von Hirsch 1995, 267–70.
21. See, eg, Husak 1992, Chs. 2 and 3.
22. Habermas 1971, 252 et seq. This point – that penal communications cannot be *herrschaftsfrei* – is developed in Hassemer 1981, 121 f.
23. See further, Hörnle and von Hirsch 1998, 94 f.
24. See discussion accompanying notes 16–18 above.
25. See more fully on this last point, Hörnle and von Hirsch 1998, 91–99.
26. For such a perspective on penal censure, see Schuenemann 1998, 109.
27. Gardner 1998a.
28. Kleinig 1992; see also Bottoms 1998.
29. See text accompanying notes 7–9 above.
30. von Hirsch 1993, 12 et seq; see also Narayan 1993.
31. Bottoms 1998, 81–82.
32. Christie 1980.
33. Such a heightened interest in restorative justice, for example, is developing among Catholic communities in Northern Ireland. See McEvoy and Mika 2002.

3

Proportionate Sentences for Juvenile Offenders

3.1 Introduction

There now are much greater contrasts among Western countries' approaches to juvenile justice than among those for adult criminal justice. Some countries (most notably, Sweden) have a justice system for juveniles with a strong emphasis on proportionality of sentence. Youthful offenders are tried in the same courts as adult offenders, and the severity of their sentences depends principally (as it does in Sweden for adults) on the degree of seriousness of the actor's criminal offence. The salient difference in Sweden's treatment of juvenile offenders lies in the penalty levels: the onerousness of juveniles' sentences is substantially scaled down.[1] Other European jurisdictions adopt a sharply contrasting approach: Scotland has instituted a rehabilitatively-oriented juvenile justice scheme in which offence seriousness (in principle, at least) has little or no importance.[2] Other countries, including England,[3] have hybrid systems employing a mixed set of aims. This divergence suggests that it may be worth considering further what the aims of juvenile sentencing should be: and particularly what the role of proportionality of sentence should be as applied to young offenders.

There have been, in the Anglo-American literature of juvenile justice (and particularly in the writings of two of America's leading juvenile-justice scholars, Franklin Zimring[4] and Barry Feld[5]) suggestions that greater emphasis should, as a matter of fairness, be given to the degree of seriousness of a juvenile offender's criminal conduct, and less to predictions of his likelihood of returning to crime and his supposed receptiveness to treatment. Much of this literature also advocates that proportionate sentences for juveniles should be scaled well below those applicable to adult offenders, as is already the case in Sweden.

The question we should consider in this chapter is how sanctions for juvenile offenders should be structured, if a proportionalist sentencing rationale were carried over to the juvenile justice system. Should sentences for juveniles, particularly, reflect significant reductions in severity as compared with proportionate sentences for similar crimes imposed on adults; and if so, why?

For purposes of analysis, we begin with a hypothetical sentencing scheme for adults, based on the principle of proportionate, deserved sentences. In such a scheme – which is of the kind the present volume advocates – penalties would be graded according to the seriousness of the offences involved, with only a modest adjustment for previous convictions. The underlying rationale would emphasize penal censure rather than 'paying back' the offender for his offence, so that levels of deprivation visited on offenders would not need to approximate the degree of suffering experienced by victims. The scheme thus could employ moderate penalties, well below those prevailing (for example) in England today.

The question to be addressed here is how such a desert-based scheme should be altered, if extended to juvenile offenders. Juvenile offenders, for purposes of the present analysis, would be those whose ages run from the minimum age of criminal responsibility (which is 14 in many Western European jurisdictions, but now 10 in England) to the age of legal adulthood (say, 18). The thesis we shall be defending is that, in applying a policy of proportionate sentencing to juveniles, substantial overall penalty reductions are called for, with the amount of those reductions graded according to the young offender's age.[6] The issue then becomes *why* there should be such severity-reductions for juveniles. The available literature refers to three kinds of reasons, relating to (1) juveniles' lesser culpability; (2) criminal sanctions' greater 'punitive bite' when applied to juveniles; and (3) the notion of adolescence as a 'time of testing'. Each of these three purported reasons will be examined in the light of desert theory.

3.2 Culpability

One argument for reduced punishments concerns juveniles' lesser degree of culpability. If a 15-year old commits burglary, or if a 35-year old commits it, the harmful consequences of the act are the same; but what may be different is the ascription of culpability: the juvenile appears to act with less personal fault in committing the act, making the behaviour less serious. Thus there should be less punishment for the crime, because it becomes less serious compared to the same criminal act committed by an adult.

The question then becomes, *why* is culpability reduced? Two kinds of arguments have been put forward: (1) a *cognitive* claim, that juveniles have less capacity to assess and appreciate the harmful consequences of their criminal actions; and (2) a claim concerning *volitional controls*, that they have had less opportunity to develop impulse control and resist peer pressures to offend. This provides a useful general framework, but more analysis is needed of *why* these factors should be permitted to count as culpability-reducing. For a legally competent adult, insufficiently developed appreciation-of-consequences or impulse-controls are not ordinarily considered grounds for ascribing reduced culpability. Why should it be otherwise for juveniles?

3.2.1 Cognitive factors

The cognitive claim relates to juveniles' more limited capacity to grasp the harmful consequences of their actions. Adolescents, it is said, 'have not acquired the capacity to realise as fully as adults the consequences of their actions'.[7] But what kind of capacities are being referred to here?

This deficiency of knowledge would not ordinarily concern those consequences that constitute the defining elements of the crime. Many commonplace offences committed by juveniles are *mens rea* crimes, requiring purpose or knowledge on the part of the defendant. Knowledge of the defining elements, for such crimes, is a prerequisite of criminal liability. For residential burglary, for example, a person satisfies the conduct-requirements of the offence if he enters the dwelling of another as a trespasser and takes items of personal property belonging to that person. He must, however, be aware that the dwelling and those items are not his own; and must, when entering the dwelling, have had the intention to steal or commit another offence.[8] If he does not understand such matters, he is not committing burglary at all. However, simple knowledge of this kind is something that most juveniles are capable of having. A 15-year old, when he breaks into a flat and steals a television set, can easily grasp that the flat is someone else's and that the television is not properly his for the taking.

In what other respects, then, might the juvenile be said to have less comprehension of a criminal act's harmful consequences? Perhaps, the reduced awareness concerns the character and importance of the interests which the prohibition is designed to protect – interests which often are not specified as defining elements of the crime. The offence of residential burglary is defined in terms of unauthorized entry into the dwelling of another for purposes of committing a theft or other offence. But what interests are thereby protected? Prevention of theft could not be the sole aim, as that is dealt with by other criminal prohibitions. Prevention of trespass into the homeowner's real property also cannot be a sufficient explanation, as trespass is not itself a criminal offence in most English-speaking jurisdictions. The paramount interests relate instead to the occupant's personal privacy and the sense of personal security.[9] It is with respect to consequences of this kind that juveniles' understanding may be partially inadequate. While the 15-year old house burglar may know that he enters his victim's flat unlawfully and wrongfully takes that person's television set, he may well have less grasp of how those actions affront the person's legitimate sense of the dwelling as personal space, and of how his entry might make that person feel vulnerable and insecure. And even if he grasps these matters intellectually, he still may not properly *appreciate* them – that is, have a sense of (say) what it might feel like to have one's privacy thus invaded.

What remains to be explained, however, is why this kind of incomplete understanding of the relevant interests should affect the ascription of culpability. For adults, it usually is not considered exculpating or even mitigating: the 25-year old house burglar who thinks he is merely trespassing and stealing items of property is not considered to merit less punishment in virtue of the fact that he fails to understand or appreciate the character of the privacy invasion that his conduct involves. We demand of a competent adult a minimal general understanding of other persons' basic interests, and of how various kinds of criminal conduct intrude upon such interests.[10] Lack of understanding of such matters constitutes just a failure to have the relevant moral standards, and should not be extenuating; the house burglar who lacks this kind of comprehension would not be regarded as preferable, morally speaking, to the burglar who does understand and enters and steals anyway.

If the conclusion should be different for juveniles, it must be because we ought to have different normative expectations for them. Young adolescents, the argument runs, cannot reasonably be expected to have a fully fledged comprehension of what other people's basic interests are and how typical crimes affect those interests – because achieving this kind of understanding is a *developmental* process. It takes a greater degree of moral sophistication to appreciate how house burglary affects someone's sense of privacy, than to know that it is impermissible to take that person's TV set. Developing that understanding calls for cognitive skills and capacities for moral reasoning which develop over time – precisely during the period of adolescence with which we are concerned. A 14 or 15-year old has had less opportunity to develop the understanding of other people's interests that we reasonably may demand of an adult.

This brings us to the critical point of whether these cognitive arguments are descriptive or normative ones. If descriptive, then claims to reduced culpability would depend on empirical evidence of a juvenile offender's reduced comprehension of consequences.[11] But that degree of understanding varies greatly within a given age group: a clever 15-year old will have a better grasp of such matters than a dull one – or even, than a dull adult. A descriptive approach thus would lead to diverse treatment of young persons of the same age, and would call making elusive judgements about the degree of moral insight a given adolescent has.[12] It would also lead to the strange result of punishing children with greater moral sophistication more severely,[a] a difficulty that has been apparent already in the

[a] Such a result seems strange because a youth's degree of appreciation of the harmful consequences of his conduct may depend not only on his innate abilities and his opportunities but (at least to some degree) also on his own efforts at learning to comprehend others' interests. To

application of the (recently-repealed) English rule of *doli incapax*.[b] Above all, a purely descriptive approach would fail to explain why limited understanding of consequences *should* affect culpability.

The claim of reduced culpability must thus be one that has normative elements. It is not just that adolescents tend in fact to have a less full understanding of criminal acts' harmful consequences; but, rather, that this should be reflected in what we may reasonably demand of them, given the degree to which such understanding depends on experience, learning, and capacities for moral reasoning that need to develop in adolescence over time.

In such an account, it is appropriate to employ age-based gradations. Because opportunities to develop cognitively are related to age, fuller comprehension may be expected of 17-year old adolescents than of 14-year olds. A graded scale may thus be established in which there would be a reduction in severity based on age, and it would be greatest for those nearest to the minimum age of responsibility (say, 14).[13] What such a scale reflects are moral expectations, not actual patterns of development among individuals. There will be variations in how much a particular 14-year old, vis-à-vis a particular 17-year old, actually grasps the typical harmful consequences of burglarizing someone's home. But more may be demanded of the 17-year old, because he has had more time to grow toward adulthood.

3.2.2 Volitional controls

The other aspect of culpability concerns *volitional controls*. Adolescents tend to be less able to postpone gratification, to restrain themselves from acting out of feelings of anger and aggression, and to resist peer pressures.[14] It is harder to say 'No' to peers, when one is only 14 or 15.

With respect to this dimension, however, the relevant normative expectations become still more important: it must be asked why lesser self-control *should* be culpability-reducing. For adults, this characteristic should not ordinarily serve to mitigate fault. Were an adult criminal defendant to assert that his penalty should be diminished because of his deficient command of his impulses, we ordinarily would regard this to be a moral failing which did not render his conduct any less reprehensible. It is

the extent that he succeeds in increasing his comprehension, it seems odd to penalize his efforts by holding him to a higher fault standard and thus punishing him more severely.

[b] Under English law until 1998, a child between the ages of 10 and 14 could be held criminally responsible if the prosecution, in addition to establishing the elements of the crime, met a burden of showing that the child knew that the conduct was wrong. In the Crime and Disorder Act 1998, s. 34, this rule was eliminated. Instead of using the repeal of the *doli incapax* rule to raise the age of responsibility to 14, however, the Act reduced that age for all juvenile offenders to the troublingly low level of 10 years, see Bottoms and Dignan 2004.

only if these deficiencies are based on significant mental or emotional disabilities that a claim for mitigation of punishment could be sustained.[c] Why should the conclusion be otherwise for adolescents?

Self-control, as other aspects of moral development, is a *learned* capacity, and childhood and adolescence is the period during which it is learned. Angels might have self-discipline from the moment of their creation, but we should not expect children to be born with similar virtues. It is through cognitive and emotional growth, interaction with others, and exposure to social norms that such capacities are gained; and this can be expected to develop not just in childhood, but also throughout adolescence. The adolescent who offends has had less time and opportunity to develop impulse-control and ability to resist the urgings of peers than the adult man or woman, which is why these factors properly should bear on the degree of culpability ascribed to him or her. And as with the cognitive dimension discussed previously, the expectations we should have should vary with age. As the adolescent approaches the age of adulthood, it is right to expect a higher level of self-control.

3.2.3 Youth 'discount' or individualized assessment?

If culpability factors suggest reduced penalties for juveniles, should this involve categorical penalty reductions or individual determinations of culpability? The principle we have suggested earlier (3.2.1) is one of categorical, age-related reductions. While actual appreciation of consequences varies considerably among youths of the same age, the degree of appreciation that we *should* demand should depend on age: we may rightly expect more comprehension and self-control from the 17-year old youth than a 14-year old, so that the 17-year old's penalty reduction would be smaller. The principle is thus one of gradually diminishing sentence reductions, as the age of adulthood approaches.[d]

Aside from the categorical, age-related reductions, juveniles should also be entitled to individualized claims in mitigation of kinds that adults could assert. A young offender may, for example, merit punishment somewhat

[c] Thus under Swedish sentencing law, it is deemed a mitigating factor that the defendant '...because of mental abnormality or strong emotional inducement or other cause, had a reduced capacity to control his behaviour', Swedish Penal Code, ch. 29, s. 3.2.

[d] How this is to be accomplished, technically, depends on the type of sentencing standards used. In a jurisdiction with numerical sentencing guidelines, these could be modified in order to apply to juveniles. To reflect juvenile offenders' reduced culpability, the guidelines' seriousness-ratings could be suitably scaled down. To reflect the concern about 'punitive bite', the sanctions set forth in the sentencing grid could be reduced. A variety of techniques could be used to implement differential adjustments dependent on age – including, for example, separate guidelines for different age categories. In a system utilizing statutory sentencing principles, such as Sweden's, the scaling down of punishment for juveniles, and the differential adjustment for different ages, would have to be more a matter for qualitative judgements.

below the level normally appropriate for his age if he was provoked by the victim's own misconduct.[e]

What requires further exploration is whether there should be any special, individualized grounds for sentence reduction that hold for adolescents only. Even if we should not try generally to make individualized assessments of moral development, certain particular types of situations might be recognized where children have been confronted with unusually grave impediments to developing comprehension or self-control. Taking such an approach would necessitate further reflection on what kinds of special circumstances should warrant such mitigation; and whether these should be treated as culpability-reducing or as compassion-based 'equity' concerns similar to those we discuss below in Appendix 1.

3.3 Punitive Bite

A second line of argument for penalty reductions that appears in the literature relates to 'punitive bite'. A given penalty is said to be more onerous when suffered by a child than by an adult. Young people, assertedly, are psychologically less resilient, and their punishments interfere more with opportunities for education and personal development.[15]

Such claims, however, raise the question of what conception of punitive bite should be used. A possible perspective is subjectivist: that severity of a penalty depends on how unpleasant it is experienced as being. Punishments thus are more onerous when applied to adolescents simply because they feel them to be more unpleasant. Such a subjectivist conception of severity would have disturbing consequences, however. It could permit much variation among offenders of any given age. Some 15-year olds are tough, others are tender: should greater deprivations be visited on the tough ones, on grounds that they would feel them less keenly? Measuring the degree of punitiveness by personal sensitivities of particular offenders would have troublesome social implications, to the extent that toughness and degree of enurement to deprivation are related to social class. The approach also would not comport well with how the severity of punishment is gauged for adults. It is commonly assumed that the onerousness of (say) a term of imprisonment should depend chiefly on such 'objective' factors as its duration and (possibly but more controversially) the kind of conditions prevailing in the institution, rather than on the defendant's personal sensitivities to the deprivations of punishment.[f]

[e] Sweden's sentencing statute, for example, generally recognizes provocation as a mitigating circumstance (see Swedish Penal Code, ch. 29, s. 3.1); for discussion of provocation as a culpability-reducing factor, see von Hirsch and Jareborg 1987; Narayan and von Hirsch 1996.

[f] There may be some exceptions on account of special types of vulnerability that typify certain groups of offenders – such as the aged and the ill; see Appendix 1 below.

The subjectivist view of penal severity strikes us, also, as being misconceived in principle. What makes punishments more or less severe is not so much identifiable sensations (that may vary considerably from person to person) but, rather, the extent to which those sanctions interfere with important interests that people have. Interests are not merely subjective: they consist of resources over which persons have legitimate claims.[16] The severity of imprisonment depends not just on its 'feeling bad' in some immediate sense, but on its interfering with such important interests as freedom of movement, privacy, personal autonomy in daily activities, and the right to choose one's associates (see more fully, 9.5.2). It thus would be preferable to apply an interests-analysis to the assessment of punitive bite. Penalties should be ranked in severity according to the degree of importance of the interests affected, and the extent to which the penalty intrudes upon such interests. The importance of those interests, we suggest elsewhere in the volume, may then be gauged by the degree to which they affect an ordinary person's 'living standard' – that is, the resources that such a person should ordinarily need to conduct a satisfactory life (see 9.5.2; Appendix 3).

Adopting such an interest-analysis means that the assessment of severity is not made dependent on the preferences and sensitivities of particular individuals. The living-standard, in the sense just referred to, refers to the means and capabilities that normally should be important for living a good existence. If a given interest is important in this sense, it would warrant a high rating – notwithstanding that some persons might find it less important or choose to go without it. Imprisonment thus qualifies as a severe penalty in virtue of the interests in freedom of movement, privacy and autonomy it takes away. This judgement, moreover, is in significant part a normative and not just a descriptive one. It is not just that many people happen to like being free to move about, to enjoy a modicum of privacy, and to have control over their daily activities – and hence detest being imprisoned. It is, rather, that such interests *should* be regarded as important for persons in a free society, and hence that imprisonment should be regarded as being very burdensome.

How would this interest-analysis bear on gauging punitive bite for juveniles? Young people, it may be argued, have certain special interests; and punishments are more onerous for them because of their intrusion upon those interests. There are, first, certain *developmental interests*. Ordinarily, there are critical opportunities and experiences that need be provided between the ages of 14 and 18. A youth requires adequate schooling and learning opportunities; needs to be in a reasonably nurturing atmosphere such as that of a family; requires exposure to adequate role models; and needs to be able to begin to develop ties to friends and associates who can be trusted. These are not mere preferences, but real interests: a young person *should* have such resources in order to mature adequately. Punishments are thus more onerous for adolescents because of the way they tend to compromise these kinds of interests. This is most obviously true of imprisonment – which tends to stunt learning opportunities, provide a hostile rather than a nurturing atmosphere, offers few role models or destructive ones; and fosters attitudes of distrust. If punishments are thus more onerous when undergone by juveniles, proportionality would require that they be reduced.

A second kind of interest relates to *capacity for self-esteem*. Given the censuring connotations of punishment, being punished is hard on a person's self-esteem. It is difficult for anyone to undergo being punished without having his sense of self adversely affected; but the difficulty is greater for juveniles, especially as they enter adolescence. It is characteristic of adolescents that their self-esteem, their sense of self as worthwhile persons having the potential for a better future, tends to be more fragile (and can reasonably be expected to be more fragile) than that of adults. Again, this is a normative and not just a descriptive matter. Developing a robust conception of self, one that is resilient yet capable of coping with the criticism of others, is a product of maturation and experience. It is thus appropriate to expect, for juveniles, a lesser degree of psychological resilience in the face of being punished than we should be able to expect of adults. Such normative judgements, again, are age-related. The younger the offender is, the less resilience can reasonably be demanded of him.

3.4 A Special 'Tolerance' for Juveniles?

The literature on proportionate sanctions for juveniles touches mainly upon the foregoing issues of culpability and punitive bite. Juveniles are to be punished less because they are less culpable, and because punishments are more onerous for them. This still assumes, however, that the conventions between linking severity and seriousness are unchanged. Where the crimes (adjusting for culpability factors) have similar seriousness-ratings, and where the penalties (adjusting for juveniles' greater vulnerability) should have the same severity-ratings, then juveniles and adults would receive equivalent punishments.

But might a further step be worth taking? Might not there be different conventions linking severity of punishment with seriousness of crimes for juveniles than for adults? That would constitute a real claim that young persons warrant less: that there should be different and milder punishment conventions for juvenile offenders, even after one has taken into account differences in culpability and in punitive 'bite'. For the reasons to be elaborated next, we believe that there is a justification within proportionality theory for arguing that adolescents should thus have less punishment. We begin, however, by examining a consequentialist approach that leads in the same direction.

3.4.1 Adolescence as a time for 'testing limits'

Youth, we know, is a time for experimentation; that is, for weaning oneself away from adult authority, for learning to live autonomously, for testing limits. As a result, it is a time for making misjudgements, including those that harm others. Franklin Zimring likens this period of life to the period when a driver obtains a learner's permit: we know that he will drive less well than an experienced driver and hence is more likely to do harm, but we permit him to drive anyway (although, perhaps, with specified restrictions) because it is only through doing so that he can become an adequate driver.[17] Giving scope to juveniles for this process of experimentation, Zimring argues, is particularly important for a free society. We do not wish to train young persons to perform predetermined social roles, in the manner of traditional cultures. Instead, we wish to help them learn to make their own life choices. That requires us to permit adolescents actually to make such choices, and to our taking the risks inevitably involved.

If these are the risks of permitting adolescents to experiment with acting autonomously, how do we deal with the harms that we know may well result? The sensible response is one of cutting losses – of, in Zimring's words, 'keeping to a minimum the harm we inflict on [young offenders] when they have abused opportunities in ways that harm the community'.[18] Punishment policy for juveniles should be designed to 'preserve the life choices for those who make serious mistakes'.[19] This is a gamble: that a juvenile who does abuse such opportunities will, as he matures, learn better how to live autonomously (as most, although not all, do); and therefore that he should not be unduly burdened with the penal consequences of his earlier bad choices.

One way of reducing that burden is to adopt punishment standards for juveniles that are less stringent than those for adults: even after controlling for differences in culpability and punitive bite, we should utilize milder severity conventions. In punishing less, it is hoped that we will preserve better the young person's opportunities and prospects – and thus permit him to live freely as an adult, carrying fewer burdens from his earlier mistakes. This approach is usually combined with a reference to the importance of other means of support and direction for the young, notably through family and social networks.

To what extent does this line of argument support reduced punishment levels for juveniles? There are several matters which need clarification. One concerns the consequences that can be expected of such a reduction. Can it be said that rates of juvenile crime will be lower if a milder punishment scale is adopted? It might variously have been argued that, on one hand, milder sanctions will cause juveniles to identify themselves less as criminals and hence offend less frequently; and, on the other hand, that such reduced sanctions might diminish marginal deterrent effects and hence permit crime to increase. These potential effects cannot be gauged with even a modicum of confidence, however, given the limited current knowledge of deterrence and other crime-prevention effects.[20]

Any claim about beneficial effects of reducing the penalty scale for youthful offenders should focus, instead, on how punishment affects ordinary processes of growing up. Living autonomously involves not only making choices but being held accountable by others for those choices. Part of that accountability, a proportionalist sentencing rationale assumes, is undergoing penal censure for the legal wrongdoing. Punishment, however, also tends to interrupt the ordinary routines and developmental opportunities of growing up. A way of holding young persons accountable while seeking to reduce damage to their life prospects is to punish them proportionately for their crimes, but to adopt less stringent penalty levels for adolescents – as well as emphasizing the importance of familial and other social support networks.

We accept the general thrust of Zimring's argument that adolescence is a time for experimentation and the testing of limits, and that this should be reflected in the state's response to youth offending. But whereas Zimring uses it to construct an argument relating to the beneficial (or less injurious) consequences of reducing punishment levels, we need to explain why there are *proportionalist* reasons for scaling down penalties. These reasons are elaborated next.

3.4.2 'Tolerance' as grounds for scaling down punishments: The first-offender discount

In determining an offender's proportionate sentence, the primary factors are the seriousness of the criminal offence, and the degree of severity of the punishment. These dimensions, as applied to juvenile offenders, have already been addressed in this chapter. In certain contexts, however, there is an additional consideration, of what we call a partial tolerance.[21] The tolerance does not address offence seriousness but, rather, how much penal censure should attach to conduct of a given degree of seriousness. The idea of the partial tolerance is that, in certain situations, we should entertain a certain degree of sympathy for the predicament of those punished – and hence utilize more forgiving standards of blame.

Elsewhere, we have applied this notion of a partial tolerance in a different context, namely, in order to argue for a modest discount in the punishments of (adult) first offenders (see 9.6). This suggested first-offender discount in the punishments of first offenders is also not based on a claim of reduced culpability; it applies to the first offender who appears to be fully culpable – for example, to have been quite aware of the wrongfulness of his conduct. The essence of the claim is even if the first offence reflects no less culpability, the offender should be judged by less stringent standards. The partial tolerance for the first offender rests on the notion of a *lapse*. A transgression (even of penal statutes) is to be judged less stringently when it occurs against a background of prior compliance. The idea is that even an ordinarily well-behaved person can have his moral inhibitions fail in a moment of wilfulness or weakness. Such a lapse reflects a kind of human frailty for which there should be some scaling-down of the censuring response.

This tolerance is, however, a temporary one: it is granted for the first offender, diminishes for a second or third offence, and then (or soon thereafter) is lost; repeated offending no longer qualifies as a mere lapse. This temporary character is crucial, as it assures that offenders will ultimately be held fully accountable for their actions without any tolerance-based discount.

3.4.3 Should a 'tolerance' thesis be applied to juveniles?

Should a comparable perspective be carried over to punishment norms for juveniles, in order to justify generally milder punishment conventions? Not directly: the particulars of the argument would have to run differently. The notion of adolescence as a time of testing, just discussed, provides another reason for granting a partial tolerance. Why does it do so? It is not just that adolescents are more liable to overstep legal limits, but rather, that the situation in which they are placed – of being encouraged to begin making autonomous choices – prompts experimentation on their part and hence the overstepping of bounds. If young persons are supposed to 'try out' making their own decisions, notwithstanding the harmful choices that may foreseeably ensue, then there should be some sympathy for failures, and those should be judged by a less stringent standard.

A few features of this argument are worth noting. First, it is different from the claim made earlier in this chapter that juvenile offenders are less culpable. This tolerance argument is not reducible to claims, for example, about lesser understanding of consequences. It is rather that young persons, when given the opportunity of trying to live autonomously, may often make the wrong choices – including wrongs for which they know the harmful consequences, and which they could well have avoided making. Learning to make choices carries with it the risk of making *bad* choices.

Second, the tolerance should *generally* be available to youthful offenders; it should not be the kind of mitigation which is accorded to this youthful offender and denied to that one, because one attracts our sympathies more than another. Any youth, in virtue of the status of adolescence, faces the predicaments of learning to live in freedom, and all should be entitled to a degree of sympathy for transgressing the limits.

Third and critically, the tolerance is *temporary*. It should be greatest in early adolescence and gradually diminish with the approach of the age of majority. This comports with the underlying rationale – that adolescence is a time for learning to live in freedom. When adulthood is reached, the person will already have had his or her opportunity to test limits, and should be treated as an adult – that is, held fully accountable.

What does this account have to do with Zimring's thesis about youth as a time for testing? His arguments, as previously noted, are concerned with the consequences for juveniles. What was needed, in order to justify penalty reduction under a proportionalist sentencing rationale, was a retrospectively-oriented reason – and that we believe we have supplied by the tolerance argument. Our thesis is that scaling down punishments is not just a matter of avoiding undesirable consequences to juveniles in the future. Rather, it is appropriate to judge juveniles by a less stringent standard, in view of the predicaments they face when learning how to live autonomously.

While this thesis resembles the first-offender discount in its reliance on a notion of 'tolerance', its criteria for application are manifestly different. The first-offender reduction depends on prior convictions and their frequency: the idea is that the first offence may be seen as a 'lapse' warranting a discount in punishment – one that diminishes with a few repetitions and then is lost. The penalty-reduction for youths constitutes another application of the general notion of judging persons less stringently in view of certain kinds of human fallibility. But this does not rely on notions of a temporary lapse, and depends on something other than offence repetitions: namely, the youthfulness of those involved. The reduction is largest at first, and diminishes as adulthood approaches. Recidivism is not the criterion here.

Because of these differing criteria, a youthful first offender may be permitted to avail himself of both discounts. Any 14-year old, for example would, on the basis of the tolerance theory for juveniles, receive a significant penalty reduction compared to that for an adult. But, if he is a first offender, he could also receive a modest discount compared to a youthful recidivist of the same age.

3.5 What Practical Difference?

In practical terms, how would our proposed scheme differ from existing juvenile-justice systems? We cannot give a general answer, given the multifariousness of juvenile-justice schemes in various jurisdictions. Our proposed approach would have considerable similarities to the

Swedish system for juveniles, but greater dissimilarities with those of other jurisdictions.

The point of departure would be a hypothetical adult sentencing system with moderate, graded penalties. Compared with those sanctions for adults, however, penalties for juvenile offenders would significantly be scaled down for the three reasons we have discussed here: culpability, punitive 'bite', and a special 'tolerance' for juveniles. The extent of the discount would be related to age.

There would be no provision comparable to 'waiver' in US juvenile courts – whereby for various (often more serious) offences, juvenile status is withdrawn and young defendants punished at adult penalty levels.[22] Degree of crime seriousness would be, on our view, reason for deciding the comparative onerousness of penalties imposed on juveniles, but not for ignoring the reasons we have set forth in this chapter for reducing penalty levels generally for juveniles.

In the US debate, the adoption of proportionate but scaled down penalties for juveniles has often been linked with proposals for abolition of a separate juvenile court.[23] But such abolition could lead to large penalty increases for juveniles, unless the adult courts were willing to scale down the penalties they apply to young offenders. Our analysis presupposes no such linkage. What should count on this analysis are the *criteria* for dispositions of juveniles – viz., the emphasis on proportionate sanctions, and the use of scaled down penalties. This could be implemented in various ways. One possible approach would be to dispense with a separate juvenile court, and have the criminal courts of general jurisdiction process juvenile cases but apply separate (and milder) sentencing standards. This is now the case in Sweden.[24] An alternative approach would be to create or preserve a separate juvenile court, but alter its sentencing criteria in the ways that we have suggested here. Alternately, there could be hybrid approaches – such as having courts of general jurisdiction operate with special juvenile divisions. It might be argued, on the one hand, that if the basic idea of proportionality applies also to juveniles, there is no further need for a separate juvenile court. On the other hand, it may appear that juveniles need special support and assistance that can best be provided by specially-trained judicial personnel. Which of these various organizational solutions is preferable may vary also among different jurisdictions, depending on their particular judicial traditions. It is important not to conflate the issues of rationale and dispositional criteria with those of judicial organization.

This chapter has, deliberately, tried to sketch an ideal scheme, designed to reflect how a desert rationale should deal with juveniles. In many jurisdictions at present, it will be difficult to achieve either the degree of emphasis on proportionality or the reduced levels of punishment that we have here proposed. But our aim here has been to specify why a desert-oriented approach should adopt different (and milder) penalty standards for juveniles. We are speaking of the direction of desired change.

Notes

1. Jareborg 1995, 110.
2. Lockyer and Stone 1998.
3. For a description of the English system, see Bottoms and Dignan 2004.
4. Zimring 1982; Zimring 1998a; Zimring 1998b.
5. See, particularly, Feld 1999, ch. 8.
6. Such a general approach, of proportionate sanctions but with age-related reductions in sentence levels, is also recommended in Feld 1999, ch. 8.
7. Ball, McCormac and Stone 1995, 115; see also, Feld 1999, 306–12; Zimring 1999, 487.
8. For a specification of the elements of the offence of burglary, see eg, American Law Institute 1962, *Model Penal Code*, sec. 221.1(1).
9. von Hirsch and Jareborg 1991, 27.
10. Husak and von Hirsch 1993, 163–65.
11. For discussion of psychological studies regarding reduced comprehension, see Feld 1999, 306–14.
12. Feld (1998, 248) points out that, '[d]evelopmental psychology does not possess reliable indicators of moral development that equate readily with criminal . . . accountability'.
13. Gradations of response based on age are also suggested in Feld 1999: 315–20.
14. Feld 1999, 309–313; see also Zimring 1998, 77–81; Zimring 1999, 487–490.
15. Ball, McCormac and Stone 1995, 116; Zedner 1998, 173.
16. See von Hirsch 2000, 79.
17. Zimring 1982, ch. 5.
18. Zimring 1982, 91.
19. Zimring 1982, 91.
20. See, eg, von Hirsch and Ashworth 1998, chs. 1–3; von Hirsch, Bottoms, Burney *et al.* 1999.
21. See 9.6.
22. In various American states, juveniles whose cases have been 'waived' to the adult court may face very severe punishments. Indeed, juveniles as young as 13 years of age have been sentenced to life imprisonment without parole (see Logan 1998).
23. See Feld 1999.
24. See Jareborg 1995, 110.

4

Extending Sentences for Dangerous Offenders?: The Bottoms–Brownsword Model

4.1 Introduction

We shall in this chapter consider whether, in a criminal sentencing system emphasizing proportionality of sentence, there should be exceptional authority to extend the sentence for especially dangerous offenders – beyond the terms commensurate with their offences. Among European countries that have adopted proportionality-oriented sentencing schemes, there is a divergence of approach on this question. Finland provides such authority to extend sentences[a] (and England did so during the last decade).[b] Sweden, however, has not adopted comparable provisions.[1]

Rather than exploring the details of such laws, we will address the issue of principle: whether a case can be made for exceptional sentence-extensions on grounds of dangerousness. For that purpose, we shall examine a model [hereafter 'B-B model'] proposed by Anthony Bottoms and Roger Brownsword.[2] These authors assume, as we do, that desert principles ordinarily should govern sentencing decisions; extending sentences for dangerous offenders would constitute a narrowly-drawn exception to this general rule of proportionate sanctions.[3] According to the B-B scheme, it would only be those convicted offenders presenting a 'vivid danger' to others who should be given a period of confinement in excess of what they deserve in virtue of the gravity of their offences.[4] We select Bottoms and Brownsword's account because these authors offer normative arguments for their proposals that are important to consider.

[a] Lappi-Seppälä 2001. The repeal of this provision is now under consideration, however.

[b] England's proportionality-oriented Criminal Justice Act 1991 provided limited authority to impose extended sentences for especially dangerous offenders; see von Hirsch and Ashworth 1996. In 2003, however, the basic provisions of the 1991 Act were replaced (see 6.2.2). The present English sentencing statute not only lists a variety of sentencing purposes, but also contains broadened authority to impose sentence extensions for high risk offenders; see Criminal Justice Act 2003, ss. 222–229; von Hirsch and Roberts 2004.

4.2 The Rationale for the B-B Model: How Convincing is it?

To provide a justification for their proposed scheme, Bottoms and Brownsword invoke Ronald Dworkin's model of rights.[5] Dworkin maintains that rights (and for present purposes, fairness constraints will be treated as rights) constitute claims against the general welfare: the right should be respected, that is, even if disregarding it would provide greater net social benefits. An example of such a fairness constraint is the requirement of proof beyond reasonable doubt in criminal trials. This is designed to avoid the injustice of convicting innocent people – and hence should apply even if a lower standard-of-proof were to provide greater aggregate crime-preventive yields, by making it easier to convict actually guilty (and still possibly criminally-inclined) persons. The principle of proportionality likewise is a fairness requirement, as such, it should be observed even at some possible sacrifice of crime-preventive effectiveness (see more fully, 9.3.3).

4.2.1 Dworkin's two grounds for derogations from fairness: which ground might be applicable?

Fairness claims, on Dworkin's analysis, are prima facie claims: they may be overridden in exceptional cases, when the countervailing concerns are of sufficient urgency.[6] He suggests two such overriding grounds. One ground is where a competing right is involved (eg, when individuals' right to privacy collides with other persons' entitlement as citizens to have access to official information). The other overriding ground is where the loss of social utility involved in maintaining the fairness constraint would be of extraordinary dimensions: when, in Dworkin's words, 'the cost to society would not simply be incremental, but would be of a degree beyond the [social] cost paid to grant the original right, a degree great enough to justify whatever assault on dignity or equality might be involved'.[7]

Of Dworkin's two possible grounds for departing from fairness requirements, Bottoms and Brownsword opt for the first (that of conflict of rights) as the purported basis for their model. The defendant's entitlement to a proportionate sentence is defeated, they assert, by the potential victim's competing 'right' not to be seriously injured by the exceptionally dangerous offender.[8] But is this correct? Granted, the prospective victim has a right vis-à-vis the prospective attacker, that the latter not infringe his personal security. But it would have strange implications to transform that claim into a victim's right *against the state*: namely, that the state provide potential victims with a rights-based guarantee of protection from criminal harm, that is capable of overriding other persons' entitlement not to be treated unfairly at the state's hands.

In this connection, it is crucial to bear in mind the question of agent responsibility: against whom is the right held, and who would directly and primarily be responsible were the victim's entitlement to personal safety infringed?[9] When the state would have to act to infringe upon one person's rights in order to protect the rights of another person, that is the true situation of conflict-of-rights of which Dworkin is speaking. But when what is being compared is an action by the *state* (in the present instance, imposing a disproportionate sentence) and an action by a *private individual* (that individual's injuring another person), this is not a situation involving conflict of rights.

When the state infringes the rights of a person, that is a wrong for which it is directly responsible. The state thus would bear the moral onus for treating a convicted offender unfairly, if it imposes a disproportionately long sentence. If, however, the offender is not given an extended sentence – and he decides to commit an offence after expiration of his normal, proportionate sentence – the wrong thus committed is one which the *offender* (and not the state) bears primary moral responsibility. Granted, the state has the duty to take reasonable steps to prevent crime. But that duty is subject to moral constraints on how the state may carry out this crime-prevention role, and unfair treatment of convicted offenders would violate such constraints.

To view the state's law-enforcement duties as 'rights' which victims hold against the state – which then may be 'balanced' against the offender's moral entitlement not to be treated unfairly – would reduce the entire analysis into a form of cost-benefit reckoning. An offender's entitlement to fair treatment then could readily be 'trumped' by crime-prevention concerns, because these now could be redenominated as purported 'rights' of potential victims. It could be argued, for example, that the proof-beyond-reasonable-doubt standard in criminal trials be diluted – because this might promote victims' 'right' not to victimized by actually guilty individuals who could be acquitted under the higher standard and might go out to commit further crimes. It ought not be permissible to legitimize such a diminution of important requirements of fairness so easily.

4.2.2 Shifting to Dworkin's second ground for derogation?

Might there be an alternative basis for the B-B model? Let us consider, for this purpose, Dworkin's second ground for derogation. This permits a requirement of fairness to be overridden, when harmful consequences of an extraordinary character otherwise would occur. This is not an issue of conflict of rights. It addresses, rather, situations where abiding by a fairness constraint (here, proportionality of sentence) might involve evil consquences of such exceptional magnitude as to warrant deviating from that constraint. We might, arguably, insist on observing proportionality requirements ordinarily, while allowing a longer-than-proportionate sentence where the case involves one of exceptionally grave injury.[10] When this is done, however, the derogation from justice involved would also need to be recognized explicitly.

What difference might this shift of rationale make? Invoking Dworkin's second argument would create a considerably higher threshold, before derogations from proportionality would become permissible. One would no longer have a rights-based reason for derogation. Instead, one would have to recognize that imposing a more-severe-than-deserved sentence would be an infringement of fairness requirements, that could no longer be supported on grounds of defending ulterior rights. It would then have to be shown that *extraordinary* losses of utility are at issue – a burden that is not easily met.

Having such a higher threshold would, we think, be a positive advantage. It would help ensure that the exception be invoked only narrowly. Bottoms and Brownsword wish to avoid wide invocation, which is why they impose their strict standard for 'vivid danger'.[11] But it is at least arguable that on Dworkin's first ('conflict-of-rights') ground, derogations could be invoked rather extensively – namely, whenever crime-prevention interests become sufficient in aggregate to 'outweigh' offenders' interests in being punished proportionately. However, on Dworkin's second ground, with its higher threshold for deviating from fairness requirements, the case for longer-than-proportionate sentences would become more difficult to sustain.[c]

4.2.3 Problems with relying on Dworkin's second ground

This alternative rationale, however, generates its own problems. Dworkin's second ground applies most readily to situations where there is a derogation from rights done in order to avert catastrophic consequences. A prime example would be the quarantine of persons infected with deadly

[c] This point should become apparent from the following illustration. Suppose that we are dealing with young, criminally-active offenders – having an apparent propensity to commit less serious crimes of violence (say, routine assaults) quite frequently. Suppose also that a significant (but not very long) stint of extra confinement could incapacitate such offenders from committing a considerable number of such crimes. On the conflict-of-rights theory, it might be argued that prospective victims have a 'right' not to be assaulted, which should be balanced against such offenders' right to no-more-than proportionate punishments. True, the prospective victim's rights are not of so high a priority here as would be the 'right' not to suffer potentially lethal violence. But the offender's fairness-claim is also less strongly infringed than by long-term confinement – because the extension of his prison term (while substantial) would be shorter than that for offenders meeting Bottoms and Brownsword's standard of 'vivid danger'. Thus when the two 'rights' are balanced aganist one another, the extension of confinement might become permissible. With this argument, however, Bottoms and Brownsword's 'vivid danger'

pandemic diseases. Quarantined persons do not deserve to lose their liberty, for it is not their fault that they are disease carriers. They are deprived of their freedom in order to protect against widespread and deadly infection. The reason for allowing quarantine is that the prevention of mass mortality is deemed paramount to concerns about justice.

Such an approach, based on Dworkin's second ground for derogation, seems plausible in the case of quarantine, because of several features. The potential harm is of extraordinary magnitude, not only in the seriousness of the possible consequences in the individual case, but also in the pervasiveness of the harm: pandemic diseases such as typhoid cause widespread mortality. The risk is immediate: members of the public will begin to be infected at present, unless prompt steps are taken to isolate carriers of the disease. Quarantine also does not involve blaming: the confined disease-carrier is not treated as though he were a wrongdoer.

These special features are no longer present, in the case of extending sentences for dangerous offenders. The risk is long-postponed and contingent: it would materialize only much later, after the offender's deserved term of sentence for his current offence has expired, and if he still remains dangerous (see further below). Such a measure has strongly condemnatory connotations, moreover: by having to serve a substantially extended prison sentence on account of his supposed future dangerousness, he is being implicitly visited with more censure. Whereas we do not treat the quarantined disease carrier as being reprehensible, we would be treating the offender who is given a lengthy sentence extension as substantially more blameworthy than someone who has committed similarly serious crimes but is not deemed dangerous.[d] In sum, Bottoms and Brownsword's extended-sentence scheme might possibly be analysed as an application of Dworkin's second ground for derogation; but there remain significant difficulties with such an extension of his theory.

test would be lost. On Dworkin's second ground, however, the case for longer-than proportionate sentences would become much harder to sustain. Failing to prevent middle-level criminal assaults would simply not be a loss of utility of sufficient magnitude to meet Dworkin's second test.

[d] A conceivable alternative could be that of treating the period of preventive confinement after the completion of the deserved sentence as something other than punishment. Para. 66 of the German Penal Code takes this approach: a convicted offender who is deemed dangerous may, after completion of the sentence for his offence, receive 'Sicherungsverwahrung': a period of confinement in a special institution, which is not supposed to be part of his sentence, but rather a kind of 'civil' restraint. This approach, however, would involve the drawback of losing the basis for an important limiting principle. Paul Robinson has suggested that more-than-proportionate sentences should be subjected to the outer constraint that the extra quantum of punishment should not be 'intolerably unjust'; Robinson 1987, 38. If the extra preventive term is deemed part of the punishment, it would be possible to provide a rationale for Robinson's suggested limit: the additional penal censure conveyed by the extra incarceration must not become wholly out of keeping with the blameworthiness of the offence; see von Hirsch 1993, 50. But if the extra time is deemed to be 'civil' and not punishment at all, then it will be more difficult to provide any kind of principled limit.

4.3 Degree of Risk and Gravity of Conviction Offence

In order to justify extending sentences for supposedly dangerous offenders, a number of further issues need to be addressed. These concern: (1) the potential harmfulness of the predicted future conduct; (2) the required degree of likelihood of the predicted harm's occurring; and (3) the degree of seriousness of the offender's offence of conviction. Let us consider these issues, successively, in terms of how they might be dealt with under the revised B-B model.

4.3.1 Degree of gravity of the predicted conduct

To make a case for extending the sentence, it is essential that the predicted conduct be of a very serious nature; unless it is, the whole logic of the scheme would be undermined. Under Dworkin's second ground for derogation, the reason for overriding the relevant fairness constraint (namely, proportionality) is the prevention of *grievous* harm. This should, at least, mean harm constituting a serious threat to affected persons' vital interests. The scheme should be limited to situations of the gravest injury: where the risk is of potentially lethal or very serious violence.

4.3.2 The degree of likelihood of the predicted conduct

How likely need it be that the offender might act violently? Bottoms and Brownsword speak of 'certainty', by which they mean that there must be a substantial risk of the predicted harm's occurring.[12] This requirement seems appropriate, in our view. If, under Dworkin's second ground, the rationale for intervention is the prevention of grievous harm, the consequences need not only be serious were they to occur, but there must be a significant likelihood of occurrence.

4.3.3 The seriousness of the conviction offence

Bottoms and Brownsword require that the offender's crime of conviction also be of a serious nature, in order to trigger a possible sentence extension on grounds of dangerousness. Specifically, they require that the conviction offence involve 'very serious violence', actual or threatened.[13] This makes intuitive sense – as a way of restricting the scope of the scheme. But what supporting reasons can be given?

Bottoms and Brownsword put forward an empirical reason: that ordinarily, the best predictor of future violent behaviour is past violent conduct. Dangerous persons tend to be those who have already shown that they are dangerous, by having committed offences of serious violence.[14] The force of this argument, however, would depend on the state of empirical knowledge: it would no longer be sustainable were future research to discover that conviction for lesser forms of assault could presage serious violent offending – provided that, say, it was accompanied by a record of earlier acts of serious violence, or by very frequent earlier assaults of certain kinds.

What other principled arguments might there be for requiring a serious conviction offence? An argument would be that the requirement of a serious conviction offence acts as a failsafe. It provides the assurance that, if someone were to transgress the criminal laws, he exposes himself to the risk of a lengthy extension of his criminal sentence only if he chooses to commit a grave act of violence – of the sort that even ordinary criminals might well be reluctant to commit. Given the uncertainties of predicting dangerousness, and the intrusiveness of the preventive measures involved, setting such a high threshold would constitute an important safeguard. It would mean, for example, that the offender need not fear such a sentence extension if he merely commits commonplace crimes, even routine assaults.

A second argument relates to proportionality. Even if a derogation from ordinary desert requirements is permissible for especially dangerous offenders, there ought still to be constraints – of the kind Paul Robinson has suggested[e] – against *gross* disproportionality of sentence. Bottoms and Brownsword's scheme may involve lengthy terms of extra confinement for those classified as dangerous. The less serious the conviction offence is (and hence the shorter the deserved term of punishment would be), the more blatantly disproportionate would such term extensions be.[f]

4.3.4 Implementation issues

Were the B-B scheme enacted into law, the foregoing three issues would need to be addressed in the implementation statute. The statute would need, for example, to address the degree of seriousness of the conviction

[e] See note d above.

[f] This point may be illustrated as follows. Suppose the offender has been convicted of a serious offence, warranting a prison term of 10 years. Suppose that it is predicted that he may remain dangerous for a 15-year period in all. The result might be, under the B-B scheme, that a five-year sentence extension might be imposed – an increase of 50 per cent. But suppose, instead, that the offender's latest crime was considerably less serious (say a simple assault), and he is being classified as dangerous because of his earlier pattern of assaultive behaviour. In that event, in view of the less serious nature of his conviction offence, his deserved term of punishment for that offence might be rather modest – say, only one year. Then, holding him for the 15 years he is estimated to remain dangerous would mean *14* extra years of preventive confinement – a huge (and manifestly disproportionate) relative increase.

offence. Merely requiring that the conviction offence constitute 'very serious' violence would be insufficiently precise, and could invite expansion of the ambit of coverage by the courts. Perhaps, it might be specified that the offence of conviction involved the actual attempted infliction of death or grave physical injury, or something to that effect; but the standard needs to be formulated with care.[g]

In resolving these questions, previously enacted schemes for extending sentences of ostensibly dangerous offenders might be examined. There have been, over the years, a variety of such schemes. In the United States, the National Council on Crime and Delinquency put forward such a proposal as early as 1963, in its 'Model Sentencing Act'.[15] England's desert-based Criminal Justice Act 1991 contained a special provision on dangerous offenders.[16] These norms vary in their drafting quality, and some involve underlying assumptions that differ from the B-B model's assumption – of a general desert rationale, with exceptional authority to extend sentence to the specially dangerous. Nevertheless, the statutory formulations might provide at least some helpful clues.

A further issue is that of procedural requirements. At a minimum, in the interests of fair procedure, there should be a separate judicial hearing before the defendant's sentence is extended; there should also be periodic judicial reviews thereafter. But what more should be needed? A judge's legal training provides him with no special skills in forecasting dangerousness, and an untrained person may be tempted to rely simply on the fact of the offender's having been convicted of a violent crime, without making sufficient further inquiry into his present condition.[h] It might be helpful to require the submission of a psychiatrist's report.[17] However, psychiatrists' opinions are likely to be useful mainly in situations where the offender's supposed dangerousness is linked with psychiatric problems – whereas the B-B scheme relates to dangerousness generally. It would be worth exploring alternative methods of providing the court with a degree of empirical confirmation for its forecasts of dangerousness. We shall not examine such issues of implementation further, however, because our main interest is the penal-theory issue: the pros and cons of extending sentences at all for supposedly dangerous offenders.

[g] Similarly, the statute should specify how serious, and how likely, the predicted conduct would need to be, in order for the offender to qualify as dangerous. Given the limitations of our predictive capacities, it would not be possible to specify a precise degree of likelihood, or to specify what legal categories the prospective violence must involve. An appropriate formulation would be needed, however, that makes it clear that only a significant risk of aggravated violence should be considered.

[h] While, as we have noted, prior acts of violence constitute the principal basis for predictions of dangerousness, other features of the offender's present condition need to be considered – for example, the presence of 'protective factors' in his current situation or environment that might reduce his propensity for violence.

4.4 Reliability of the Prediction of Dangerousness

The B-B scheme, resting as it does on predictions of violence, cannot be justified unless available forecasting methods offer a tolerably reliable way of making such predictions. How good are these forecasting methods?

Forecasting dangerousness has traditionally been undertaken primarily in the context of forensic psychiatry, where the task was to predict whether a mentally disabled offender was sufficiently at risk of engaging in violence to warrant his civil commitment. Two aspects of these psychiatric cases, however, somewhat facilitated that task. First, the risks were associated with certain psychiatric conditions which forensic psychiatrists were trained to evaluate. Second, the risks had some immediacy: the period of time in question (that is, the period of the person's detention) would commence quite soon – because ordinarily, the person could not first be given a prison sentence, in view of his mental disability. Predictions of dangerousness are, as just noted, based mainly on the individual's actual previous conduct, and tend to be more reliable in the shorter term after that conduct occurs.

Predicting dangerousness in the context of the B-B scheme would be considerably more problematic, because these two factors are absent. First, the B-B scheme extends beyond psychiatric cases to dangerous persons generally. Once one leaves the psychiatric realm, however, it becomes harder to identify the various reasons or conditions that might incline an individual to future violence. Second and more importantly, the period during which the prediction operates is much postponed: the offender must, in order to qualify under the B-B scheme, have committed a very serious offence (see above) – and hence would have to serve a lengthy deserved prison term before his stint of preventive confinement begins.[i] By then, the offender's previous acts of violence – on which the prediction must in large part rely – would have been long past.[j] Given the uncertainties about the duration of offenders' residual criminal careers and the tendency of offenders to be less criminally active as they get older, it would be hard to have much confidence in forecasts that relate to such a long-postponed period.

[i] This problem cannot be dealt with by having the term-extension for dangerousness served *before* the proportionate sentence. This is because the whole point of the B-B scheme is to prolong the sentence only where the proportionate term would not be long enough to restrain the defendant's continuing violent inclinations. (For further discussion of a proportionate sentence's also serving preventive functions, see 9.7.)

[j] Of course, the prison authorities may continue to monitor whether the offender engages in further violent behaviour during his initial, proportionate term of confinement. However, the presence or absence of violent behaviour within an institution tends to be a less useful predictor of subsequent violent behaviour after release.

In recent years, there has been further research on violence risk prediction. Has enough progress been made? Some answers to this question are suggested in a recent survey and analysis of violence risk management, by John Monahan.[18] His discussion suggests that there has been some success in making statistical forecasts of dangerousness. However, the prediction instruments he cites are designed for psychiatric cases primarily, in which the question is the offender's *present* propensity for violence. It would be more difficult to make reliable forecasts of dangerousness in the context of the B-B scheme, where that prediction concerns risks of violence at a long-postponed time, after conclusion of the deserved sentence. Indeed, few prediction studies of dangerousness utilize lengthy follow-up periods at all.[k]

4.5 Risks of Erosion of the Standard

In any sentencing statute there is always the risk that its safeguards become eroded under political pressures. However, such a risk is particularly great in the case of the B-B scheme.

A reason for this vulnerability to erosion concerns the problems of 'false negatives'. Any scheme for predicting violence – besides wrongly identifying as risks a significant number of persons who would not have offended (the false positives) – will also do the opposite. It will fail to identify a significant number of persons who subsequently *do* commit violence (the false negatives). When such persons are released and violence then ensues, this may well attract public protest. The decision-maker will face strong criticism that he could have classified such persons as dangerous and held them in prison for longer, and has acted irresponsibly in failing to do so. This will put judges under pressure to act overcautiously: to err in favour of finding any eligible defendant dangerous and extending his sentence.

There will, furthermore, be pressure on legislatures to expand the ambit of the preventive-confinement legislation. Under the scheme discussed above, the eligibility criteria would be narrowly drawn – for example, the crime of conviction would need to involve serious violence (see 4.3.3 above). Cases will arise, however, where a defendant would not qualify for the scheme because his conviction crime is not serious enough, but he

[k] Monahan (2004b) calls attention to the three principal recent statistical prediction studies of violence. All three use data drawn from samples of patients in civil psychiatric hospitals. The most sophisticated of these, the MacArthur Study, utilizes only a 20-week follow-up period after release from the facility. A second, the HCR-20, uses a two-year follow-up. Only the third, Canada's Violence Risk Appraisal Guide, utilizes somewhat longer periods. However, none of these prediction instruments is designed to make forecasts of violence at a long-postponed time.

goes on to commit acts of violence anyway after being released at the end of his proportionate sentence. Public outcry at such results will generate powerful incentives for the legislature to widen the eligibility criteria, and thus include a larger number of cases within the scheme's ambit. Such dilutions, however, will defeat the whole point of the B-B scheme, which is to make sentence extensions truly the exception.

4.6 Conclusions

Our analysis has suggested that it is possible to develop a case for Bottoms and Brownsword's scheme of extending the sentences of especially dangerous offenders, on the basis of Ronald Dworkin's rights theory (albeit a different branch of that theory than they rely upon). Doing so, however, involves stretching Dworkin's theory well beyond its most plausible ambit of application. It may also be possible to develop certain legal safeguards governing the predictions of dangerousness involved. Unsolved, however, remains the difficulty of making predictions of dangerousness that must operate during a long-postponed period, after the completion of the deserved sentence for the past violent crime. Unsolved, also, is the vulnerability of the B-B scheme's narrow criteria of application to erosion toward a wider and less defensible scope of use. Our sense is that Sweden acted wisely when, in devising their proportionality-based sentencing system, they decided not to adopt such a scheme of extra confinement for the dangerous.

Notes

1. Jareborg 1995.
2. Bottoms and Brownsword 1983; see also, Bottoms and Brownsword 1982.
3. For a general discussion of the issue of limited deviations from proportionality under a proportionalist sentencing model, see Robinson 1987, von Hirsch 1998, ch. 6.
4. Bottoms and Brownsword 1983, 17–21.
5. Dworkin 1977, ch. 7.
6. Dworkin 1977, 200.
7. Ibid.
8. Bottoms and Brownsword 1983, 16.
9. See more fully on this question of agency, Williams 1973.
10. See also, von Hirsch 1993, 51n.
11. Bottoms and Brownsword 1983, 17.
12. Bottoms and Brownsword 1983, 19–20.
13. Bottoms and Brownsword 1983, 20.
14. Ibid. If prior violent conduct is thus required, the safest way of determining that it has occurred is through a conviction, with its high standards of proof.

15. See National Council on Crime and Delinquency, 'Model Sentencing Act' ss. 5, 9, *Crime and Delinquency* 18: 335, quoted in part in von Hirsch and Ashworth 1998, 96–97.
16. Criminal Justice Act 1991, s. 2(2)(b).
17. This procedure was recommended in von Hirsch and Ashworth 1996, 178–79.
18. Monahan 2004a.

5

Proportionate Punishment and Social Deprivation

5.1 Introduction

We consider in this chapter the disposition of convicted offenders who live under circumstances of significant social deprivation. Our focus will be on those deprived persons who are not suffering from life-threatening want: they are, we are assuming, neither starving nor homeless. However, they live in substandard accommodation in deteriorated neighbourhoods; have limited and irregular incomes, poor or non-existent employment prospects, and often, weak networks of social and personal support. These persons, in other words, find themselves at the bottom of the social scale, and may have little participation in the society's ordinary working and living routines.[a] The crimes they commit are, however, not exclusively those designed to alleviate immediate want; rather, they include acquisitive crimes, involving thefts of consumer items such as cars or TVs; or expressive offences such as those involved in crimes of vandalism or assault.

How offenders of this kind should be sentenced will depend, in large part, on the sentencing rationale that is assumed to govern. We postulate, for purposes of this discussion, a desert rationale for sentencing, according to which the severity of punishments should be fairly proportionate to the seriousness of criminal offences. Such a theory at least does not *add* to the punishment imposed on deprived persons – whereas penal consequentialism may do so, to the extent that social deprivation is a sign (say) of greater likelihood of reoffending.[1] The question remains, however, whether and to what extent such persons should have their punishments *reduced*. This issue, of deserved punishment and social deprivation, is one that long has puzzled us. One of us made previous attempts to address it, once in a 1976 volume and once in 1993,[2] but we have come to view these efforts as insufficient. We make this further attempt to wrestle with this issue, with some trepidation.

[a] We are speaking here of social deprivation among persons living in countries which otherwise generally have the living standards prevailing in developed Western nations.

5.2 Reduced Culpability?

The argument for mitigation that most readily comes to mind, and which has been discussed in recent writings on the subject,[3] concerns the offender's *culpability*. Under the principle of proportionality, an offender's sentence should be reduced if the circumstances render the offence less serious, with seriousness being a matter of the conduct's degree of harmfulness and of the offender's culpability. Criminal offences become no less harmful by virtue of the fact that their perpetrators are socially deprived. But might offenders' culpability possibly be reduced, in virtue of the greater obstacles such persons face in leading law-abiding lives?

A conceivable basis for claiming reduced culpability would concern diminished capacity. The offender is deemed less responsible for his actions if his capacity to comply with the law is impaired – because, for example, of significant mental disability.[4] Ordinarily, however, it does not seem plausible to ascribe impaired volitional capacity to socially deprived defendants; and it may not be desirable to do so, since those who are treated as volitionally impaired may become subject to more onerous 'civil' restraints on liberty.

Another ground for ascribing reduced culpability relates, not to diminished volitional capacity, but to the offender's having reasons for acting that render him less than ordinarily blameworthy. The classic reason of this kind relates to excusing necessity. A person should be entirely (or partially) excused if he commits an offence against someone in order to protect vital interests of his own – for example, in order to forestall his own death or serious bodily injury through natural circumstance or at the hands of a third party.[b] We wish to withhold or mitigate blame from the person because we recognize the importance, from his perspective, of safeguarding his own vital interests. We might thus speak of not demanding saintliness from him, because saintliness consists precisely in an heroic willingness to sacrifice one's own vital interests to safeguard those of others. While admiring such willingness, we do not think that the state should impose penal censure on someone for not showing it.[5]

The difficulty is, however, that we are not dealing here with such life-threatening situations. The person who steals food because he is seriously malnourished, or unlawfully occupies an empty flat because he has no home of his own, may have an arguable (albeit still debatable)[c] ground for

[b] See German Penal Code, s. 35, which excuses criminal acts done in order to ward off an immediate and otherwise unavoidable danger to life, personal safety, or freedom. This ground becomes a mitigating circumstance, rather than a full excuse, if the actor was in part responsible for bringing the danger about.

[c] Such a claim of exoneration on ground of excusing necessity (or, in English legal parlance, duress of circumstances) could not be sustained under existing criminal law doctrines because of the requirement that the threat to the person be *imminent* and *unavoidable*. The imminence

making such a necessity-based claim. But the deprived offenders of whom we are here speaking tend not to be in quite such desperate straits, and their crimes are not of this need-alleviating kind. The young man from a bad neighbourhood who absconds with a car, or assaults a rival, would not be acting out of urgent need.

Might the grounds for culpability-reduction be expanded beyond these cases of necessity or partial necessity, in order to cover other cases where, in HLA Hart's words, 'conformity . . . was a matter of special difficulty for [the offender] as compared with . . . persons normally placed'?[6] Expanding the criteria for reduced culpability so as to cover socially deprived offenders would involve inclusion of situations where compliance would not necessarily have required the offender to forego fundamental interests of his own; but where the incentives for offending may nevertheless be substantially greater than usual. Here, compliance might be considered more than normally onerous, although it would no longer be heroic. The argument would be that, when social context is taken into account, such deprived persons do not have the same practical opportunities of choosing obedience to law as normally-situated persons, and that hence they should be deemed less blameworthy.[7]

Excuses, John Gardner has suggested,[8] involve (except in cases involving diminished capacity) situations where the offender is in a position to supply a moral reason of some kind for his actions. When the offender asserts excusing or partially excusing necessity, for example, he can advance such a ground: namely, that through his actions he was seeking to protect a resource of his own over which he has a valid claim; indeed, a resource of such importance (say, his life, health or safety) as to make it understandable in the circumstances for him to act to try to protect it. This constitutes legitimate prima facie reason for acting, even if in the circumstances it would not suffice to justify the conduct – which is why we merely excuse it. What is essential on Gardner's account, however, is that a person of reasonable self-discipline would have great difficulty in desisting in the circumstances. If the offender seriously injures someone to protect his own life from attack by a third person, it would take extraordinary fortitude to desist – which is why we are reluctant to impose penal censure on him for his act. But if he offends to protect some lesser interest of his – say, if he kills to protect an ordinary property interest – the

requirement is that the threatened harm is likely to materialize in the very near future; the unavoidability requirement concerns the lack of viable alternatives – no other (permissible) means exist to avoid the threat; see Simester and Sullivan 2004, 593–94. Classic instances of excusing necessity concern emergency situations, where these requirements are readily met. Here, however, they would not be: the undernourished offender who steals food may not be facing imminent starvation, and some alternative legal means might exist (for example, through state welfare provision) to obtain nourishment. Thus to cover the situations of socially deprived offenders who engage in need-alleviating offences, these requirements of imminence and unavoidability would need to be watered down.

claim of reduced culpability has less force, because he has failed to show as much fortitude as should be expected of him. He may have increased incentives to steal the car, or fewer disincentives to desist from doing so; but in taking the car, he is not, for example, protecting any resources of his own that are of fundamental importance.

Could the reduced-culpability thesis be sustained, then, by expanding the admissible reasons that might excuse or partially excuse the defendant's action? In the car-theft case, for example, might it be argued that the deprived individual has a legitimate interest in maintaining a standard of living beyond mere subsistence – in sharing in some of the benefits of modern life that ordinary citizens take for granted. Indeed, he may have such an interest. But in stealing the car, he is acting at the expense of someone else's rights. The problem is showing why his interest is of such importance as would require a special degree of moral fortitude for desistance. The necessity-based claim of reduced culpability becomes progressively less plausible, as the defendant's supposed interests, on the basis of which he acts, become of less central importance to his own existence.

A second problem is that culpability-reduction, on this perspective, would depend critically on the defendant's motives in committing the criminal misconduct: namely, whether and to what extent the conduct was designed to promote a supposed interest of his. Conceivably, it might be asserted (although we disagree, as just noted) that the car theft is less culpable, because the conduct promotes the defendant's interest in having a less substandard quality of life. But what of more purely expressive offences, such as vandalizing another's car, or smashing a neighbour's windows as a result of an argument? Here, the conduct does not seem to have much to do with serving the defendant's interests in better life-quality at all. The culpability-reduction thesis, in other words, does not seem to supply a general basis for reducing the punishments of deprived offenders.

5.3 Social Deprivation as a 'Compassion-Based' Mitigating Factor?

If the reduced-culpability argument is not sustainable, should that be the end of the matter? We have a sense that an accommodation should be made for deprived offenders when they face sentence. It ought therefore to be possible to formulate some kind of alternative reason why. We shall sketch such an alternative ground: one that rests sentence-reduction not on diminished culpability, but on notions of compassion. We will set forth the argument first, and then examine what some of its problems might be.

We might begin by referring to an illuminating provision of the Swedish sentencing statute.[9] That statute adopts a proportionalist perspective for sentencing, according to which the 'penal value' (seriousness) of the crime is made the principal criterion for deciding the severity of the sentence. It also lists a variety of mitigating and aggravating factors that affect the crime's seriousness in particular circumstances. The Swedish law, however, has an additional feature; it enumerates several factors – termed 'equity factors' – which are expressly said *not* to reduce the crime's penal value, but which nevertheless qualify as mitigating. Examples are the advanced age or bad health of the offender, or the lapse of an unusually long time since commission of the crime. What seems to be involved in such cases is a notion of compassion. These are cases where the crime's seriousness has not been affected, but where nevertheless there appears to be special grounds for sympathy for the defendant's predicament (see more fully, Appendix 1).

The Swedish statute does not list social deprivation as one of its factors. But our question is: might similar concerns relating to compassion – to justified sympathy for a defendant's predicament – warrant treating the socially deprived defendant less severely? The attraction of applying this kind of approach to the situation of deprived offenders is that it seems to fit more naturally with the way we ordinarily might think of such cases. The difficulty with the 'reduced-culpability' approach, we saw, is that it is far from clear that the actor acts less culpably in situations where his incentives for offending may admittedly be stronger, but where he would sacrifice no vitally important interests of his own by choosing to comply. Nevertheless, we might well think that we ought to feel more sympathy for this kind of offender: that because bad social conditions have rendered his situation more than normally difficult, this could supply a possible reason for extending a special degree of compassion.

Why, then, might there be special grounds for sympathy? There appear to be two kinds of reasons. One relates to the character of the deprived offender's diminished incentives for compliance. The other relates to a judgement that these diminished incentives reflect a *societal* failure: that no one ought to be faced with a situation where his social environment provides such poor support for ordinary law-abidingness. Let us consider each of these two reasons more fully.

5.3.1 Reduced stakes in compliance

The deprived offender, of the kind of whom we are speaking, would (as noted already) not be sacrificing his own vital interests by complying. Nevertheless, the social environment reduces the social stakes he has in abiding by the law. The ordinary person, confronted with a legal prohibition against theft or violence, is provided with normative reasons for desistance: the censure of the conduct conveyed through the penal prohibition carries with it a message that the conduct is wrongful. The law provides also a complementary prudential disincentive – namely, the disincentive provided through the threatened 'hard treatment' of violators (see Chapter 2). These direct normative imperatives and prudential disincentives, moreover, are ordinarily supplemented by important social supporting factors that, together, create significant 'stakes' in compliance. These supporting factors are of three kinds. First, there are collateral social incentives for compliance. The social environment ordinarily furnishes preferable alternative methods of acquisition and self-expression than those provided through criminal activities: if one wishes to get a fine car and acquire status, why not earn the requisite money, or engage in other activities that enhance one's social standing? The second are collateral social disincentives against violation: committing crimes and getting caught (or even being suspected of engaging in this kind of behaviour) carries with it the risk of getting a bad reputation – which can significantly damage one's standing and prospects. The third are the social standards themselves: the criminal law's norms regarding honesty and non-violence are backed by comparable informal norms in the broader social environment. (This third factor is not strictly speaking a 'stake', but it does constitute an inducement to compliance.) Through these three kinds of inducements, the ordinary person is given to understand that compliant behaviour is considered socially more acceptable, and may offer a better way of achieving his goals.

What is different, then, about a severely deprived social environment? It is that it tends to undermine or weaken these three kinds of 'stakes'. First, the social incentives to compliance are reduced: there may no longer be better lawful ways of achieving many aspirations. The young resident of a deteriorated neighbourhood who wishes to have a good car of his own will seldom be in a position to earn the money for it rather than stealing it, because his ability to get well-paying employment is so restricted. Secondly, the disincentives for violations are weakened: being convicted (and even going to jail) may no longer so clearly interfere with his social standing and prospects because these may well remain substandard anyway, and because being punished may be so commonplace among young men in his community. Finally, the local mores may be less supportive of law-abidingness, at least among his own contemporaries and peers. Compliance may be seen as naïve, and law-breaking the 'cool' option. It is these factors, rather than any direct sacrifice of vital interests which the offender must experience if he abides by the law, which create reduced incentives to law-abidance. In these settings, in other words, virtue may seem not just its own but its only reward. The compliant individual does not necessarily appear to be better situated, and more socially creditable, than the non-compliant one.

Why do these altered and weakened incentives for compliance place those affected in a predicament for which a modicum of sympathy is due, when deciding how much they should be censured through punishment when they offend? It is because we know that ordinary people, even when capable of understanding that predatory conduct is wrong, may be strongly tempted to offend nevertheless. To offset this temptation, the criminal law offers the normative moral support for law-abidingness embodied in its censuring features, and the material disincentives provided through its threatened penal deprivations (see 2.4 and 2.5). But these may too easily be disregarded – because being punished is both remote in time from the actual decision to offend, and contingent on apprehension and conviction. This, as a practical matter, makes important the 'stakes in compliance' – the social supports for law-abidingness – because they increase the ulterior practical benefits of a law-abiding life and reduce those of offending. By being denied these social supports, the deprived offender is truly in a more troubled situation, one in which the temptations to offend become harder to resist. This represents a predicament for which a degree of sympathy seems warranted; and which could become the basis for reducing the penalty. The appeal being made is thus similar to that underlying the 'equity factors' addressed in the Swedish statute just mentioned. Reasons of compassion, arguably, may under certain circumstances justify sentence reduction, even when the conduct itself is no less serious.

But how does our suggested perspective on social deprivation account for the fact that many individuals in deprived neighbourhoods remain law-abiding? It is here that it becomes important that mitigation would rest on notions of compassion rather than those of culpability. To make a case that an offender is less culpable for his crime would seem to require that almost anyone in his situation would find it extraordinarily difficult to desist – that compliance would be a matter of heroism or something akin to it. That is not so for the compassion-based account we are proposing. The deprived offender's situation is one in which the moral imperatives for not victimizing others remain; what is deficient are the collateral 'stakes' in compliance. In such a situation, more self-disciplined persons will still be able to comply, and it is only the more 'susceptible' ones who may not. Our proposed basis for mitigation is that we should have some modicum of sympathy for the latter persons, because they have been denied the social supports that might help them overcome that susceptibility.

In Anglo-American penal systems, considerations of compassion (when operative at all) have operated in a highly discretionary fashion, when the individual judge or executive official happens to feel moved by the defendant's plight. But this is not the approach that we are considering here: the exercise of compassion would not be discretionary, but regulated by sentencing standards. The Swedish provisions take this approach, by specifying various grounds for compassion that should be taken into account by the sentencer. Were social deprivation to be considered a mitigating ground, this too should be so regulated – and not left to the consciences of individual decision-makers. One would not be leaving questions of social deprivation to the sympathetic judge, or to amnesties on royal birthdays.

5.3.2 Societal failure?

It is the duty of a decent state, we assume, to provide adequate economic and social opportunities for its citizens. The existence of seriously deteriorated neighbourhoods, in which incentives to law-abidingness are so much weakened, thus represents a failure on the part of the state and the society which it represents. If this judgement is correct, it could provide further ground for sympathy with the predicament of the deprived offender. It is not merely the case that his situation makes it more difficult for him to resist temptation; it is, moreover, that this is a predicament in which he ought not to have been placed. This seems to be a case of *our* failure, as well as his.

What needs further analysis, however, is just why this societal failure would be relevant. One possibility, mentioned by R.A. Duff,[10] is that of 'unclean hands': that it may be the state's and the larger society's *fault* that social deprivation has been permitted to exist, and that fault weakens the state's moral authority to condemn and hence to punish offences.[d] This view, however, would lead to puzzling results – for what would then matter is not the degree of social deprivation itself, but the extent to which that deprivation is due to the state's dereliction. This means there would be no direct link between social deprivation and mitigation; all would depend on identifying governmental or class villainy or neglect. It would not be easy to develop doctrines or theories which enable one to identify when this kind of fault is present. In the absence of such fault, moreover, the state's standing to punish could not be called into question. It would remain possible to argue that social deprivation should mitigate punishment in places such as the United States, which appears to have given such scant recognition to its obligations to alleviate poverty; but not necessarily in Sweden or Finland which (though pockets of deprivation remain) have made more substantial efforts to address want.

If, however, the basis for mitigation is one that concerns compassion (rather than the state's standing to punish), the state's degree of malfeasance in having permitted deteriorated neighbourhoods to develop would no longer matter. What would count, instead, are the grounds for sympathy with the defendant's predicament. The state's obligation to alleviate deteriorated social conditions would be relevant to such

[d] Duff is careful to point out, however, that 'unclean hands' would actually be grounds for calling into question the authority for the state to punish at all, rather than for sentence reduction; see Duff 2001, 181–184.

grounds – for it is the state that is imposing penal censure. Even if the state had made significant efforts to alleviate want, and could not achieve much more with the resources it has available, the persistence of deprivation should remain a source of profound regret. The state is still punishing deprived defendants for misconduct of a kind that they might not so readily have committed had it been able, as ideally it should, to have eliminated the inducements to offending that social deprivation provides. That shortfall from the ideal thus provides additional grounds for sympathizing with the defendant's predicament, not only in places such as the United States, but also in those such as Sweden or Finland.

5.4 The Problem of Norm and Exception

Thus far, we have outlined the case for sentence-reduction for the socially deprived, on the basis of a 'compassion' rationale. But what would be the difficulties with such a view? The most troublesome of these, conceptually, is the problem of norm and exception.

The factors listed in the Swedish statute as equity-based mitigating grounds are clearly designed as exceptions (see Appendix 1). Ordinarily, the defendant is to receive a penalty based on the seriousness of the offence, but in exceptional circumstances the defendant should on compassionate grounds receive a mitigated sentence. Since few convicted defendants would be likely to qualify (few, for example, are apt to be old or ill when being sentenced), it is possible to maintain the norm (punishment according to the offence's degree of seriousness), and yet permit the exception (punishment reduced on compassionate grounds). With social deprivation, however, this distinction becomes harder to maintain. Even in developed Western countries, social deprivation unfortunately remains common, and criminal offending is frequently associated with it. Thus a significant proportion, or even the majority, of those convicted of certain types of offences may come from deprived backgrounds. If penalty reduction were permitted for such persons, it may well become the norm rather than the exception for certain categories of crimes.

Why should this be a problem? It is because an important function of sentencing law, under a proportionalist rationale, is to provide a public valuation of conduct: to make clear, through the law's punishment gradations, that crime *X* is to be regarded as more reprehensible than crime *Y* (see more fully, 2.6.4). If a few of those convicted of crime *X* happen to be old or ill and are given reduced sentences on that account, that still keeps intact the public norm concerning the seriousness-difference between the two offenders. But if crime *X* is of the type that is primarily or quite frequently committed by deprived offenders, and they are given significantly reduced sentences on that account, the effect could be routinely to reduce that crime's actual penalty down to near crime *Y*'s levels – thus tending to obscure the actual seriousness-difference between the two types of offences. With mitigation for first offenders and juveniles, there are also substantial numbers of offenders involved, but the mitigation of sentence is *temporary* – and disappears when the offender accumulates a sufficient number of previous convictions (see 9.6) or becomes an adult (see Chapter 3). Social deprivation, however, is likely to be a permanent condition for many of the offenders involved.

This difficulty, it should be pointed out, arises because of the particular character of the sentence-reduction ground we are discussing: one according to which the gravity of the offence is not diminished, and mitigation is allowed on compassionate grounds. Were the reduced-culpability thesis sustainable (see 5.2), this difficulty would be avoided: then, it could be maintained that deprived offenders – being less culpable – actually act less reprehensibly when they commit crime *X*, and hence *deserve* the reduced punishment. Mitigation, far from providing a confusing public valuation of the conduct, would provide the appropriate valuation. But on the compassion-based rationale, it is not being asserted that the conduct is less reprehensible, and yet many offenders would receive a reduced sentence that would imply an altered valuation of the conduct. On a desert theory, for reasons discussed earlier (2.6.4), providing reasonably unambiguous public valuations is a function of the criminal sanction of considerable importance. To the extent that a scheme of mitigation for deprived offenders obscures or complicates such valuations, that will militate against such a scheme.

5.5 Formulating the Standard

Reducing sentences for deprived offenders would also involve a number of significant practical difficulties. One of these is that of developing adequate guidance on when sentence reduction would be appropriate. Merely authorizing sentencing judges to decide when an offender qualifies as being sufficiently deprived would lead to highly variable results, given judges' differing outlooks on this highly charged question. Providing generalized statutory guidance would be an alternative possibility – with mitigation being permitted when, say, the defendant has been found to suffer from exceptional and sustained deprivation. Such a formulation might well keep the scope of mitigation quite narrow, however; whereas broadening the formulation's scope would bring back problems of variable application. Yet another possibility would be categorical grants of mitigation, such as those suggested by Barbara Hudson;[11] these would authorize sentence reduction when, say, the defendant comes from a neighbourhood showing specified indicia of deprivation, or when the crime is of a type that is frequently committed by deprived offenders. Such an approach, however, is likely to be both over- and under-inclusive: relying on crime type, for example, would bring in non-deprived offenders committing those kinds of offences, while excluding deprived offenders who commit other crimes. A somewhat preferable solution might be to adopt a generally formulated qualitative standard which judges would be called upon to apply; but which is augmented by some explicit guiding principles which make use of the idea of the living standard (see 9.5.1 and Appendix 3) as the measure for assessing social deprivation. But with any of the foregoing solutions, gauging when deprivation is sufficient to warrant mitigation would remain a troublesome task.

5.6 Political Obstacles: Is Mitigation Feasible?

The greatest practical difficulty is a political one: getting social deprivation adopted as a mitigating ground is likely to encounter formidable political obstacles. In a country with strong traditions of a *Sozialstaat* and relatively small residual pockets of deprivation, there might conceivably be sufficient sympathy for the deprived few to permit adoption of such a mitigating factor. Here, also, the limited number of persons who could claim mitigation would alleviate the problem of norm and exception, of which we have just spoken.

However, in Britain and in most other Western countries, poverty is much more extensive, and the poor constitute a substantial portion of the caseload of the criminal justice system (especially for certain types of offences). Here, the possibility of a large number of indigent but criminally active offenders 'getting away' with reduced punishment would be likely to generate so much popular indignation as to create insuperable political obstacles against making social deprivation a mitigating ground. Yet it is precisely in such circumstances that the need for a scheme of mitigation would seem, normatively speaking, to be most urgently needed.

5.7 Drawing the Balance: Mitigation for the Socially Deprived?

Mitigating the punishments of deprived offenders will continue to present a conundrum for sentencing and for desert theory. On one hand, a case can be made for mitigation, albeit on a different theory than previous discussions have explored: namely, one based on notions of compassion. However, such a theory becomes problematical when punishment's public-valuation function is taken into consideration. The practical obstacles to adopting a scheme of mitigation, moreover, are also likely to be substantial in any Western jurisdiction, and be nearly insuperable in jurisdictions with significant levels of deprivation and deep public concerns about crime. We thus doubt (albeit with considerable sense of unease) that such a scheme of mitigation can ultimately be defensible or workable – at least in places where social deprivation is extensive.

5.8 What if Deprived Offenders' Punishments were not Reduced?

Suppose that a jurisdiction has implemented a proportionality-based sentencing scheme but has, for the reasons just cited, decided not to opt for sentence-reduction for the socially deprived. Would this vitiate the scheme as a just way of sentencing offenders? Some writers have suggested so. A desert theory, their argument runs, aims to achieve justice. A sentencing system that fails to make proper adjustment for social deprivation is not really just. If justice cannot thus fully be achieved, the whole aim of desert theory collapses.[12]

The reply to this critique that most readily comes to mind would point to its all-or-nothing character: that either a proportionalist sentencing approach must achieve complete justice or else, if it falls short in any significant respect, it should be dismissed as having failed and the pretence of being fair should be abandoned. But a proportionality-oriented system – even if it made no adjustment for the socially deprived – would remain one which promotes justice in other vital respects and would be considerably more equitable than one that rests (say) primarily on deterrent or incapacitative aims.[13]

A further response is suggested by our arguments in this chapter. On our view, the basis for granting mitigation would not be that of reduced culpability – but rather, one of compassion. Were reduced culpability at issue, failure to grant mitigation would constitute a derogation from fairness: deprived offenders, by being punished as much as others, would actually be penalized more than they deserved, in view of the reduced blameworthiness of their actions.[e] But if culpability is not seen as reduced, this problem is alleviated. The system would not be vulnerable to the charge of injustice, but rather to having failed to temper justice with compassion as much as might be wished.

[e] Were the derogation not great, moreover, the scheme could still be defensible on the basis of a 'modified' desert model. Suppose that the deserved sentence, within a given system, for a given type of crime were, presumptively, *X* months. Suppose it were assumed that social deprivation were considered culpability-reducing, and hence that the appropriate sentence for the socially deprived individuals convicted of this crime were *X-minus n* months. If these offenders were denied this discount, they would be getting *n* months more than they deserved. So long as *n* represents a proportionately modest amount, however, such a deviation might be defensible on the basis of the modified desert model discussed in 9.8; Appendix 2.

Would our conclusions mean that nothing needs to be done to address social deprivation? Surely not. It should remain a high priority, as already mentioned, for the state to maintain social programmes for alleviating want. Within the criminal justice system, moreover, there also are steps to be taken. Provisions of substantive criminal law need to be reviewed, to eliminate or revise provisions that discriminate against the indigent or against racial minorities (as aspects of existing drugs legislation now do).[14] In sentencing, a general scaling down of penalty levels, which we recommend elsewhere in this book,[15] would reduce the suffering inflicted on the deprived offenders, who tend to be more likely targets of penal interventions. What remains debatable here is only whether, when in a scheme of proportionate sentences, there should be provision for sentence-reduction specially aimed at socially deprived defendants.

Notes

1. See more fully, von Hirsch 1976, ch. 17.
2. von Hirsch 1976, ch. 17; von Hirsch 1993, 106–8. In recent years, the topic has come to receive attention from other authors; see particularly, the collection of essays in Heffernan and Kleinig 2000 and also, Hudson 1998; Hudson 1995. The influential essay that first raised the issue of desert and social deprivations is Murphy 1973.
3. See, eg, von Hirsch 1999; cf. Morse 2001.
4. See, eg, German Penal Code, ss. 20–21.
5. See Gardner 1998a; Morse 2000; von Hirsch 1985.
6. Hart 1968, 17.
7. See, eg, Hudson 1998.
8. Gardner 1998a.
9. Swedish Penal Code, ch. 30, s. 5. The factors listed in the Swedish statute are discussed in Appendix 3.
10. Duff 1999, 61–68; von Hirsch 1999, 73–74, Duff 2001, 181–84.
11. See Hudson 1995.
12. Tonry 1994.
13. von Hirsch 1993, Epilogue.
14. See, eg, Tonry 1995, ch. 3.
15. See 9.4; see also, von Hirsch 1993, ch. 5.

6

Proportionality and Punitiveness?

6.1 Desert Theory as Leading to Punitiveness: The Desert-Severity Hypothesis

In the course of their critique of contemporary theories of punishment, the influential criminologist John Braithwaite and his co-author Philip Pettit assert that the adoption of the proportionality principle and desert theory leads almost inevitably to increased levels of punitiveness:

> When you play the game of criminal justice on the field of retribution, you play it on the home ground of conservative law-and-order politicians. You give full rein to those who play to the sense of normality of the majority, urging them to tyrannize the minority. Once all the players agree that retribution, or giving people what they deserve, is the rationale for punishment, the genteel visions of retributivists count for nought.[1]

This is not an isolated claim. Similar assertions may be found in the work of Nils Christie[2] and Michael Tonry.[3] In David Garland's analysis of recent developments in crime control and criminal justice, moreover, the following assertion is made:

> In the last 20 years, however, we have seen the reappearance of 'just deserts' retribution as a generalized policy goal in the US and the UK, initially prompted by the perceived unfairness of individualized sentencing. This development has certainly prompted the concern for proportionality and fixed sentencing for which its liberal proponents had hoped. But it has also re-established the legitimacy of an explicitly retributive discourse, which in turn, had made it easier for politicians and legislatures to openly express punitive sentencing and to enact more draconian laws.[4]

Garland does not assert that desert theory should bear sole responsibility for these trends, for he refers to the rise of the victim (and of victim-based organizations in the US), and to the advent of penal populism. But he does suggest that the emergence of desert theory in sentencing has had an historical connection with trends toward increasing penal severity that have tended to dominate criminal justice policy at the turn of the millennium.[5] Garland takes the view that this was an unintended consequence; Braithwaite and Pettit seem to say, however, that even if unintended it was a natural consequence that should have been foreseen and (presumably) have led to the abandonment of desert rationales by those genuinely favouring reductions in punishment levels.

In the present chapter, we examine this 'desert-severity claim' (hereafter the 'D-S' claim). It is apparent that such a view has different strains. For Garland it is a historical viewpoint about the development of penal policy in certain English-speaking jurisdictions in recent decades, and it does not include any assertion that adoption of a desert model would lead inevitably to greater severity. For Braithwaite and Pettit it is also expressed as a historical claim, but is presented as a kind of historical inevitability – that reliance on ideas about deserved punishment is almost bound to result in severer punishments, in most jurisdictions.

6.2 Does the Desert Model Justify or Lead to Greater Severity?

In this section, we begin by examining the implications that desert theory, constructed along the lines set out in this book, has for severity of punishment. We then look into the effects of current desert-based sentencing schemes in various jurisdictions on severity levels. Lastly, we point to some misconceptions about desert theory that might have made the D-S hypothesis look plausible.

6.2.1 Implications of desert theory for severity of punishment

A number of features of proportionality theory point to why it supports moderate sanctions, not harsh ones. First, there is the theory's emphasis on offenders and potential offenders as rights-bearing citizens. The entire structure of modern desert theory is one that views offenders and potential offenders as *persons*, whose capacity for moral judgement is to be respected, and whose rights are to be taken seriously. All penal interventions therefore call for justification, in terms of both the fairness of making an intervention and the fairness of the degree of onerousness of the proposed intervention (see Chapter 2).

A second important feature is desert theory's rejection of talionic versions of retributivism, and its emphasis on the censuring features of the criminal sanction. A traditional talionic view of retributivism would point to very severe penalties for serious crimes, as the penalty should visit as much suffering on the offender as he did on his victim. This talionic perspective, however, is explicitly rejected by modern desert theorists, as the discussion elsewhere in this volume makes clear (Chapter 2). The basis of proportionality is not the return of suffering for suffering, but rather penal censure; and the latter conception allows substantial reductions in overall sentence severity, so long as penalties express the requisite disapproval of criminal behaviour (see 9.4).

A third restraining influence is the theory's scepticism about deterrence or incapacitation as the basis for deciding on the severity of sentences. The desert rationale sketched in this volume makes limited use of deterrence in explaining why the criminal sanction (with its deprivations) should be established, instead of a purely symbolic censuring response (see 2.5). However, the rationale substantially restricts the use of deterrence and incapacitation as grounds for deciding the comparative severities of punishment (9.3.3). This rules out a variety of sentencing strategies that have been used to raise punishment levels – such as escalating punishments for persistent offenders, on grounds that such offenders have disregarded previous penal messages, and thus need tougher responses in order to intimidate them from reoffending.

Finally, the theory expressly offers reasons for limiting overall severity. The censuring features in punishment, the argument runs, constitute a normative appeal for desistance from crime: that mistreating others should be avoided because it is wrong. If levels of punishment become unduly severe, however, the resulting threat of drastic responses will tend to 'drown out' any such moral reasons for desistance supplied by the law's censuring features, and render the system one predominantly based on intimidation – and thus unsuitable for a citizenry to whom the state should show respect as citizens deemed capable of moral deliberation (9.4). Conceptions such as this one clearly militate in favour of moderate levels of penalties.

6.2.2 Do desert-oriented sentencing systems, as actually adopted, tend to be more punitive?

The foregoing suggests that desert theory in its developed form does not support higher penalties. Now, we must consider the reality of systems that have implemented a proportionality-based approach: what has happened in practice? Were the D-S hypothesis correct, it could be expected that policymakers, when implementing a desert-oriented model, would tend to opt for substantially increased levels of punitiveness. Has this occurred?

The first systematic adoption of proportionality theory is to be found in Finland. Amendments to its Penal Code enacted in 1976 were designed to make seriousness of the offence the primary criterion for determining sentence, and to introduce an approach to sentencing that 'stress[es] the neo-classical values of equality and proportionality'; the law also aimed at reducing the overall severity of sanctions.[6] Subsequent to this change, punishment levels in Finland have declined dramatically, so that the country moved in two decades from being virtually the most punitive nation in Western Europe to being one of the least punitive. The magnitude of this shift is suggested by the fact that between 1975 and 1997 the Finnish prison population declined by 50 per cent, from 116 to 58 per 100,000 of the population.[7] The Finnish experience would seem plainly inconsistent with the D-S hypothesis.

A second example, also from Scandinavia, is provided by the Swedish sentencing reform enacted in 1988. This introduced into the Swedish Criminal Code a complex set of provisions, centring on the requirement that courts impose sentence on the basis of the 'penal value' (ie, seriousness) of the offence. Until 1992, the effect of these measures was to reduce slightly the use of imprisonment.[8] In that year, the then incoming conservative government proposed certain toughening changes primarily related to drink-driving, that resulted in small increases in sentence levels during the mid-1990s. The international statistics for that decade as a whole show, however, that at its end the Swedish 'imprisonment rate' was 64 per 100,000 (seven percentage points higher than the figure of 57 for 1990), but declining again in the late 1990s.[9] It would scarcely seem the case that the small (and in significant part temporary) increase in severity brought about in 1992 could be regarded as confirmation of the desert-severity hypothesis. Sweden remains among the Western European countries that make the most sparing use of imprisonment.[a]

The Finnish and Swedish examples demonstrate that, *pace* Braithwaite and Pettit, and also *pace* Christie,[10] adoption of desert and proportionality as guiding principles does not lead to greater severity. Braithwaite and Pettit might argue that their discussion was really confined to English-speaking countries. If so (and they did not thus qualify their assertions), then their claim would come close to Garland's – that in the UK and US the rise of desert theory made it easier for politicians and legislatures to support more punitive sentencing.[11]

A few jurisdictions in the United States have introduced proportionality-based sentencing in a systematic fashion: most notably, Minnesota and Washington state, which have adopted numerical sentencing guidelines in which the central determinant of the presumptive sentence is the offence of conviction. The degree of reliance on imprisonment tends in these states to be modest by American standards, with Minnesota's having the next-lowest per capita prison population in the nation.[12] In contrast, certain other US states have espoused law-and-order approaches that have led to steep increases in prison populations over the last two and a half decades.[b] This has been accomplished largely by the adoption of

[a] By 2001, these imprisonment rates for Finland and Sweden did not change significantly.

[b] Based on 1997 figures, the five states with the highest per capita rates of imprisonment were (in order) Texas, Louisiana, Oklahoma, South Carolina and Nevada. In none of these states, was there significant interest in adopting presumptive sentencing guidelines based on a desert model; see, Beckett and Western 2001.

mandatory minimum sentences for a wide variety of crimes – and especially, severe mandatory minima for repeat offenders. Perhaps the most draconian of the latter measures is California's 'three strikes' law, which mandates a 25-year minimum prison sentence for a third felony conviction (including a third conviction for various intermediate and lesser offences).[13] The US Supreme Court, in upholding the constitutionality of this statute, recently confirmed a minimum *50-year* sentence for the theft of 11 blank videotapes valued at under $150.[14] As we argue below, the driving force behind these laws may be found in a mixture of incapacitative and deterrent rationales, and appeals to popular resentment against lawbreakers. Not only would the desert rationale provide no support for such sentences, but it would militate strongly against them – because they involve disproportionate emphasis on the offender's prior criminal record, and manifestly excessive severity in relation to the (often not serious) offence of conviction.

Turning to England and Wales, the Criminal Justice Act of 1991 was the most comprehensive sentencing statute for many years. It was preceded by a government policy document that proposed 'a new legislative framework for sentencing based on the seriousness of the offence or just deserts'. The proposals aimed explicitly at reducing reliance on imprisonment, and especially at diminishing the large number of repetitive property offenders sentenced to prison – with the report stating that 'imprisonment can be an expensive way of making bad people worse'.[15] The one exception to this policy concerned offenders predicted to be especially dangerous, in respect of whom a different rationale (incapacitation) was employed.[16] But for ordinary offenders, the Act provided that sentence severity should be 'commensurate with the seriousness of the offence'.

The English judiciary did not welcome this legislation, because it imposed restrictions on the exercise of 'their' sentencing discretion. Within weeks of the Act's implementation the Court of Appeal delivered a judgment that significantly undermined the proportionality principle by interpreting it to refer to the penalty 'commensurate with the punishment *and deterrence* that the seriousness of the offence requires'.[17] This subversion of the 1991 Act's key provision, reinstating deterrence as a sentencing aim when the clear intention had been to remove it, was followed in 1993 by new legislation to remove or water down other provisions of the 1991 Act on prior criminal record, multiple offences, unit fines and other matters.[18]

After these changes, the English courts tended to revert to their previous practices, and politicians increasingly supported much tougher measures – proclaiming that 'prison works' and calling for the introduction of mandatory sentences. There came a tide of 'law and order' rhetoric, particularly from the then Home Secretary Michael Howard, leading to the adoption of the Crime (Sentences) Act 1997, which imposed mandatory minimum sentences for a number of significant offence categories, including drug offences and burglary, purportedly on incapacitative and deterrent grounds.[19]

After taking office in 1997, the Labour government continued to distance itself from the proportionality principle. When commissioning a review of the sentencing framework, it assumed the failure of the desert approach. The ensuing government-sponsored Halliday Report (2001) expressed considerable scepticism about deterrent and incapacitative rationales for sentencing, but proposed a significantly weakened version of the proportionality principle: that 'the severity of punishment should reflect the seriousness of the offence [*and*] of the offender's criminal history'.[20] The recently enacted Criminal Justice Act 2003 calls upon the courts to have regard to five purposes of sentencing (deserved punishment, deterrence, incapacitation, rehabilitation, and reparation to victims), without indicating the comparative weight that should be given to these differing aims.[21] The seriousness of the offence of conviction is to remain relevant, but courts will be required to treat previous convictions as rendering an offence substantially more serious if they are considered to be 'relevant' and recent. How much influence the proportionality principle will retain is difficult to predict, as it will depend on the guidelines which a newly-established sentencing commission (the 'Sentencing Guidelines Council') has been commissioned to issue.[22] But it is apparent that, at least among government ministers and officials, support for proportionate sentencing has markedly diminished.

However, the English experience, far from confirming the desert-severity claim, appears to do just the opposite. Were the D-S claim correct, one would have expected there to have been a large increase in overall penalty levels, but within a graded system of sanctions based chiefly on offence seriousness. Instead, as law-and-order perspectives gained strength, the government showed increasing hostility to the proportionality requirements of the 1991 Act and its underlying philosophy. In the period before the Criminal Justice Bill 2003, the government was vocal in its criticism of the proportionality provisions of the 1991 Act, as unduly lenient to repeat property offenders – and ultimately came up with a statutory scheme with a shopping list of purposes and enhanced recidivism premiums.

6.2.3 Whence the desert-severity hypothesis?

It seems from the evidence just set out that in the jurisdictions that have explicitly embraced proportionality theory, this did not generate large sentence increases: a causal relationship between desert and increased severity cannot be discerned. This leads us to speculate on why the D-S claim has appeared so alluring to some thinkers on contemporary criminal justice.

One possible factor is the historical identification of desert with talionic theories. Before the mid-1970s when modern desert theories emerged, the idea of deserved punishment was given minimal attention by English-speaking penologists. It was assumed that desert – usually denominated as 'retribution' – was a retrograde notion, reflecting the traditional talionic idea that the offender should be made to suffer as much as his victim. The possibility that desert requirements could rest on another basis (of censure) that did not require tit-for-tat suffering was not taken into account. When modern, censure-based desert theory did emerge, many still identified desert with the talionism which it was actually designed to supplant.

A second influence seems to be one of historical association. Desert theory first made its appearance in the American penological literature of the 1970s;[23] and sentencing policy in a number of US jurisdictions since that time has strongly been associated with severity. It has therefore been assumed that desert theory must be responsible for the rise in punitiveness. As is typically true of 'after therefore because' styles of inference, this overlooks a great deal: for example, that the 1970s desert literature was influenced by strongly liberal assumptions, whereas proposals to escalate penalties came from the political and penological right, and were usually allied to deterrent or incapacitative rationales; and that the proportionality-oriented schemes actually adopted tended to be in US jurisdictions that have resisted the general American trend to escalated severity, or else tended to be in the more liberal European states such as Sweden and Finland in which penal-populist pressures were more muted.

Another source of belief in a desert/severity link has been an identification of a proportionalist sentencing approach with rigid numerical guidelines schemes allowing little room for mitigation – a theme emphasized by Nils Christie.[24] Actually, the desert-oriented sentencing schemes that utilize numerical guidelines, such as Minnesota's, allow considerable leeway for reducing sentences on account of culpability-related mitigating factors.[25] Bars to sentence mitigation are mainly characteristic of mandatory sentence schemes that (for reasons to be noted shortly) cannot be rationalized on proportionality grounds. Europe's proportionality-oriented schemes, such as those of Finland and Sweden, rely on general statutory principles, and not on numerical guidance at all. These latter schemes also grant substantial leeway both for culpability-related mitigating factors, and (as noted earlier) certain other 'equity' factors.[26]

A final idea underlying the D-S claim consists of an identification of moderation in penal policy with 'penal welfarism' (that is, rehabilitatively-oriented penology). Although penal welfarism was not infrequently used to justify long-term confinement of potential recidivists,[27] its prevailing effect on policies in the 1960s and early '70s probably was to act as a restraining influence on penalty levels. However, penal-welfarism advocates and desert theorists appear actually to have shared a commitment to limiting the use of severe punishments, although they sought to achieve this by different means. When the treatment model began to lose influence in the early '80s, it was in part replaced in the succeeding decade by the desert model, also having liberal assumptions, but more modest aspirations about the state's capacity to reshape criminals. A balanced view of sentencing reform efforts in this period would characterize both the treatment model and its successor, the proportionality model, as different versions of liberal reform ideology.

An example of these trends is provided by Sweden, which scaled its penalties down to the present level in the '60s and '70s. At that time, emphasis was placed on rehabilitation and reduction of use of imprisonment.[28] Later, in the late 1970s and the 1980s when interest began to develop in proportionalist approaches, it was not suggested that sentence levels should be raised above those achieved in the rehabilitative era, but only that sentencing should be made fairer and more predictable by introducing proportionality criteria.[29] As we have shown earlier in this chapter, Sweden's adoption of proportionality in 1989 did not produce a return to higher penalty levels.

6.3 What have been the Main Influences Leading to Penalty Escalation?

If a proportionalist sentencing rationale does not lead to tougher penalties in countries where that has taken place, what other influences might be fostering such trends?

6.3.1 Academic support for toughening sentencing policy

A few modern criminologists have supported stringent sentencing policies, but definitely not on desert grounds. They tend to base their proposals on crime-preventive grounds of deterrence or incapacitation.

The leading spokesman of this approach has been the American criminologist James Q. Wilson.[30] He has favoured mandatory minimum prison sentences as a deterrent, and longer sentences for high-risk criminals as an incapacitant.[31] Another proponent has been the conservative writer and publicist, Charles Murray. In a 1997 publication that appears to have influenced the UK government's views, he suggests that the steep penalty increases that took place in the US in the 1980s and 1990s were in large part responsible for declining crime rates there; and that Britain should adopt similar policies, if it wished to cut crime rates.[32]

Writers such as these view a proportionalist sentencing outlook with overt suspicion. Wilson has asserted that desert should be considered only in setting the broadest outer limits on permissible punishments, and that sentence levels within those bounds should be decided on crime-control grounds.[33] Considering his enthusiasm for 'selective incapacitation' strategies that would make the offender's sentence turn mainly on his estimated likelihood of future reoffending, his repudiation of a desert model (which would bar such substantial inequalities in the punishment of those convicted of similar crimes) is scarcely surprising. (Another conservative penologist, Ernst van den Haag, went still further and asserted that crime prevention should be the *sole* ground for deciding sentence, and that no desert-based limits whatever should apply – since the convicted offender has 'waived' claims to fair treatment through his knowing decision to infringe the law.)[34] The academic advocates of tough penalties, in other words, do not fly proportionalist colours.

Why, however, do these penologists not try to achieve tougher penalties espousing a stringent version of retributivism? Why not set high the anchoring points of the penalty scale – so that the entire range of sanctions is onerous and penalties in the middle and top of the range are very severe indeed? Adopting this tactic would require ignoring previously mentioned arguments that proportionalists such as ourselves put forward for keeping the penalty range on the modest side; but sanctions might still be ranked according to crime-seriousness, only at higher degrees of punitiveness.

There are two reasons why conservative penologists would have little interest in such a strategy. One is that they would not be impressed by the fairness claims that underlie proportionality requirements – since they tend to regard offenders as undesirables to be controlled, rather than as rights-bearing moral agents. A second, and perhaps more compelling reason is that adopting this tactic would rule out a variety of seemingly more attractive prevention strategies, including Wilson's two favourites, namely, targetting tougher sentences against 'high risk' recidivists,[35] and adopting substantially increased penalties for petty incivilities – on grounds that doing so will help alleviate neighbourhood deterioration and its resulting crime.[36] A toughened but graded penalty system, in other words, would be viewed by them as removing too many arrows from the law enforcement quiver.

6.3.2 Measures adopted to increase severity

What measures typically are adopted in order to increase punishment levels? It is unusual to see an all-round escalation of maximum sentences or an all-round introduction of minimum sentences (although the Federal Sentencing Guidelines in the United States were designed to increase actual sentence levels overall).[37] The strategy is usually more selective and four approaches are principally relied upon. As will become apparent, none of these approaches comports well with a policy of scaled penalties, based on offence seriousness.

Selective increases of statutory maximum penalties. These measures are often political responses to concerns expressed in the mass media. Recent examples in England and Wales are increased maximum penalties for drug importation and for causing death by dangerous driving.[38] How much these changes alter actual severity levels may vary, depending on judges' willingness to invoke the higher ranges of the permissible sentence. Such a policy, however, would militate against maintaining proportionality – as it allows a widened leeway for individual judges to impose differing degrees of severity for similar cases.

Mandatory minimum sentences for specified categories of offences. In England and Wales, two recent examples (both from the Criminal Justice Act 2003) are the five-year mandatory minimum sentence for crimes committed by offenders carrying firearms, and extremely lengthy minimum tariff periods for offenders sentenced to life imprisonment for murder.[39] In the United States, there are numerous examples of mandatory minimum sentences for drink driving, weapons possession, drug dealing.[40] In proportionality terms, such policies are problematic. If the minimum sentences are set high, they will tend to be disproportionate to offence seriousness. Selecting certain offences for minimum levels of punishment will also cause them to be more severely punished than other crimes of comparable seriousness for which judges retain discretion to punish below such prescribed levels. Further, this approach manifestly restricts a court's ability to reduce sentences to reflect diminished culpability.

Mandatory minimum sentences for specified types of persistent offenders. Some of the best-known of these mandatory minima involve gross infringement of proportionality requirements. This is true, as noted earlier, of California's 'three strikes and you're out' law that mandates a 25-year minimum for the third conviction of various types of lesser and intermediate-level offences. In English law there is a mandatory sentence of life imprisonment for the conviction of specified 'sexual' or 'violent' offences (although this is subject to a court-imposed exception requiring the court to consider the offender's dangerousness to the public before imposing the life sentence).[41] Some of these purported 'sexual or violent' crimes are actually not grave offences – such as attempts at robbery involving toy weapons.[42] There are also mandatory minimum prison terms of seven years for a third offence of drug dealing, and of three years for a third offence of domestic burglary.[43] While, in proportionality terms, these sanctions are less horrendous than California's three-strikes sentences, they still are problematic because they give the criminal record so much greater comparative weight than the proportionality rationale would support.

Across-the-board sentence premiums for persistent offenders. We have noted that this was a recommendation of the Halliday Report for England and Wales in 2001.[44] The Criminal Justice Act 2003 requires the court to treat each 'recent and relevant' previous conviction as an aggravating factor.[45] The intention is to increase sentences for persistent offenders above their present levels, although the extent of the permitted increase will depend on the Sentencing Guidelines Council's guidelines. The larger the recidivist premium becomes, the more this conflicts with the proportionality principle's requirement that the seriousness of the conviction offence should be the main determinant.[46]

The upshot of this survey of techniques recently used for increasing sentence levels should be clear enough. Not only are these techniques not called for under a desert rationale, but they tend actually to infringe the requirements of proportionality – and in some instances, such as California-style mandatory minimums, do so blatantly. Measures such as these quite evidently are little influenced by proportionality concerns.

6.3.3 Why proportionalist sentencing is not attractive for the law-and-order ethos

A proportionalist sentencing model, as just noted, has held little appeal for the academic advocates of increased penalty levels. Policy-makers favouring tough responses to crime tend to show a comparable or greater scepticism, as was made recently clear in the 2001 UK Government White Paper – which explicitly calls for a rejection of the proportionality-oriented philosophy of the Criminal Justice Act 1991.[47]

The reasons for this hostility to proportionalism in sentencing are easy enough to discern. Politicians advocating toughened sanctions suspect strongly the desert model's emphasis on fairness to the offender; the concern instead should be, as former Home Secretary David Blunkett frequently asserted, for the interests of victims and potential victims. The desert model's constraints on severity for lesser repeat offenders is also suspect, since this would restrict tougher policies against 'persistent' offending (again, a theme much emphasized by Blunkett.)[48] And finally, there is a strong preference for sentencing strategies aimed at 'public reassurance' – where the latter seems to be a mixture of promising more effective crime control and evincing an attitude of strong hostility to law-breakers.

6.3.4 Penal populism and the appeal to public resentment

The law-and-order ethos involves not only support for sharp increases in penalties, but also escalated rhetoric concerning crime and criminals. Convicted criminals are to be subjected to drastic sanctions, in view of their supposed depravity and their status as moral outlaws. This approach tends to utilize what Arie Freiberg[49] terms 'forfeiture': convicted offenders are deemed to have excluded themselves from the body politic, and forfeited claims to be treated as citizens entitled to equitable treatment.[c] In one version of law-and-order, offenders are to be subjected to degrading penalties as an expression of community indignation at their crimes.[50] Because the offender is granted so little moral standing, such penal responses could disregard the degree of blameworthiness of the offender's conduct, as well as any claims he might have to dignified treatment; what counts, instead, is giving vent to citizens' animus at criminals and their behaviour.

With penal populism, substantive penal goals generally receive little serious attention. Proportionality of sentence is jettisoned, as we have just pointed out. There likewise tends to be little real concern with crime-prevention effects (notwithstanding rhetorical claims about 'prison works' and suchlike). Symptomatic is the fact that law-and-order measures are seldom accompanied by significant efforts to estimate their likely crime-preventive impact. Thus the former British Home Secretary, Michael Howard, when introducing his version of three strikes in the mid-1990s (providing for substantial mandatory sentences for third-time burglars and drug dealers),[51] asserted in his accompanying White Paper that these measures would reduce the rates of burglary and drug dealing by 20 per cent.[52] No supporting evidence was developed or offered, however, for this figure.

If penal populism does not seriously aim at achieving proportionality or reducing crime, what aims does it have? Its primary goal, in our view, is to mobilize and exploit resentment at crime or criminals.[53] In England, for example, Home Secretary Michael Howard's campaign that 'prison works' in the early 1990s became a useful unifying theme for an otherwise divided Conservative Party. The current Labour Government has been making efforts to toughen sentencing policy further – as well as pursuing drastic measures against other supposed 'undesirables', such as persons engaged in non-criminal 'antisocial behaviour' and asylum seekers. Occasionally, these policies are accompanied by an explicit admission that they are primarily concerned with popular animus against crime and criminals.[d]

[c] Charles Murray has thus recently asserted that those charged with serious or repeated crimes should be deemed 'outlaws'. While he speaks of 'retributivism', it is a bizarre species of retributivism in which previous arrests (not resulting in conviction) would count toward the severity of the sanction. See Murray 2004.

[d] The former British Home Secretary, David Blunkett, thus recently asserted that severe policies on immigration, security and law-and-order may be necessary to retain alienated voters

Where law-and-order dominates the debate on crime, meaningful sentencing reform becomes difficult to accomplish. Congress passed legislation in the mid-1980s creating a US Sentencing Commission to write guidelines for sentences in federal cases.[54] By the time the Reagan-appointed members of the Commission were drafting its standards, law and order had become a much-emphasized theme for the Administration and Congress. A study by Anthony Doob[55] shows the results. The Federal Sentencing Guidelines adopt no consistent penal philosophy. There is, however, one clear (and clearly intended) effect of the guidelines: that of large increases in penalty levels.

At this point it is timely to revisit the D-S claim, this time in the form (not dissimilar to those considered above) of the contention by David Rothman[56] that the liberal reform efforts of the 1970s – particularly the liberals' espousal of explicit guidance for sentencing decisions – has legitimated restraints on sentencing discretion; and that such restraints have since been used to increase penalties. In the absence of such reforms, he argues, sentencing might still be discretionary today, and hence not so readily escalated.[57]

In actual fact, the principal technique for raising sentence levels throughout the United States has been the mandatory minimum sentence, which is in no sense a by-product of liberal reforms. The mandatory minimum was effectively initiated by the Rockefeller drug laws adopted in New York at the outset of the 1970s, but before desert theory and sentencing guidelines became influential.[58] Rothman's thesis appears to rest on the assumption that the penological right can seek to achieve its aims only by taking advantage of liberal reforms and turning them to its own purposes. If something goes amiss, it must be because liberals unwisely have espoused one particular kind of reform rather than another. This perspective, however, overestimates the extent to which progressive reformers control the criminal justice agenda. Penal populism has not needed liberal reforms to legitimate its quest for harsher punishment. The appeal is to loathing and fear of criminals, and the policy mechanisms can be quite varied – ranging from a policy of denouncing 'lenient' judges to enactment of mandatory-minimum and habitual-offender laws. 'Three-strikes-and-you're-out' legislation is not a co-optation of some benevolently minded penal measure; it draws its force, instead, from popular images of habitually violent offenders.

Later in his book, Garland offers an account of the law-and-order ethos, which he terms 'the criminology of the other'.[59] That account is essentially consistent with our own, just-described perspective on this phenomenon.

who otherwise could be tempted to support for extremist political groups (such as the British National Party). The troubling implication is that mainstream politicians need to offer repressive policies, of a character that might placate constituencies potentially sympathetic with radical right-wing solutions. See Blunkett 2003.

Faced with the increasingly apparent difficulties in implementing ambitious crime-prevention policies successfully, he asserts, the state tends to adopt a bifurcated approach to criminal justice. Some contemporary criminal policies treat crime as a concomitant of ordinary life which is to be dealt with by a variety of everyday environmental constraints (such as public television surveillance, and entry-controls in public space) that would make the commission of offences more inconvenient or less profitable. Such policies appear to concede that criminals are 'like us', and that the state has relatively modest crime-prevention capabilities. Other criminal policies adopt the opposite stance, however: of pursuing repressive policy initiatives that mark out criminals as undesirable 'others' and that reaffirm (symbolically, at least) the state's power to put a stop to crime. Sophisticated as this account is, it has little to do with the supposed effects of retributively-oriented discourses to which he refers at the outset of his book. Garland now is treating law-and-order as a reactive and symbolic stance, designed to reassure citizens that the state is protecting them from crime, and to express resentment of criminals on their behalf.

6.4 Conclusion

If our arguments in this chapter are correct, the D-S claim is unsustainable. Whereas the D-S hypothesis asserts that the emergence of desert theory has encouraged politicians and legislatures to express openly punitive attitudes and to enact more draconian laws, we have pointed to other sources of punitive rhetoric and policies that have had a far stronger influence. We have shown also that desert theory has been accompanied by moderation in levels of punitiveness in the jurisdictions where it has been adopted systematically.

Does this mean, however, that any jurisdiction may proceed with proportionality-oriented reforms, if policymakers are convinced by their merits? Not necessarily: much will depend on the character of the particular jurisdiction, and the implementation strategies used. In a jurisdiction where law-and-order politics have become strongly influential, severe difficulties will be encountered in adopting or preserving proportionalist sentencing schemes. The reason is evident from what has been said here already: the law-and-order ethos is inconsistent with basic assumptions of desert theory, including the latter's emphasis on horizontal equity and on limitation of severe punishments. In such an atmosphere, however, the failure of the reform is likely to take a different form than the proponents of the D-S claim suppose. Instead of a graduated tariff of harsh penalties being adopted, a desert-oriented scheme will simply fail to obtain approval or, as in England, suffer diminishing political support some time after adoption. Instead, a plethora of mandatory minimum sentences and presumptions favouring severity is apt to emerge in its stead. Thus the proponents of the D-S claim have failed to produce concrete evidence that it is the espousal of a desert-oriented model of sentencing, rather than other influences such as those mentioned here, that has fuelled penalty escalation in jurisdictions where this has occurred.

In places where the political atmosphere is somewhat more propitious, proportionalist sentencing reforms have a greater chance of obtaining approval or (as is evident in Sweden or Finland) of surviving once approved. But even here, reformers need to proceed with some caution. Questions of penal reform have doubtless become increasingly contentious in most Western democracies, and reform strategies need to take this into account. Sometimes, it may be preferable to adopt gradualist reform tactics. In Germany, for example, the Criminal Code already provides that the sentence should principally be based on the 'fault' of the offender[60] – and such a provision could be reinterpreted to place an increased emphasis on the degree of seriousness of the offence in deciding the penalty's severity.[61] Ambitious and comprehensive sentencing schemes ('cathedral building' in the words of a knowledgeable Swedish colleague) should be approached with a degree of caution.

Perhaps the greatest damage done by the D-S hypothesis has been its tendency to short-circuit debate over sentencing reform. When the desert rationale first emerged in the 1970s, it was accompanied by a substantive critique of traditional preventively oriented sentencing conceptions, and a systematic case in favour of the desert model. We think the latter model continues to have much to offer, as the other chapters of this volume suggest. If we are mistaken, however, it must be for *substantive* reasons why this model is deficient and why alternative conceptions would be preferable; it cannot be on account of unsupported claims that desert is unavoidably linked with greater punitiveness.

Notes

1. Braithwaite and Pettit 1990, 15–16.
2. Christie 2000, ch. 10.
3. Tonry (1996, 14) states that 'while most academic proponents of desert theories favour overall reduction in the severity of punishments, the result has been both to make punishments more severe and to create disparities as extreme as any that existed under indeterminate sentencing.'
4. Garland 2001, 9.
5. Garland 2001, 9.
6. Lappi-Seppälä 2001, 122.
7. Lappi-Seppälä 2001, 102–106.
8. See generally Jareborg 1995.
9. Barclay and Tavares 1999, 3.

10. Christie, somewhat strangely, uses Finland and Sweden as two examples in favour of the D-S claim: see Christie 2000, 26ff, 48ff and 99.
11. See text at n. 4 above.
12. Beckett and Western 2001.
13. Zimring, Hawkins and Kamin 2001.
14. *Lockyer v Andrade* (2003) 123 S.Ct. 1166; see also *Ewing v California* (2003) 123 S.Ct. 1179.
15. Home Office 1990, paras 2.3, 1.6 and 2.7.
16. Criminal Justice Act 1991, s. 2(2)B; see Wasik and von Hirsch 1994.
17. *Cunningham* (1993) 14 Cr App R (S) 44: for full discussion of this decision and its consequences, see Ashworth 2000, 86–87.
18. Criminal Justice Act 1993.
19. Crime (Sentences) Act 1997.
20. Home Office 2001b, para. 2.8.
21. Criminal Justice Act 2003, s. 142; for a critical analysis of these provisions, see von Hirsch and Roberts 2004.
22. von Hirsch and Roberts 2004, 646–7, 651–2.
23. See, eg, von Hirsch 1976; Kleinig 1973.
24. Christie 2000, chs. 7–10.
25. See von Hirsch, Knapp and Tonry 1987, 102–105.
26. Jareborg 1995, 106–8, 109–10.
27. American Friends Service Committee 1971, ch. 5.
28. In particular, the Swedish Minister of Justice Lennart Geigier campaigned in favour of this shift of emphasis.
29. Brottsförebyggarde Rådet 1977; Heckscher, Snare, Takala and Vestergaard 1980.
30. See particularly Wilson 1975; Wilson 1983.
31. Wilson 1983, ch. 8.
32. Murray 1997.
33. Wilson 1983, ch. 8.
34. van den Haag 1981.
35. Wilson 1983, ch. 8.
36. Wilson and Kelling 1982.
37. Doob 1995.
38. Criminal Justice Act 2003, ss. 284 and 285.
39. Criminal Justice Act 2003, ss. 287 and 269.
40. Tonry 1996, ch. 5.
41. *Offen (No.2)* [2001] 1 Cr App R 372: the Criminal Justice Act 2003 replaces this sentence with a new 'dangerousness' provision, see Criminal Justice Act 2003, ss. 222–229.
42. Compare *Offen* (last note) with *Buckland* [2000] Cr App R (S) 207.
43. Crime (Sentences) Act 1997.
44. Home Office 2001b, 2.21–2.20.
45. Criminal Justice Act 2003, s. 143(2); for critical analysis, see von Hirsch and Roberts 2004, 647–652.
46. See von Hirsch 2002, Roberts 2002; von Hirsch and Roberts 2004.
47. Home Office 2001a, para. 2.62: 'the current sentencing framework is too narrowly focused on the specific offence for which the offender is before the court'.

48. Home Office 2002.
49. Freiberg 2001, 41.
50. Kahan 1996.
51. Crime (Sentences) Act 1997.
52. Home Office 1996, 54–55.
53. See more fully von Hirsch and Ashworth 1998, ch. 9.
54. Doob 1995.
55. Ibid.
56. Rothman 2003.
57. Rothman's examples of the impact of sentencing guidelines are highly selective. He disregards state guidelines systems (such as Minnesota's) that have made serious efforts to limit rises in imprisonment levels.
58. Tonry 1996, ch. 5.
59. Garland 2001, 184–186.
60. German Penal Code, Par. 46.
61. Hörnle 1999, Part 5; von Hirsch and Jareborg 1991, ch. 8.

7

Proportionality and the 'Penance' Perspective

7.1 Introduction

With Antony Duff, the leading exponent of the 'penance' perspective on punishment, desert theorists such as ourselves share a *communicative* view of the criminal sanction: punishment, we believe, should be conceptualized as an expression of censure. Penal censure has important moral functions that are not reducible to crime prevention. A response to criminal wrongdoing that conveys disapprobation gives the individual the opportunity to respond in ways that are typically those of an agent capable of moral deliberation: to recognize the wrongfulness of the action; to feel remorse; to express regret; to make efforts to desist in future – or else, to try to give reasons why the conduct was not actually wrong. A purely prudential sanction, aimed at preventing crime and not embodying blame, would fail to provide this recognition of the defendant as a person capable of moral deliberation.

On our view, the disapproval conveyed by the sanction should serve only as an *appeal* to the offender to respond in the manner just described. We do not advocate a penance theory, according to which the aim of the sanction would be actually to seek to generate in the offender specified sentiments of shame, repentance and the like. Duff, however, does offer a penance theory. On his view, the objective of punishment is to bring the criminal to repent of his wrongdoing, and to provide a vehicle through which he may 'work through' and express his penitent understanding.

Let us explain this difference a little further. Punishment conveys censure, but does so in a special way – through visitation of deprivation ('hard treatment') on the offender. That deprivation is the vehicle through which the blame is expressed. But why use *this* vehicle, rather than simply expressing blame in symbolic fashion? It is on this latter issue that we part company with Duff.

We have argued earlier in this book (Chapter 2) that the reason for having the hard-treatment element in punishment has in part to do with prevention: with helping to keep predatory behaviour within tolerable limits. The hard-treatment element furnishes a prudential reason for obedience to those who might find themselves insufficiently motivated by the penal censure's moral appeal; but this should support rather than replace the normative reasons for desisting from crime conveyed by penal censure – that is, provide an additional reason for compliance to those who are capable of recognizing the law's moral demands, but are also tempted to flout them.

Duff rejects this partially prevention-based argument for the hard treatment in punishment. Penal hard treatment, in his view, should serve as a vehicle for the offender's developing a penitent understanding of his wrong.[1] One of us has previously criticized that view – arguing that while imposing penances would be a legitimate function in a monastery, it should not be the business of the state in a liberal society.[2] Duff has responded, and developed his view more fully, in a number of recent writings.[3] In this chapter, we reply, and sketch our reservations about the penance perspective more fully.

7.2 The Aims of Penance: Communication or Expiation?

Duff claims that, on his penance perspective, punishment can be accounted for wholly in communicative terms. But what moral functions do penances involve, and to what extent are they communicative?

One function, of which Duff speaks, is that of *forcing the offender's attention*: the unpleasantness of the sanction may compel the actor to attend to the disapproval visited through the sanction.[4] The moral logic of this function needs explanation, however. Ordinarily, when *A* visits disapprobation on *B* for some moral failing, it is up to *B* to decide whether or not to pay attention; *A* is not entitled to use coercive means to get *B* to attend properly. Coercive attention-getting is warranted only when *A* holds a special position of moral authority over *B*. Perhaps, an abbot has such authority over his charges, in view of his special role as their spiritual mentor, and in view of the fact that they have submitted themselves to his authority. Whether the *state* has that authority, however, is more questionable, as we shall argue below. But at least, attention-getting is a communicative role, and thus can be part of a communicative theory of state punishment (provided that the state can be shown to have the requisite authority).

A second function for a penance may be that of *providing an appropriate psychological setting for the offender's experiencing certain feelings of shame and remorse*. The material discomforts of the penance might be seen as a way of evoking the moral discomfort that the penitent offender should feel.[5] This, too, gives hard treatment a communicative character – of doing something to try to induce the offender to think and feel in a certain way.

A third possible function of penances is that of *expiation*, but that is a different matter. Expiation involves more than creating the right psychological setting; it involves the idea that undergoing certain discomforts is the *proper* manner through which repentance ought to be experienced and achieved. The deprivations of the punishment are not just ways of evoking regret for the deed; but are seen as required (that is, *morally* required) for the purging of guilt. This function does make the link to hard treatment necessary rather than contingent: even the already penitent offender needs to undergo some painful experience to 'work through' his penance. However, it is far from clear whether and why this is a communicative function. Moral communication involves conveying a normative judgement to someone: perhaps, trying to persuade him of the correctness of that judgement; and perhaps, also, trying to get him to feel emotions that comport with that judgement. But if all that could occur without the imposition of hard treatment, it is far from clear what further *communicative* role necessitates offenders actually having to suffer the pains of expiation.

Duff suggests that the expiatory pains offer the offender the opportunity to communicate *back* to the community his penitent understanding of the wrong: the penalty, he states, may be viewed as constituting a kind of 'forceful and weighty apology'.[6] But in what sense does the defendant's undergoing the deprivations of punishment serve as a communication on his part? Those deprivations may take a form (fines or imprisonment, for example) that do not purport to be apologetic.[a] Moreover, the offender has no choice but to undergo such deprivations; treating the expiatory pains of punishment as a kind of enforced apology thus raises the problem of compulsory attitudinizing – which may be viewed as a form of demeaning treatment.[b] It is thus our suspicion that the expiation is not a communicative function at all. It seems, rather, to reflect the traditional retributive notion that suffering is needed to 'wipe clean' the moral blemish of the wrongdoing.

Even if an account of expiation and its moral functions could be satisfactorily provided, there remains the key question of whether this is a proper function of the state. Perhaps an abbot may be entitled to impose penances designed to make erring novices expiate their sins. But why may the *state* do the same to its citizens in a free society?

7.3 Standing to Impose Penances and the State's Role

Duff mentions two dimensions of 'moral standing', namely, (1) that the censurer has the requisite relationship to the actor to make the

[a] Recently, Duff (2001, 111) concedes this point, saying that even if some offenders could be induced to become more active participants in their punishment, for others, 'punishments will in the end be simply inflicted on [those] who refuse to obey penal requirements themselves'.

[b] von Hirsch 1993, ch. 9 (83–84). Duff replies (2001, 110) that the offender is not forced to *mean* what he thus is required to express, but this reply scarcely suffices: what is degrading about compulsory attitudinizing is precisely being compelled to express what one does not mean.

wrongfulness of the latter's conduct his proper business; and (2) 'clean hands' – that the censuring agency is not disqualified through his own misconduct from standing in judgement on the actor.[7] There is, however, a third dimension of standing that Duff does not address and that is crucial for present purposes: namely, that of how deeply the censurer may properly involve himself in the feelings and attitudes of the offender, in order to bring about a morally appropriate response. That may depend on his relationship to the wrongdoer.

Consider simple everyday acts of reprobation: someone has acted inconsiderately toward me, and I respond in a critical manner. How far I may properly go in trying to elicit the morally appropriate response from him depends on the character of our relationship. If a stranger negligently steps on my foot, I may respond expressing my disapprobation (eg by telling him not to be so careless); but it would be inappropriate of me to ask him why he acted in this inconsiderate manner, whether he feels regret, and so forth. If he were a close friend, however, I might have standing to make such further inquiries.

This dimension of standing also affects the appropriateness of imposing penances. There is no doubt the head of a monastic community has standing to visit a penance upon an erring monk, since his function is to attend to the moral welfare of his charges. For a university disciplinary committee to undertake this role, however, would be questionable. Yes, the committee is entitled to censure a faculty member who has misconducted himself, after the proper procedures have been undergone; and in appropriate cases the response may properly embody some form of deprivation – say, a period of suspension. It would also be hoped that the penalty might elicit in him sentiments of regret, or the like. But if the committee characterized the sanction as a penance whose discomforts provide the vehicle for achieving a penitent understanding, one might well think they had overstepped their proper role.[c]

Duff concedes that the state operates differently from a monastic institution, in that membership is not optional; that the shared values underlying the criminal law are conduct-related and more restricted in scope, and that the state is not properly concerned with the person's own spiritual good per se.[8] Notwithstanding these differences, however, he still seems to wish to give the state an abbot-like function of imposing penances. Our essential objection remains that this ascribes to the state a role beyond its proper standing (in the sense of that term just suggested), given its function and its relationship to citizens.

[c] Duff responds (1999b, 84–5) that departmental colleagues might legitimately seek to elicit penitential attitudes from an erring member. Conceivably, this might be appropriate for a very small, tightly-knit department – in virtue of its character as such. But in larger institutional contexts (for example, that of a university-wide disciplinary committee) this would seem a strange role.

Duff does attempt[9] to make his position more consistent with liberalism by imposing two kinds of side-constraints on penances: (1) a limitation of scope: penances may be imposed only for conduct threatening certain basic values of peaceable social coexistence, and (2) a limitation of method: penances may not involve bringing about penitent attitudes through coercion. The second limitation is implicit anyway in any proper notion of a penance: the abbot wants to bring forth the person's *own* penitent attitudes, not brainwash him. The first limitation also seems insufficient, as it does not address the standing issue spoken of here: that even with respect to significantly harmful conduct, the function of which Duff speaks appears to go beyond the state's proper remit. It would scarcely be reassuring if a university disciplinary committee sought to impose penances, but only for specified kinds of unprofessional conduct.

7.4 Penances and the State's Role: Some Hypotheticals

What more can be said on this issue of the state's standing to impose penances? Two hypotheticals might help to bring the differences between penances and state-administered punishments into sharper relief.

(1) Suppose a penalty system, with quite moderate sanction levels, were instituted in a hypothetical state and that (given the relatively peaceable character of the populace) it sufficed to help maintain low rates of offending. Suppose, however, that an in-depth survey of convicted offenders were to disclose that the sanctions had little success in eliciting from them sentiments of shame, repentance and the like; and that to the extent that such persons desisted from reoffending, that was mainly due to growing older, or to motives of wishing to avoid the unpleasantness and stigma of further punishment. From a desert theorist's perspective such as our own, this scenario would represent a modest success. The sanctions reflect and give public expression to a moral valuation of the conduct. Offenders are being treated as moral agents, by being given the opportunity of responding as such agents should. And the prudential disincentive embodied in the hard treatment has some apparent effect and yet is not so severe as to 'drown out' the censuring message.[10] While one may well regret that actual offenders are so seldom penitent, this would not suffice to warrant a judgement of failure.[d]

[d] Duff (1999b, 86–7) suggests that it is inconsistent to suggest, in this scenario, that punished offenders would be sufficiently capable of reflecting on the wrongfulness of their actions to make a censuring response appropriate; and yet so seldom actually to become penitent when punished. We do not see the inconsistency, given that choice (and rather painful choice, at that) is involved in making use of one's moral capacities to develop a penitential stance about one's past behaviour. A person might opt not to respond in this fashion, because (say) of his reluctance to admit the error of his ways, or because of his unfavourable attitudes towards the authorities administering the penances.

On Duff's perspective, however, this outcome would have to be deemed a failure – because the penalties, intended as penances, so seldom elicited the desired penitential response.[e] Now, if a comparable scenario occurred in a monastery, the abbot would quite rightly be concerned that he was failing. But it would seem strange to carry over such a judgement to a liberal state, whose central mission seems so centrally concerned with conduct (see 2.6).

(2) Consider a yet more peaceable society, in which punishment hardly seems needed to prevent crime at all. Offending is relatively rare, being kept in check by people's moral inhibitions, by fear of the social stigma associated with having been discovered to have offended, and possibly, by civil remedies. In their effects on the incidence of harmful behaviour, there would not be much difference between instituting a system of state punishments and relying instead only on civil remedies plus informal social controls. Suppose, however, that there was occasional offending in this society, and that something more than symbolic censure – some measure of hard treatment – was needed to help the few actual offenders achieve a penitent understanding of their misdeeds. Should one, then, insist on punishment with its attendant deprivations?

On our view, the answer would emphatically be negative. The justification for punishment would fall away, since hard treatment would not generally be required to help people overcome the temptations of offending (see 2.5.2). On Duff's view, however, a system of punishments would seem to be called for – simply to provide penances for those few persons who do offend.

In the context of the monastic institution, this latter conclusion would make sense. If there were any infractions of monastic discipline, even if rare, it would be the abbot's duty to attend to the consciences of those involved, and institute the purifying process of penance to help them achieve repentance. But for a liberal state, this would seem a bizarre conclusion. Duff does assert, as noted earlier, that the state should not be concerned with conscience or moral attitudes per se, but only with these as expressed through harmful conduct. But the present hypothetical should bring into relief why this concession is not enough. We are speaking of harmful conduct here, but the question remains what aspect of the conduct should be the state's main concern. In a situation where crime prevention is no longer significantly at issue, we cannot see why it should be the business of the state to establish so coercive and burdensome an institution as punishment, merely to help a few wrongdoers to expiate their wrongs.

[e] True, Duff points out that penances need not *always* succeed in eliciting penitence from the wrongdoers on whom they are imposed (2001, 121–25). But if the institution of state-imposed penance almost *never* induced the desired response from offenders, it would be questionable whether it was performing what he characterizes as its main function.

7.5 Rehabilitation and Penance

Offender rehabilitation in earlier decades tended to steer clear from attempts to convey moral judgements to offenders about their conduct. The offender would be enlisted in a programme designed to improve his skills or resolve his psychological difficulties; his offence and its injurious character, however, was seldom discussed. Now, this reticence is being questioned. Changing the offender's behaviour, recent thinking about rehabilitation holds, may call for talking to the offender about what he has done, discussing the reasons why he did it, encouraging him to consider other persons' interests, and trying to get him to understand why his behaviour failed to do so.[11] Confronting the offender with his behaviour is again coming to be seen as a legitimate and important aspect of rehabilitation.

In cruder versions, such strategies have been conceived in purely consequentialist terms: how much the offender is to be 'shamed' would depend solely on what will work to prevent reoffending.[12] Desert theorists, however, see these strategies as constrained by strong proportionality limits: the duration and degree of onerousness of the sanction (including its treatment elements) should depend on the gravity of the offence.[13] Thus restricted, these newer rehabilitation methods can be made consistent with a proportionality-oriented sentencing theory.[14]

But why is confronting the offender morally the legitimate business of the state? The seeming answer would be that this helps induce offenders to refrain from reoffending. It is thus a crime-prevention aim, and crime prevention is a legitimate state function, within appropriate desert constraints.[15] In contrast with the scepticism of recent decades, researchers have recently been cautiously optimistic about the effectiveness of certain rehabilitation programmes: that programmes, carefully targeted to amenable offenders, might in specified types of cases work to a modest extent to reduce recidivism.[16]

However, matters are not quite so simple, as becomes apparent when we consider recent research on another crime-prevention aim, incapacitation. That research has suggested that – even if imprisonment does 'work' in the sense of preventing the imprisoned offender from reoffending while he is confined – it still may not be of much use in reducing the public's net exposure to crime. Locking up the potential recidivist will not necessarily put others significantly less at risk, if (for example) there are large numbers of other potential offenders not currently in confinement who can replace his criminal activities. Incapacitation research thus has come to focus increasingly on the issue of *net* effects on crime.[17] Were this question of net preventive impact asked of rehabilitation, the implications could be disturbing. If treatment works only for certain selected types of offenders carefully screened for amenability,[18] then the numbers of persons thus 'cured' might simply be too few to have a substantial impact on the incidence of crime. In that case, rehabilitation would not 'work' as a conventional crime-prevention strategy.

However, rehabilitation still may have a more modest preventive role: even if net crime rates are not affected, inducing to offender refrain from reoffending would spare potential victims from harm at *his* hands. It may also serve a somewhat different end, closer to the old notion of 'reforming' offenders: that of inducing them to live different lives. On this perspective, a predatory lifestyle is a bad way of living – bad not only in its destructive effects on victims, but in the values that it embodies. Inducing offenders to give up this kind of life and to treat others decently might arguably (albeit controversially)[f] be seen as worthwhile, even if no net crime-preventive impact ensues.

Were one to go this far, would one have embraced Duff's position? One would be utilizing means of which he speaks – namely, using the vehicle of hard treatment to confront the offender, and to bring about a recognition of wrongdoing and efforts to change. And a possible aim of the intervention seems close to his: namely, moral reform of the offender.

Nevertheless, one would still be a long way from Duff. First, reform of the offender, in the scenario just mentioned, is not being offered as the primary rationale for the whole penal system, but merely as an incidence of a penal system which principally derives its justification from other grounds. The main reasons for punishing could still be those of our suggested kind, of conveying censure and providing a disincentive against criminal behaviour. The constraints applicable to punishments – namely, those of proportionality – derive from this basic rationale.[19] If the criminal sanction fails or is not needed to promote these basic aims, then (as the above hypotheticals have indicated) it should not be retained – not even to 'reform' some offenders. Offender reform, in the sense just described, is thus only a derivative activity of the criminal justice system.[g]

Second, offender rehabilitation, even of the kind that involves confronting the offender about his offence behaviour, has aims that are narrower and more clearly prevention-focused than Duff's penances, for several reasons. (1) Calling upon the offender to address the reasons for his offending, under a rehabilitative approach, is only *a* treatment modality, to be evaluated alongside other treatment techniques. (2) Even when the offender is asked to address his criminal conduct, the emphasis tends to be oriented mainly to the future – to pragmatic concerns of making him

[f] It might be objected that this is a species of moral paternalism, since the aim is in part to promote the moral wellbeing of the offender himself. However, the conduct with which the rehabilitative intervention is concerned is of a kind that is injurious to others.

[g] That is also why one would be entitled to retain the penal system even if relatively few offenders could be successfully reformed – why one can legitimately take the risk of failure of treatment. With Duff's rationale, however, systematic failure of offender-reform efforts would put the legitimacy of the whole system into question (see 7.4 above).

understand why his self-control failed him when he offended and of helping him develop techniques (such as 'anger management') that could assist him in controlling himself better in future – rather than on his expiating his past offence as an end in itself. (3) Crucially, these rehabilitative techniques are subject to an effectiveness requirement: they should be employed only to the extent that their effects in preventing reoffending can be empirically confirmed. This makes it likely that the techniques would be imposed only on a limited group of subcategories of amenable offenders, rather than on all offenders as a matter of course.

With Duff's penances, none of these limitations would operate. *All* offenders presumably would have to undergo a regime of penances. It is claimed by Duff that the offender's undergoing a penance would, if successful, involve desistance from further offending. However, the use of such penances would not be contingent on their being tested empirically and being shown to be successful in reducing recidivism – since its rationale remains in substantial part a deontological one. The penance thus has a different basis and much more sweeping applicability than rehabilitation (even in the sense of offender 'reform') would have.

7.6 The Constitutive Grounds for State Punishment

Our own view of the state and its proper functions goes well beyond the restricted contractualist liberalism which Duff seems to wish to attribute to desert theorists.[20] It admits that sentences may (so long as they observe proportionality constraints) seek a variety of objectives, including that of trying to reform offenders by fashioning sanctions designed to help them recognize the wrongfulness of their conduct. But functions such as these presuppose the legitimacy of the criminal sanction – and that legitimacy should rest on more restricted claims.

The justification for the criminal sanction concerns its *constitutive* grounds: the reasons why such an institution should exist at all. Those constitutive grounds should concern certain *public* functions: of expressing a valuation of certain kinds of (harmful) conduct, and of providing a (modest) disincentive to it. The character of and grounds for such public valuation have been addressed already, in Chapter 2.

These basic expressive and preventative functions are matters which concern the character of the minimum norms for peaceable coexistence, and their enforcement. If the institution of the criminal sanction were incapable of carrying out these public functions (or if those functions could be performed without having to resort to the intrusive features of punishment) then that institution would lose its *raison d'être*. In that event, the pains of punishment could not be sustained solely on the grounds that they help it function as a penance for certain wrongdoers.

Our just-stated claim about constitutive grounds is designed to address only certain coercive state institutions. The assumption is that, in a free society, such institutions should exist only where necessary for certain fairly narrowly circumscribed purposes, including those just described. Where sustainable on those grounds, these coercive institutions might also be given certain *supplemental* functions, perhaps concerned in part with the offender's 'reform'. But the latter functions cannot alone support the existence of the criminal sanction. This perspective also should not restrict the availability of a plethora of state and communal institutions aimed at providing resources to citizens and encouraging cooperation among them. It is not the idea of a minimal state on which these arguments rest, but a certain minimalism concerning state *coercion*.

On this perspective concerning state coercive institutions, would the imposition of penances be a proper function of the state? Declaring a given type of conduct punishable would be appropriate, as this provides both a disincentive against the conduct and a public valuation that the conduct is blameworthy and ought to be eschewed. Punishing a convicted offender would likewise be appropriate, as this involves the imposition of formal public penal censure of someone, for conduct that has been proscribed and is deemed blameworthy. But making the offender undergo the pains of punishment as a means for his expiating his crime (of 'working through' his guilt through suffering) seems too private and variable an experience to the basis of support for a major state institution, especially in those situations where this cannot be shown empirically to be linked with preventing the offender's reoffending.

A proponent of the penance perspective might reply that he simply has a wider conception than we of the possible aims of coercive state institutions. What, then, might be lost by such a wider conception – that is, what identifiable undesirable side effects might there be in making penance the principal aim for state punishment? It is possible, we think, to identify two kinds of undesirable effects: a dilution of proportionality requirements, and the risk of undue intrusiveness. Let us address these next, in turn.

7.7 Dilution of Proportionality Requirements

It is common ground between Duff and ourselves that the principle of proportionality of sentence is of central importance: punishments should be proportionate in their severity to the seriousness of the crime. On both our views and his, this principle derives from the censuring features of punishment: if punishment conveys blame, then the quantum of punishment should depend on the degree of blameworthiness (ie seriousness) of the offender's criminal conduct.[21]

However, the criteria for proportionality appear to operate differently according to the two perspectives. The desert perspective calls for a somewhat demanding standard of proportionality: conduct of approximately equal reprehensibleness should be punished with roughly comparable severity, and penalties should be ranked according to crime seriousness. With criminal prohibitions seen as public admonitions, and sanctions as public acts of censure, what counts is the degree of blameworthiness of the offence, and the degree of disapproval conveyed through the severity of the sanction. This conception, as mentioned above, can still allow rehabilitative efforts that are designed to confront the offender about his offence: to foster awareness of wrongdoing on his part, in order to encourage desistance from further offending. But given the preeminently public nature of the sanction, and the public character of its constitutive grounds, the degree of seriousness of the offence should act as a strong constraint on how severely the offender may be punished in order to achieve such reformative effects. The offender may not, for example, be held in a given penal regime for a significantly longer period than others convicted of similarly blameworthy offences, even were the extra time helpful in inducing 'reform' on his part.

Duff also calls for proportionality in punishment, and thus opposes any tactic of confining the offender indefinitely until he repents.[22] But his penance rationale would significantly dilute proportionality requirements. Suppose Offender *A* has 'thicker skin' than Offender *B*, and hence would require a more onerous penance in order to bring about a penitent understanding of his act. Since Duff's view under the imposition of penances is the *constitutive* aim of the criminal sanction, this presumably would call for punishing *A* more severely than *B*. Indeed, he makes this explicitly permissible in a recent volume,[23] by propounding a version of proportionality that would serve as a 'negative' (ie, limiting) principle: it would only impose upper and lower limits (albeit significant ones) on the onerousness of punishments.[h] This he proposes to implement through a guideline structure based on 'zones of discretion': the sentencer would be free to choose the type and degree of onerousness of the sanction within specified upper and lower limits provided by the seriousness of the

[h] Duff defends such a 'range' model in part on grounds of the difficulty of comparing with exactitude the severity of different types of crime or the severity of different types of punishments (2001, 137–39). Were that the main reason, however, one should still try to do one's best to observe horizontal equity standards. When crimes are of the same type and thus easily comparable in seriousness, parity of sentence would remain essential. When crimes are of different types and not so easily comparable, it would be appropriate to seek approximate parity. This is definitely not Duff's approach, however: his 'zones of discretion' scheme would allow penalties of substantially differing degrees of severity for crimes of comparable seriousness, even when such seriousness-comparisons would be easy to make.

crime.[24] Duff does not view such an approach as a limited (but, arguably, permissible[25]) derogation from proportionality requirements. Instead, imposing differential amounts of punishments on the two offenders – at least, when the differences are not so great – would be treated on his view as involving no moral cost at all.

In the context of a monastery, this latter conclusion would seem acceptable. Suppose Novice *C* and Novice *D* commit sins of comparable gravity, and the abbot (in view of their differences in character and sensitivity) subjects *C* to the more onerous penance. Were *C* to have the temerity to complain that he has been unfairly treated, the abbot might rightly respond that penances are concerned with helping to promote a penitent response and induce expiation, and that the differences in their treatment were designed to help bring about such responses.

Such differentiation seems misplaced, however, in the context of state-imposed punishment, given its public character. Criminal statutes are published, and trials are open to all, with verdicts and sentences publicly announced. These features are no happenstance of Anglo-American legal tradition, but should derive ultimately from legal punishment's central function as public valuation (see 2.6.4). The severity of punishment thus implies a public judgement about the degree of blameworthiness of the conduct: to punish *A* more than *B* for crimes of an apparently similar nature would imply that there was something about *A*'s conduct – perhaps, some element of added culpability – that made it worse. It is from these features that strong requirements of horizontal equity should arise. When the state, as an institution purportedly representing us all, imposes a sanction that publicly implies that someone's conduct is reprehensible – and is worse than someone else's – that should entitle him to demand an account of why it is worse. Yet the variations in sanction allowed by Duff's account may have nothing to do with the conduct's being worse; but rather, only to do with the offender's personal degree of amenability to penitential regimes.

To downgrade horizontal equity, as Duff would do, would call for a diminished emphasis on punishment's role as public valuation: to suggest that the state, in its punitive role, has functions more akin to a religious institution, with its emphasis on personal salvation; and less to do with conveying public judgements concerning the degree of reprehensibleness of conduct. Yet strangely, Duff in his recent book explicitly stresses the criminal sanction's role of providing a public valuation of conduct.[26] The apparent tension between that perspective, and Duff's view of punishment as penance, is not adequately resolved.[i]

[i] This tension is made all the more apparent through his discussion, elsewhere in his recent book, of imposing penances on already repentant offenders (Duff 2001, 118–21). There he says there should be no mitigation of such offenders' punishments, because reducing the penalty would conflict with the public communicative functions of punishment.

7.8 Expiatory Sanctions' Potential Intrusiveness

When an abbot exposes an expiatory penalty upon an erring novice, he is entitled to pursue 'deep' inquiries into the latter's thoughts and feelings, to help assure that he is responding to his penance in a properly penitential way. 'It's none of your business what I feel!' is not a response the novice should be entitled to make, as his deepest feelings and attitudes are precisely the abbot's business as the person in charge of the novice's spiritual development.

Transferring these functions to the state would be profoundly problematic, however. The state represents citizens having a variety of differing outlooks on how to think and live. An individual has no assurance that the authorities are in deeper sympathy with his aspirations and values. Moreover, there is no exit. For communal institutions claiming extensive authority over members' moral and spiritual lives, this possibility is crucial. If our novice becomes disenchanted with the moral demands his abbot is making on him, and with the perspectives and routines of his monastic order, he may safeguard his sense of personal integrity by quitting. A state is not a voluntary association in this sense. It represents the framework within which people live their whole lives. The possibility of exit is far more restricted: emigration would ordinarily involve uprooting the whole of a person's life – and may not even be a possibility, if immigration to other countries is restricted.

Duff's response is that penance in the context of state punishment is different from that in a monastery, because a much more restricted aspect of the person's life is under consideration.[27] It is not any 'impure' thought or deed that can invite punishment, but only certain conduct that is injurious to others and prescribed by law on that account. On a censuring perspective in punishment, this would be a satisfactory answer: one may be penalized (and thereby be censured) only if one does certain injurious things; and the penal censure serves just to give one the opportunity to respond by feeling shame or regret; and there is no occasion for pursuing deeper inquiries about whether one is truly expiating one's wrong. But if expiation becomes the central purpose of the sanction, as it is on Duff's perspective, then such deeper inquiries would seem a virtual inevitability. Even if criminalization were restricted to harmful behaviour, it would seem to become necessary, once an offender is facing sentence for such conduct, to explore the offender's moral attitudes to ascertain what form of sanction might have the best expiatory effect; and to inquire into the state of his feelings as he undergoes the punishment. This could be undertaken even when there was no empirically verifiable grounds for believing that it would enhance the rehabilitative impact of the sentence.

Could this difficulty be overcome, however, by adopting appropriate side-constraints – against, for example, intrusive attitudinal inquiries? On a desert rationale, this could be helpful, as a limit on rehabilitative interventions. Since rehabilitation, as we just noted, would serve merely a supplementary penal function, not as central to the whole purpose of punishment, workable limits might be placed on unduly searching scrutiny for rehabilitative ends. On a penance perspective, however, offender attitudes become central. If the very point of the penal process is to induce certain attitudes in the punished offender, it will be far more difficult to develop adequate restrictions on scrutiny of offender attitudes.

Duff treats the foregoing objection, concerning the potential intrusiveness of penances, as a conventional claim of privacy. He replies that an offender's criminal actions constitute a manifestation of certain contemptuous or disrespectful attitudes toward others, so that the state's legitimate concern with censuring criminal behaviour extends to addressing such attitudes.[28] Conventional privacy claims, however, have a different logic. One begins with an assumedly legitimate state role such as crime prevention through offender rehabilitation. It is then claimed that the carrying out of this role is limited by the defendant's entitlement to protection of his private life from undue scrutiny. While that entitlement may preclude certain kinds of intrusive inquiries into the personal, there is likely to be a considerable remaining scope for the state's looking into the offender's reasons for offending, as part of its rehabilitative efforts. Rehabilitation, however, is straightforwardly within the state's proper remit, as a method of preventing harm; and it has considerably narrower and more modest aims than the imposition of penances (see 7.5). It thus cannot be assumed that a penance-oriented scheme may properly be pursued except to the extent it is restricted by specific, rather narrowly drawn privacy constraints – for the legitimacy of penances as a state function is precisely what is at issue here.

7.9 'Community' to the Rescue?

To overcome objections to the penance perspective such as these, Duff invokes the idea of 'community'. While a conventional liberal might object to the state's concerning itself with the offender's deeper moral attitudes, Duff describes himself as a communitarian, and it is his notion of community which, supposedly, supplies the warrant for an expiatory conception of punishment.[j]

[j] An earlier essay of Duff's makes this link explicit (Duff 1999a). His recent book does not contain such strong assertions, but the link remains apparent. He devotes an entire chapter to his conception of community (Duff 2001, ch. 2). In the logic of his argument, the introduction of the idea of community provides an important part of his justification for state-imposed penances.

In his recent volume,[29] Duff gives an account of his view of the state as a political community. He likens this to an academic community. An academic community, he suggests, is defined by a commitment to certain shared values, such as those of scholarship. Members assess each other's performance in terms of these shared values; and feel called upon to cooperate in performing certain teaching and administrative duties in order to further them. The university has certain formal structures and disciplinary rules, that these shared values largely define. This community holds its authority, however, only over certain aspects of its members' lives – primarily, those to do with scholarship. The political community, Duff asserts, likewise is defined through commitment to certain shared values – those, for example, of freedom, autonomy, and mutual regard and respect. Its formal structure, the state, derives its power from these values. It, too, holds its authority only over certain aspects of its members' lives.

What is notable about this account of community is its modesty. What counts is the adoption of certain specific values. If a university has shared values of scholarship that define its activities, that constitutes it as a scholarly community. If a liberal state embodies certain shared liberal values, that renders it a community and should define its powers. Given these very modest definitions, it would not seem controversial to consider the university as a scholarly community, or the state as constituting a certain community of liberal values. There is nothing in this limited account, however, that would warrant granting the community more sweeping authority over its members – for example, giving it powers of deeper inquiry into members' moral attitudes.

When Duff treats the notion of community as giving warrant to expiatory functions in punishment, however, his 'community' suddenly seems to grow muscle. It would no longer suffice to assert that the state is defined through a commitment to liberal values, as those values do not justify (indeed, they militate against) such an intrusive conception of sanctioning. What gives the monastery its strong disciplinary powers is not the mere fact that it is a close-knit community, but that it is a community of a certain kind, whose stated values have to do with spiritual welfare of its members and with submission to the moral authority of superiors. Thus the appeal to community in no way advances the case for expiatory punishments. And a liberal could agree that the state should embody a community of shared values in the restricted sense in which Duff initially suggests, without in any way being compelled to grant this 'community' the more far-reaching role of imposing expiatory punishments.[k]

[k] In dealing with the restraint of dangerous offenders, Duff (1998; 2001, 170–174) gives notions of community still more muscle. He argues that highly dangerous offenders might be held well beyond the term of punishment deserved by the seriousness of their offences. If these individuals have perpetrated serious acts of violence, he suggests, this represents so grave a derogation of the political community's values as to warrant their expulsion – and that

The authority of a community to impose sanctions on its members should depend straightforwardly on the values that it is assumed to embody, and on the constraints of liberty and fairness that are assumed to apply to it. If an academic community is legitimately entitled to expel plagiarists, this derives from the community's particular role in policing minimum requirements of scholarship. If an abbot is entitled to impose penances on his charges, that depends not on the order's character as a community, but on the fact that assumed values of this particular community are strongly focused on its members' spiritual wellbeing and on the wide spiritual authority conferred upon the order's superiors. If the values of the political community are those which Duff initially describes – those concerned with freedom, autonomy, and mutual respect – then it is far from obvious how those values could support expiatory punishments. In that event, Duff's notion of 'community' does not itself provide any added leverage for deriving the power to improve penances.

7.10 What Practical Difference?

Much of our foregoing differences with Duff revolve around our diverging conceptions of the state and its relations with its citizens: our traditional liberal one, as contrasted with his more 'communitarian' one. While those issues are of interest from the perspective of political and penal philosophy, how much difference do they actually make for practical sentencing policy? In many of its salient substantive aspects, Duff's sentencing model is not dissimilar to ours: in the central role that he gives to penal censure, in his insistence on moderate sanction levels, and his reliance on proportionality as an important criterion for deciding comparative sentence severities. Behind these similarities lies a shared perspective on offenders and potential offenders as agents capable of moral deliberation, and an emphasis on fairness concerns. With these similarities, why do the differences discussed in this chapter matter? Might it not, indeed, be

'expulsion', he adds, may take the form of long-term preventative confinement. Against this scheme, several specific objections come to mind. First, the scheme would infringe even Duff's somewhat watered-down proportionality requirements: the offender could receive *much* more than the seriousness of his offence would warrant – but he does not even recognize this as a derogation from what is deserved. (Compare our view in Ch. 4, where we expressly treat sentence extension on grounds of dangerousness as a derogation from proportionality.) Secondly, expulsion of citizens does not seem to be a legitimate power of a liberal state: even under present law in most Western countries, they may not be deported for the most heinous crimes. Third, long-term confinement is in no sense an 'expulsion': an expellee may at least exercise his freedom of action in the place to which he is expelled, whereas the long-term prisoner is denied his autonomy altogether. What is most problematic about the proposal, however, is that his account of the state as a community representing certain liberal values in no way supports the notion that its most recalcitrant members may be 'expelled' through long-term incarceration. Duff (2001, 173–4) more recently has recognized some difficulties with his proposal, and states that he has become 'uneasy' with it.

suggested that our emphasis on our differences is actually misplaced? If the practical implications of the two theories for sentencing policy are similar, and if the divergences mainly concern differing 'deeper' conceptions of state power, might this not be a cause of celebration rather than alarm? Could it not be a sign of the robustness of the proportionalist sentencing model, that it can be derived from varying, but still basically liberal, conceptions of the state?

To answer these questions, it would need to be examined whether Duff's theory has troublesome implications for practical sentencing policy that would not arise on our conception. In the preceding discussion in this chapter, we have identified two potentially problematic areas: first, the dilution of proportionality requirements (7.7); and second, the possibility of intrusive and wide-ranging inquiries into what punished offenders think and feel while undergoing their penances (7.8). Both of these, however, are *potential* difficulties. Whereas the desert rationale has actually been implemented in a number of jurisdictions (see 6.2), we still have little idea of how Duff would wish his scheme to operate when applied in a (far from ideal) contemporary democratic state. This is because Duff does not attempt systematically to 'model' the application of his theory in a contemporary criminal justice system. Thus it remains uncertain how his scheme might actually address these two potential problem areas.

With the first issue, concerning proportionality requirements, Duff has provided us a hint – in his proposal for sentencing guidelines utilizing 'zones of discretion' (see 7.7). But as he put forward this scheme as just an example, however, we need to know more about what firm limits (if any) he would insist upon concerning deviations from horizontal equity requirements.

On the second issue, the uncertainty is greater still. Even if Duff would allow an ideal state to undertake wide-ranging inquiries into punished offenders' feelings and attitudes, might he wish to impose firmer limits on such inquiries in the context of the far-from-ideal political and penal systems that operate in modern Western states? Arguably, penal authorities' lack of sympathy with lawbreakers in actual penal systems would make such limits desirable, even if they were thought not to be appropriate for an ideal state. We thus would need to know more about what Duff thinks the constraints on inquiry into offender attitudes should be, in the context of an actual, contemporary society.

Notes

1. Duff 1986, ch. 9.
2. von Hirsch 1993, ch. 8; von Hirsch 1999.
3. Duff 1999a; Duff 2001, especially chs. 3 and 4.
4. Duff 2001, 108.

5. Duff 2001, 107–8.
6. Duff 2001, 109–112.
7. Duff 1999a, 61–64; see also Duff 2001, 181–84.
8. Duff 1999a, 53–54.
9. Duff 1999a, 52.
10. See 9.4; von Hirsch 1993, ch. 5.
11. Rex 1998.
12. See Braithwaite's (1989) view of 'reintegrative shaming'; for a critique of his view, see von Hirsch 1993, 71–72.
13. See, eg, Rex 1998.
14. For how treatment efforts can be made consistent with a desert model through observance of proportionality constraints, see von Hirsch 1993, ch. 7, Rex 1998, and this volume, 9.7. Certain limits on the modalities of treatment are also called for and designed to assure that they are not intrusive or demeaning – for example, a bar against forcing the offender to express attitudes or views to which he does not subscribe; see von Hirsch 1993, ch. 9.
15. See Ch. 2.
16. See 1.2.2. Note, however, the recent setbacks to this optimistic perspective, generated by unfavourable results in some recent studies, see ibid.
17. See von Hirsch and Ashworth 1998, 113–127.
18. Rehabilitation research indicated that successes tend to occur *selectively*, for treatment modalities targeted to particular subgroups, selected for amenability, von Hirsch and Ashworth 1998, 27–28.
19. See 9.2.
20. See Duff 1999a, 56–57.
21. See 9.2; Duff 2001, 132.
22. Duff 1999a, 52; Duff 2001, 137–39.
23. Duff 2001, 137–41, 156–58.
24. Duff 2001, 137–41. Duff derives this guideline scheme from proposals by Michael Tonry, devised for the latter's rather different theory of 'limiting retributivism'; see Tonry 1997; Tonry 1998; see also Appendix 2, below.
25. See von Hirsch 1993, ch. 6, and Appendix 2, on permissible deviations from proportionality.
26. Duff 2001, 60–66.
27. Duff 2001, 125–129.
28. Duff 2001, 128.
29. Duff 2001, ch. 2.

8

Restorative Justice: A 'Making Amends' Model?

(*Co-author: Clifford Shearing*)

We turn, in this chapter, to considering a set of ideas that have gained considerable recent influence: Restorative Justice ('RJ'). RJ typically involves processes by which offender and victim meet to negotiate a disposition involving some kind of 'reparative' or 'restorative' task. The question we address, is why invoke schemes of this kind, and subject to what limitations?

Much of the existing (and now quite voluminous) literature concerning RJ suffers from unduly sweeping definition of aims and insufficient specifications of limits. We shall examine whether these might be defined more clearly, and how they would compare with those of a desert rationale. The chapter brings together three authors, two (von Hirsch and Ashworth) of whom support desert-oriented approaches and a third (Shearing) who has been exploring alternatives to traditional criminal justice processes.

We shall proceed by sketching and analysing a particular conception for RJ, which we term the 'making amends' model. We will describe the model, and then try to draw out some of its implications – regarding modalities and techniques for achieving its stated rationale, criteria for evaluating success or failure, and possible requirements concerning proportionality. We shall then examine two ways the model might be implemented: first, ambitiously, as a comprehensive scheme aimed at replacing the criminal sentencing system; and second, more modestly, as a scheme for a specified range of cases, within the broader framework of a proportionality-oriented sentencing system.

We make no ambitious claims on behalf of this 'making amends' model. It can, at best, reflect some but not all of the aspirations discussed in the RJ literature; and two of the present authors continue to have doubts concerning the model, which we will sketch at the end. We wish, rather, to make heuristic use of our model, to suggest how RJ's aims and possible scope might be specified more clearly.

We shall be addressing RJ as it applies to criminal offending – that is, to conduct that has been found violative of a state's criminal prohibitions. Some writers (eg, Braithwaite[1]) suggest that restorative approaches might be extended beyond crime to deal with other social and political problems, but we shall not be discussing such matters.

8.1 RJ's Stated Aims and Limits: Problems of Coherence

We begin our analysis by setting forth an 'internal' critique of restorative justice – namely, one that does not depend on strong ulterior (particularly, desert-based) assumptions. The aim of this critique is to scrutinize RJ in its own terms: to ask whether RJ conceptions, as usually represented, constitute a coherent theory capable of providing meaningful guidance.

8.1.1 The critique

The internal critique of which we are speaking points to a number of problematic features of RJ. These include the following:

- *Multiple and unclear goals*: The advocates of restorative justice put forward a variety of stated RJ goals: that, for example, the victim be 'restored'; the offender be made to recognize his wrong; the 'conflict' between victim and offender be healed; the breach of the citizens' sense of trust in each other be repaired; the community be reassured against further criminal behaviour on the offender's part; and fear of crime be diminished.[2] The goals may be ambitiously but vaguely formulated: for example, that the aim is to 'repair' the harm done by the criminal act, but without specifying to what extent this should involve repairing the consequential harms or should involve a normative response of some kind. Multiple goals may be put forward simultaneously, without priorities among them being specified.[a] Some purported goals appear to have analogical rather than literal meaning. Restorative processes are supposed, for example, to resolve the 'conflict' between offender and victim;[3] but crimes are different from disputes in that the offender seldom claims to be entitled to what he takes – so what 'dispute' is being resolved?[b] RJ processes are said to 'restore' the bonds of community frayed through the offence, but it is not explained what kinds of bonds have been damaged or how this restoration is to take place. Such overbreadth and vagueness of purpose dilutes the guidance that RJ conceptions can provide.

[a] See, eg Pettit and Braithwaite 1993, with the multiple proposed aims of giving recognition to the wrongdoing; recompensing the victim; reducing crime, and reducing fear of crime.

[b] The idea of 'conflict', moreover, also carries no implication that either party has *wronged* the other (see 8.2.6 below).

An injunction to seek numerous imprecisely delineated goals tells us little about what particular aims should be pursued, or how these ends may be achieved.

- *Underspecified means and modalities*: Not enough has been done to specify the particular means for achieving the various RJ objectives – other than to assert that these would emerge through a deliberative process in which offender and victim participate. When, say, a 'group conference' involving the offender and his victim meets to deal with a particular offence, what kind of interventions ought it ordinarily decide upon? When would monetary compensation to the victim be preferable, and when would something else be? If an apology by the offender is desired, when would this be desirable and when would it be likely to be counterproductive? With multiple and vaguely delineated goals, the means and modalities for achieving them have been difficult to identify.
- *Few or no dispositional criteria*: RJ proceedings tend to be largely discretionary: it is up to the parties of the proceeding to decide in the individual case what would be 'best'. Granted, there may be certain stated minimum requirements – such as that the participants must agree to a proposed outcome before it may take effect; and there may also be certain jurisdictional limits – for example, a ceiling on amounts of compensation. But within these wide bounds, an RJ proceeding may largely be free, in practice, to pursue any aim (including quite traditional ones such as rehabilitation or deterrence); and to choose nearly any means it wishes to achieve such aims.
- *Dangling standards for evaluation*: RJ programmes have been evaluated by a variety of criteria, including participant 'satisfaction' and impact on recidivism. Yet it is seldom explained how these criteria are related to the purposes to be achieved – again, not surprisingly, considering the multiplicity and imprecision of the stated goals.
- *Absent or unclear limiting principles*: The limits on the degree of onerousness of RJ interventions are unspecified or underspecified. There is debate among RJ theorists about whether there should be any proportionality constraints based on the seriousness of the offence.[4] Among those RJ advocates who believe there should be such constraints, their character and rationale have been given little searching analysis.[5]

In response to criticism of this kind, it is sometimes asserted that RJ is only in its early stages; that it develops its aims inductively from practice; and that it emphasizes procedural values rather than predefined substantive goals. None of these responses strike us as being adequate. RJ is no longer in its infancy; it has been influential for more than a decade and a half, and some of its texts go back a quarter-century.[6] While developing goals inductively is a possible way of proceeding, this approach succeeds only if well-defined and consistent goals eventually *do* emerge, as they have not done thus far. Procedural values, however, cannot be free-standing: the procedure must be *for* something. Having crimes dealt with through interaction between victim and offender has value only if it is possible to specify what goals such a procedure could accomplish.

8.1.2 Is RJ primarily an expression of aspirations?

The characteristics just cited, a critic might argue, could suggest that RJ is primarily *aspirational* in character – serving to express wishes or hopes rather than to adopt substantive goals that are designed to guide the choice of dispositions. True, RJ's stated aspirations are somewhat different than those of traditional pre-1980s discretionary sentencing schemes (which also relied on multiple and possibly conflicting goals)[c] in that RJ's purported goals have more to do with 'healing', 'conflict resolution' and the like. There is also a shift on who officiates: it would no longer be the judge, but rather the offender, victim and possibly certain other community representatives. But the function of RJ, on this interpretation, would be to express what it is hoped might be accomplished, ranging from resolving the 'conflict' between offender and victim to reducing fear of crime in the community generally. There would be no need to choose among the ambitious and varying goals, because they are all worth desiring and the RJ process and its dispositions serve to express these desiderata.

What is wrong with such an aspirational approach? Someone might wish to defend it along the following lines: something needs to be done about criminal offending, but what exactly should be done is difficult to decide and may not make much difference in its consequences for public safety. So why not have a discretionary response that expresses chiefly what we *wish* would occur? RJ advocates, however, do not view their efforts as merely expressing aspirations: they see themselves as serious reformers, wishing to implement better ways of dealing with criminal offenders. Something substantive needs to be accomplished through RJ, that goes beyond involving offenders and victims in decisions, and expressing through the disposition the desire that various good ends be achieved.

[c] Traditional, discretionary sentencing schemes claimed to promote rehabilitation, deterrence, incapacitation and 'denunciation' of criminal conduct. However, no priority was set among these differing and potentially conflicting goals, few criteria were provided for deciding individual cases, and there were scant constraints on individual decision-makers' discretion. Such an approach might arguably be understood as expressing aspirations rather than seeking to achieve substantive goals; see von Hirsch 2001a, 410–412.

8.1.3 The need for specifying aims and limits

How might one respond to the foregoing critique? One way would be to try to specify aims and limits more fully: to develop a coherent and consistent formulation of RJ's aims and related processes, that includes protections to help ensure that basic liberal democratic values are not compromised. Good reasons – ones suitable for the public sphere in a modern democratic society – would need to be specified to justify RJ interventions. Such a specification calls at least for the following:

- Consistent and adequately prioritized goals for RJ;
- Adequate specification of means-ends relationships: why should a given set of goals call for given kinds of responses?
- Guidance for deciding individual cases that relate to goals and known means;
- Evaluation criteria, the use of which can be justified in terms of their relevance to the restated goals;
- Adequate fairness constraints on the severity of dispositions.

To see whether such a restatement of RJ is possible, we shall conduct a thought experiment. It is to try to sketch a particular conceptual model for restorative justice, and examine whether it might satisfy these requirements of rationality better.

8.2 A Possible RJ Model: 'Making Amends'

The RJ model which we shall describe is one that involves the notion of 'making amends'. In the limited space available, our sketch will necessarily be incomplete, but, we hope, sufficient to convey the concepts involved.

8.2.1 The 'making amends' model

The 'making amends' model constitutes a response negotiated between the offender and his victim, which involves (1) the implicit or explicit acknowledgement of fault and (2) an apologetic stance on the part of the offender, ordinarily conveyed through his having to undertake a reparative task.[7]

The model differs from the conception of punishment developed by desert theorists. In a desert model, penal censure is *authoritatively* conveyed through the imposition of punishment. Its aim, in part, is to convey censure which the offender, as a moral agent, should consider in evaluating his own conduct and deciding how to behave in future. That model involves a form of moral discourse but not a negotiated one: *A*, the punishing agent (typically the state), determines certain types of actions to be wrong, and adopts legal norms prohibiting such conduct and prescribing sanctions that convey disapproval for the conduct. If *X*, an actor, engages in the conduct, he will suffer the sanction and thereby be subjected to the disapproval. He, as well as others, may take this into account in evaluating their conduct (see Chapter 2).

The 'making amends' model is also a form of moral discourse, but one which is closer to informal moral discourse in everyday life. In this kind of response, the victim's role is deemed central. The procedure is a *negotiated* process between offender and victim,[8] leading to a response that conveys acknowledgement of fault and the undertaking of a reparative task reflecting that acknowledgement. The reparative features of the sanction do not literally heal or 'take back' the wrong. Rather, they constitute a way of showing concern for the victim's interests, on the part of a person (the offender) whose lack of respect and concern was expressed, precisely, in his act of wrongdoing.

While the negotiated and discursive character of this response differs from the authoritative model of deserved punishment, the model is 'retributive' in the sense that it is a response to *past* wrongdoing: making amends is a way of conveying an apologetic stance for a misdeed that has occurred. Granted, if the process works as intended, there will also be beneficial consequences: the offender may (and it is hoped will) come to feel more empathy with his victim and others, and thus be less inclined to offend in future; and the victim may become less resentful and alienated from the offender. But these consequences are not the sole point of the exercise, so that the making-amends response does not fail whenever they do not materialize – just as an apology becomes no less appropriate because the offended individual is unwilling to accept it.

If 'making amends' were thus made the focus of RJ, would this have to be the exclusive aim? Not necessarily; other goals might also be pursued, provided this were done consistently with a primarily making-amends focus. (Providing support for the offender to help him avoid reoffending, for example, could be such a supplemental end, if done in such a manner that comports with the appropriate making of amends for the offence.)[9] How such supplemental goals could be taken into account would call for further analysis, however, and could complicate our model. Thus, for the sake of simplicity, we shall limit our discussion to the sole end of making amends.

8.2.2 The RJ intervention as an imposition

Among RJ theorists, there has been considerable divergence of view whether restorative responses are or are not 'punishments'.[10] What should be clear, however, is that the making-amends model, even if it differs in significant respects from traditional punishment, is one involving an *imposition*. It is so in two important respects. First, calling for acknowledgement of fault involves adverse judgements about the offender and his behaviour. Second, any disposition that results from the process will ordinarily deprive the offender of certain important interests: his property, if he must pay compensation; some of his freedom of action, if he must undertake a reparative task.

To say that an imposition is involved is no criticism: indeed, the adverse judgement and the burdens to be undertaken by the offender are central to the aims of the scheme. Acknowledging that we are speaking of impositions means, however, that a burden of justification must be met: good reasons need to be supplied for why the offender must suffer these burdens, and fairness requirements need to be observed to ensure that the burdens are justly imposed.

The character of making amends as an imposition cannot be avoided on grounds that the offender's 'consent' is required, for the offender cannot choose simply to have nothing happen to him. If he refuses his consent, he will have to face whatever alternative sanctioning system awaits the nonconsenting: a traditional criminal trial, or else possibly, John Braithwaite's suggested scheme of deterrent or incapacitative sanctions.[11] He may have reason to fear that those latter responses would (at best) be no less unpleasant.

When a negotiated procedure results in someone's being deprived of important interests, an imposition is involved – notwithstanding that the person agrees to participate in the negotiations. In criminal justice contexts, this is obvious: being sentenced to prison as a result of a plea- or sentence-bargain involves an imposition, and no less so because the person might have refused the bargain and faced the alternative legal consequences. The point holds also for restorative processes. So long as the offender engages in the process, it is that process – and not something else – which is responsible for any resulting deprivation he must suffer. It does not matter that the offender could have withdrawn from the process, and then had to face an alternative sanctioning system.

8.2.3 Modalities and guidance

The 'making amends' model represents a particular set of aims, that should influence the modalities of RJ intervention: only certain kinds of intervention are likely to be helpful in promoting the model's aims. The making of restitution to the victim as a way of acknowledging fault could be a legitimate way of making amends. Purely unpleasant sanctions might serve other (for example, deterrent) purposes, but not this purpose. There should thus be some explicit principles suggesting what kind of dispositions might be appropriate, and what kind might not be. Leaving this purely to the discretion of particular participants is likely to lead to dispositions which, if capable of being rationalized at all, could be so on grounds having little or nothing to do with the making of amends.

Even for those types of dispositions which appear generally to be appropriate to this model, it would be helpful to provide further guidance on specific means and techniques employed. What kind of making-amends response might help victim and offender understand that an expression of regret is involved? What kind is likely to bring the parties towards reconciliation and a better understanding? What kinds of rituals and dispositions are likely to be counterproductive? As RJ programmes are tried and evaluated, there should develop some understanding on such matters, and individual decision-making groups should have available explicit guidance reflecting that knowledge. Calling for such guidance will mean that some norm- or rule-generating process needs to provide it, and will mean that the guidance will need to be set forth in some useful and readily available form.

8.2.4 Scope of application of the model

The making-amends model is most readily addressed to situations in which there is an identifiable person who is the offender, another identifiable person who is the victim, and a victimizing act which infringes the latter's rights. A typical case which seems to suit this model is one where *X* unprovokedly enters and vandalizes *Y*'s flat. Here, there is an act of wrongdoing against someone, which would seem to warrant an apologetic response by the actor to the victim, conveyed in some act of making of amends.

There are, however, a variety of cases which seem less well suited to this kind of response. One less 'suitable' category, in our judgement, would consist of crimes in which there are no individual victims. If *A* is charged with tax evasion, there is no person to whom he can convey an apologetic stance via some kind of restitutionary act. Saying the 'community' is the victim here is not illuminating.

There are also types of cases in which the appropriateness of an RJ approach should be a matter for further debate. An example are crimes in which an individual 'victim' has been injured or threatened with injury, but in which this is a response to previous wrongful behaviour on the victim's part directed against the present perpetrator. *X* has beaten up *Y* last Saturday night, and now *Y* beats up *X* this Saturday night, is apprehended, and is placed before a group conference. In such cases it is less clear who should apologize to whom; or whether mutual apologies would be desirable. Having a more clearly stated set of goals – in our suggested model of making amends – might help resolve whether a restorative approach would be appropriate here.

8.2.5 Evaluation criteria

Criteria for assessing the success of RJ programmes tend at present to 'dangle': reasons are not provided why a given evaluation norm, rather than others, is being employed. Let us, however, examine some possible evaluation criteria, in the light of the 'making amends' model's aims.

Recidivism reduction. Reduction in the rate of reoffending is a criterion often used in evaluating RJ programmes. The results have been mixed.[12] But why should this be the basis of evaluation?

One possible claim is that reduced recidivism would show that RJ is an effective crime-preventive tool. Even if crime prevention were deemed the desideratum, however, that depends not on reducing recidivism per se, but on reducing citizens' net exposure to criminal victimization. The debate over 'selective incapacitation' in the 1980s has made clear that reducing net victimization rates depends on more than lowering the number of convicted offenders who return to crime. Other critical facts affecting crime rates include: (1) the number of new entrants into criminal activity and the number of those successfully avoiding detection and conviction; (2) the estimated length of the residual criminal careers of convicted offenders, and the frequency with which they could have been expected to offend; (3) the extent to which the crimes involved are committed by co-offenders, some of whom remain apprehended and continue active offending.[13] Issues such as these are generally not addressed in the RJ evaluation literature.

Another (in our view more plausible) claim, would be that desisting from further crime is part of the making-amends process. An aspect of the offender's conveying a regretful stance for criminal behaviour is his making efforts to refrain from offending in future – and recidivism rates measure that. The difficulty remains, however, that lowered recidivism may be motivated not by regret on the part of the offender elicited by the making-amends procedure, but rather by a variety of ulterior factors. Even if young offenders are unimpressed by the substance of the RJ proceeding, they might still desist from reoffending if they find it sufficiently tiresome – so that special deterrence, rather than anything having to do with making amends, would be the major influence. Thus one would need evaluation techniques that help separate out these various possible effects.[d]

[d] In response, it might be asserted that the offenders' possible reasons for desisting from further crime would not matter, so long as they do desist. This, however, would be treating making amends simply as a crime reduction technique. Lowered recidivism might possibly be achievable by various strategies quite different from the making of amends – such as traditional incapacitative techniques. Were recidivism-prevention the main criterion for success, much would depend which approach – the making of amends or something quite different – proved the most efficient.

'*Satisfaction*'. Satisfaction on the part of those participating in the RJ processes has also been used as a test of success.[14] But why should 'satisfaction' be the measure? A possible explanation is that the making-amends process, if it operates as it is supposed to, will lead to an accommodation between offender and victim from which both might derive satisfaction. However, it would be necessary to consider what else might yield comparable satisfaction. Often, the research compares RJ proceedings with traditional court procedures, and finds that participants are more satisfied by RJ.[15] But this may derive, in part, from the fact that RJ procedures are more friendly and informal, and give the participants more time and scope to discuss what has happened to them. Court procedures using traditional sentencing conceptions (say, of desert), might also evince a more satisfied response, if operated in a fashion that is less rushed, and gives more scope to the parties' explanations. If 'satisfaction' is to be a valid success measure, it would thus seem necessary to undertake comparisons of that kind.

'*Meeting of minds*'. In recent research, Kathleen Daly uses as a measure of success whether, as a result of the procedure, the parties come to appreciate each other's perspectives better, and develop more empathy for one another. This does seem to be an appropriate evaluation norm for the making-amends model, one whose express aim is to achieve a degree of reconciliation between offender and victim. But, as Daly notes, the occurrence rate of this phenomenon is relatively modest.[16]

8.2.6 The role of proportionality

There exists considerable disagreement, among RJ proponents, about the need for proportionality constraints. Some RJ advocates, such as Braithwaite, suggest that these should be jettisoned entirely[17] (although he recently seems to have modified his position somewhat).[18] Others, such as Dignan, suggest that there should be some proportionality limits.[19] However, the grounds for and character of such limits have been little addressed in the RJ literature.

Outer proportionality requirements, that bar the use of severe penalties for lesser crimes, are minimal requirements of fairness that any modern liberal state should recognize. Indeed, a ban on grossly disproportionate penalties is constitutionally required in some jurisdictions.[20]

The interesting question is whether there should be proportionality requirements going beyond these minimal ones. For a punishment system, the argument for proportionality requirements is straightforward enough: such a system utilizes responses that involve *censure*, and the severity of the sanction signifies the degree of censure conveyed. Consequently, the severity of sanctions should fairly reflect the degree of comparative blameworthiness of the conduct (see Chapter 2; 9.3).

Could comparable reasons be used to support proportionality requirements in a making-amends model? A possible argument might run as follows. An essential feature of the making-amends model is that the procedure and its sanctions are designed to express a moral evaluation of the conduct. The victim, it is assumed, has been *wronged* by the offender, and the procedure aims at giving adequate recognition to that wrongdoing. In tort law, there is no such aim: the point of tort is mainly to decide who should bear the loss, the actor or the injured party; fault is deemed a ground – but not an exclusive one – for shifting the burden of loss to the actor. The making of amends, however, is much more than a loss-shifting device: its point is to provide a means through which the wrongdoer conveys to his victim a recognition of wrongdoing. If such a moral evaluation of the conduct is thus centrally involved, the response should bear some reasonable relationship to how reprehensible the conduct can fairly be characterized as being.

The foregoing point holds already for simple verbal apologies in everyday life. Suppose *X* negligently steps on *Y*'s toes, and says that he is sorry to have hurt her. Suppose, however, that *Y* insists that this is not enough; that *X* must admit that his conduct has not merely been clumsy but extraordinarily reprehensible. *X* could rightly be entitled to resist such a suggestion; to say that while he was wrong to have hurt *Y*, the injury was not great, and his fault was one of mere negligence; and hence, that the wrong was relatively minor. *A*'s apology should not be required to overstate his degree of fault.

This argument extends to the making-amends model, where what is to be negotiated is not just a verbal apology, but a burden undertaken by the offender that is designed to convey that apologetic stance. If the basis for the imposition lies in its recognition of wrongdoing, its degree of onerousness necessarily conveys how reprehensible the conduct is treated as being. This implied valuation should, then, bear a reasonable relation to the actual degree of reprehensibleness of the conduct – that is, to its seriousness. The upshot is a requirement of proportionality. (It should be noted, moreover, that this requirement has not been 'externally' derived from traditional criminal-justice principles; it derives from the logic of making-amends itself.)

In this kind of negotiated disposition, however, it would not seem feasible to import the kind of rigorous ordinal-proportionality requirements that a desert model envisions for criminal punishments (see 9.3.2). This is because considerable leeway would be needed for the parties to choose a disposition that they feel conveys regret in a satisfactory manner. We will return below to the question of how large this leeway might need to be.

8.2.7 Is the 'making amends' model conceptually coherent?

Our critique at the outset questioned whether RJ, as it is usually formulated, is a meaningful rationale at all. RJ's multiple and unclear goals, its under-specified conception of means and modalities, its lack of dispositional standards and fairness limits, its dangling measures of success – these all seem to point to a lack of coherent conception. The question we posed was whether an RJ model could be formulated that avoids these deficiencies.

The making-amends model, in our view, does seem to provide a modicum of conceptual coherence. It seeks to achieve, not all conceivable desiderata, but a particular, interrelated and mutually consistent set of them: namely, the conducting of a dialogue between offender and victim about the former's wrongdoing; the expression by the wrongdoer to his victim of an acknowledgement of fault, carried out through a reparative act; and the opportunity given to the victim to accept that expression of regret and thus possibly to achieve some measure of reconciliation. This model resembles in important respects moral dialogue that is carried out in everyday life, and that can be described directly and without reliance on metaphors such as 'healing' and the like.

The model also helps yield some norms of application. It points toward particular kinds of interventions, and standards of use; it provides some guidance regarding scope of application – that is, regarding the kind of cases for which this approach would or would not be suitable; it suggests what kind of evaluation criteria should be used to judge success or failure; and it tells us something about the standards of fairness – particularly, of proportionality – that should be utilized. A 'making amends' model thus might be seen as seeking substantive ends, and not merely as constituting the expression of aspirations. Adopting a model such as this one involves, however, certain trade-offs, for the model focuses on some possible goals, and not others. The making-amends model is victim/offender focused: it is conceived as a certain kind of discursive interchange between them. As a result, other possible goals would necessarily be given less emphasis, if any: the model, for example, is not explicitly aimed at maximizing crime-control effects, or reducing the fear of crime, or the like. This kind of trade-off is inevitable: trying to accomplish all goals simultaneously is tantamount to having no meaningful goals at all.

8.3 Some Queries about the 'Making Amends' Model

That the making-amends model is conceptually coherent does not necessarily mean it is right. A number of substantial problems exist, which need to be considered next.

8.3.1 Impartiality of decision-makers

A fair procedure for determining the offender's guilt is, of course, essential. Although most defendants tend to plead guilty anyway, those who plead not guilty should have access to a court in order to determine this. The processes of RJ should be reserved for those who have either pleaded or been found guilty.

Impartiality of the decision-maker remains an issue, however, at the dispositional stages after guilt has been established. In an RJ group conference, two of the central participants – the victim and the offender – are clearly not impartial. (While there may also be an impartial facilitator at the proceeding, his role is likely to be primarily advisory.) It would not be possible to remove the parties from having a central role in deciding the disposition of the case, as much of the point of the procedure lies in giving them this role.

It might be argued that impartiality need no longer be a concern where the sanction is not one imposed externally by an official, but rather negotiated in a process in which the offender is a participant. If the offender feels that he is not being treated fairly, he can withdraw. The feasibility of withdrawing, however, depends on what alternative processes and possible dispositions would then await him. He may have reasons for feeling that he must participate, for fear of facing something worse. The lack of impartiality thus remains a drawback of the model.

8.3.2 The problem of the role of attitude

A ban on compulsory attitudinizing is an important safeguard of the human dignity of offenders: it is demeaning to be compelled to express views or attitudes that one may not actually hold.[21] In the criminal process, this safeguard is not always observed: parole boards, for example, sometimes are known to insist on a showing of penitent attitudes, before granting parole release. But in punishment, the expressed attitudes of the offender are not of the essence; what matters is the authoritative expression of penal censure by the state through the sanction. Thus it should be possible to adopt principles designed to guard against trying to force the offender to manifest any particular set of attitudes. On our suggested making-amends model, however, this issue becomes more difficult; here, the whole point is to negotiate a disposition that is meant to convey an acknowledgement of fault. Attitude and its expression thus become central.

It might be possible, on a making-amends model, to try to protect against the cruder kinds of compulsory attitudinizing. If the offender is browbeaten into making an apology, that is no real apology at all. The problem lies, however, in the more subtle pressures to express the 'right' attitudes – since those attitudes make so much difference for the process.

Two kinds of constraints might help to alleviate this problem. One would be a bar against requiring rituals of self-abasement (such as making a convicted thief wear an 'I am a thief' T-shirt). The other would be limits on attitudinal inquiries in the proceedings: the parties would negotiate on a disposition having an expressive form, but direct inquiries would not be permitted about what the offender actually believes or feels. Nevertheless, these are palliatives: the offender may still feel under pressure to express attitudes of repentance which he does not hold, in order to obtain agreement on a favourable disposition.

8.3.3 'Privatization'

A desert model treats punishment as a way of providing a *public* valuation of crime. The sanction is seen as an authoritative response by the state, that conveys censure to the offender – seen as a person capable of moral deliberation. The state's response serves also, through its implied public censure, to express a public evaluation – that certain kinds of conduct are injurious and reprehensible (see 2.6.4).

This public valuation has certain important normative functions. It conveys to the offender and potential offenders, and also to victims and potential victims, the message that the behaviour is deemed to be wrong in a certain degree. While the actual primary injury may be to a particular victim, the conduct is treated as infringing standards of the conduct of the larger body politic. In providing that public acknowledgement of wrongdoing, the state gives public recognition to the value of the rights involved, and makes a moral (rather than purely prudential) appeal to citizens that they should desist from the conduct.[22]

Using RJ to deal with victimizing criminal behaviour would tend to *privatize* the response. The crime is treated primarily as an affront to the particular victim, and the procedure and its sanctions serve as a means by which the actor conveys to him regret for that affront. Additional actors – for example, the community representative at the hearing – would act primarily as facilitators for the process. Notwithstanding frequent references in the restorative-justice literature to themes about 'community',[23] the procedure would chiefly reflect the perspectives of the immediately interested parties.

An important drawback of this kind of privatization is that it tends to blur the distinction between wronging and harming. On a wronging conception, the severity of the sanction should reflect how reprehensible the conduct is deemed to be. Harm is an important element in determining the conduct's degree of blameworthiness, but culpability is also vitally important – for example, the degree of foreseeability of the harm, the kind of intent involved, and the presence of any partially excusing conditions. Conventional depictions of RJ tend to blur this distinction, by describing RJ as largely focused on consequentialist goals such as 'repairing' the harm or resolving the 'conflict'.[24] The making-amends model, as we have seen, more clearly treats the conduct as wrongdoing, and the response as a way of acknowledging the wrong. But if the procedure leaves decisions primarily to individual offenders and their victims, the emphasis may too easily shift in practice from one of wronging to that of harming. What will come to matter is not so much how culpable the offender was in committing his wrong, but the particulars concerning how much the victim has been made to suffer. We shall return to this theme of privatization and its implications below.

8.4 'Making Amends' as a Replacement for Criminal Justice?

Some of the RJ literature proposes the ambitious goal of having RJ largely or entirely replace traditional criminal justice. The institution of legal punishment is said to be fundamentally flawed, and should be supplanted by a restorative justice approach.[25]

If RJ, with making amends as its aim, were to replace criminal justice, how might such a system be constituted? An informal, negotiated process involving the victim and offender, aimed at the acknowledgement of fault and the undertaking of a reparative task, would become the *primary* response to victimizing criminal behaviour. The procedure would apply not only to juvenile offenders but, after judicial adjudication of guilt,[26] to adult offenders as well. RJ's scope might thus extend to a wide variety of cases, ranging from petty thefts to serious violent offences. With this increase in scope would come wider dispositional powers (including possibly, the power to impose incarcerative dispositions for serious offences).[27] The formal criminal justice system would be relegated to the status of a 'back up' system, applying to cases deemed unsuitable to the making of amends, and to persons who fail to co-operate with RJ processes. What concerns would such a scheme raise?

8.4.1 Regulating discretion

Earlier in this chapter, we suggested the need for guidance concerning what kinds of procedures and dispositions would help implement a making-amends model. Today's RJ proceedings tend, however, to be largely discretionary, with only limited external controls. If the ambit of RJ is expanded so that it becomes the response of first resort for most victimizing offences, this discretion would potentially be expanded still further. In order to deal with more serious cases, for example, the range of permissible sanctions would have to be widened substantially. This would make still more urgent the need for dispositional norms.

Yet for such an expanded system of 'free standing' RJ, discretion would become much more difficult to regulate. The primary decision-makers would be lay persons not trained in applying and interpreting explicit norms. The legal system's usual way of policing the application of sentencing criteria – namely, having an appellate tribunal review the decision and possibly revise the disposition – would also be awkward to apply, because what matters is not just the disposition but the discursive process through which offender and victim reach it.[e] As a result, it would become harder to formulate and implement norms and review procedures that would help assure that the process serves to achieve making-amends goals, and does so in an equitable manner.

8.4.2 Uncooperative offenders

Establishing a free-standing RJ system raises the question of what is to be done with uncooperative offenders. There are three types of persons potentially involved: those who refuse to participate in an RJ proceeding or who do not consent to the resulting disposition; those who agree to undertake a reparative task, but then fail to carry it out; and those who repeatedly reoffend, after previous RJ dispositions.[28] The third category, of recidivists, is likely to be quite large – and would remain so, even if RJ were to have some success in reducing recidivism rates.

Some RJ theorists have proposed strongly consequentialist responses, designed to strengthen incentives to participate, or to help combat recidivist crime. Braithwaite, for example, recommends a system of deterrent and incapacitative back-up sanctions.[29] Schemes of this kind would be open to two serious objections. One concerns fair treatment: purely incapacitative sanctions for recidivist offenders, for example, may involve disproportionately severe responses.[30] The other objection relates to the adverse effect on the integrity of the making-amends process. The more the offender's default would involve risk of deterrent or incapacitative sanctions, the more offenders will feel compelled to participate in RJ on purely cautionary grounds and the less genuine any purported efforts at making amends are likely to be.

[e] If a court is given the power to overrule an RJ conference's decisions, for example, it will have to order a new proceeding, or alter the decision agreed upon by the parties. Either approach would interfere with RJ's role as a discursive process through which the parties agree on the disposition. Alternatively, the facilitator could be given a larger role in explaining the range and limits of what the parties may agree upon; but then the question remains of enforcing such directives against unwilling parties.

An alternative possible approach would be to retain a system of proportionate penal sanctions for those who do not cooperate. But this would seem to defeat the aims of advocates of RJ who wish to see it replacing criminal justice. If defaults are numerous, it would be necessary to create a large-scale desert based 'shadow' criminal justice system to deal with them.

8.4.3 Routinization

Making RJ the response of first resort would involve, given high rates of victimizing crimes in most Western countries, shifting much of the large caseloads dealt with by the courts to RJ forums. It is these large caseloads that have contributed so much to the routinization of criminal justice, with its assembly-line procedures and truncated opportunities for meaningful discourse. This is problematic enough for the criminal justice system, as it can make for the remote, cut-and-dried character of criminal proceedings. But criminal sentencing is not essentially dialogic in character, whereas RJ is. On a 'making amends' model, as we have seen, adequate communication and the reaching of understanding between the parties are central to the process. Here, routinization undercuts the whole point of the procedure.

The Canberra RISE Project found that the average length of court hearings in the sample studied varied between seven and 27 minutes, depending on the type of case involved. Restorative conferences lasted much longer, averaging between 60 and 94 minutes.[31] The longer duration doubtless gives a better opportunity to disclose the background to the case, and to permit offenders, victims and their supporters to put forward their perspectives on the event. But with large caseloads, will it be feasible to provide restorative hearings lasting between one to one and a half hours? If calendar pressures shrink the time available down to the ten or twenty minutes with which courts have to make do, that would scarcely suffice for adequate restorative processes.

8.4.4 Aggravating the 'privatization' problem

If restorative proceedings are made the primary response to criminal behaviour, the problem of 'privatization' spoken of earlier will be aggravated. After a finding of guilt by the courts, the focus shifts to a victim-centred negotiating process in which the victim's individual degree of hurt is likely to become central. Consider the case of a relatively routine assault against a victim who turns out to be somewhat more than usually vulnerable. A 'wronging' perspective, which the making-amends model purportedly would adopt, would focus on the offender's intent and how foreseeable the injuries were – thus ordinarily permitting the offence to be treated as having only a modest degree of seriousness. Suppose, however, that such cases are dealt with restoratively. What will then matter more is satisfying the victim's sense of grievance – which will be strongly influenced by the actual injuries he has sustained. The focus will tend to shift from 'see the wrong that you have done' to 'see how I have been made to suffer' – which in this kind of case would point to a more severe response.

A related drawback of this kind of privatization concerns the watering down of horizontal equity requirements. When the response to crime is thus privatized, what will become important is the *parties*' sense of wrongfulness of the behaviour, and of the disposition appropriate thereto; and if different negotiating pairs perceive these matters differently, so be it. Proportionality constraints – which we have said should be part of a making-amends model – could come mainly to constrain proposed dispositions which involve manifestly unreasonable views of the wrongfulness of the conduct.

8.5 'Making Amends' within a Proportionalist Sentencing System?

An alternative to the comprehensive RJ scheme just discussed would be to give restorative approaches, using a making-amends rationale, a more modest role within a larger structure provided by a proportionalist sentencing system.

How might such a scheme be constructed? We might begin by positing a hypothetical sentencing system, based on the principle of proportionate sentences. Penalties would be graded according to the seriousness of the offence, with limited adjustments for previous convictions. Such a system would then be modified by introducing a 'making amends' scheme of limited scope. This would apply to a specified range of victimizing offences – say, certain types of property offences not involving significant violent behaviour. In such cases, guilt or innocence would continue to be determined by the courts, with traditional procedural safeguards. Upon a determination of guilt, the case would be referred to a victim-offender conference, with a facilitator presiding, which would seek a negotiated disposition – based on the making-amends rationale sketched above. The dispositions would be deemed to be punishments, however, and hence subject to proportionality constraints. These latter constraints, however, would be loosened somewhat (although not a great deal) to allow participants some added leeway for agreeing upon a disposition. Would such a more limited scheme of making amends fare better?

8.5.1 Less routinization

Routinization may become somewhat less of a problem. With an RJ system of more limited scope, it will become possible to target this scheme to types of cases for which it appears most suitable. This targeting will also help limit the caseload, so that the system does not become overloaded and negotiations excessively truncated. Much will depend, however, on the scope of the eligibility requirements. Hence, this tension: keeping caseloads down points to narrower eligibility requirements – which, however, would reduce RJ's role. Expanding the eligibility requirements would make RJ become more important, but would increase caseloads and hence aggravate routinization.

In such a scheme, non-cooperative offenders would be returned to the penal system, to receive the appropriate proportionate sanction. Any adjustment in the sanction for recidivists, for example, would be based on the system's general principles regarding recidivism (see 9.6). As the penal system would itself be an intact sanctioning system, and not a mere repository for persons who refuse to participate in an alternative scheme considered preferable, it could operate reasonably equitably.

8.5.2 'Privatization' and horizontal equity

This more limited scheme would also alleviate the 'privatization' problem of which we have just spoken. While the making-amends process would aim at a meeting of the minds between the parties, the relevant standards – especially the proportionality limits – would ultimately be public standards, that represent not just the views of the parties but wider public understandings concerning the degree of blameworthiness of the conduct.

A potential objection to placing RJ within a proportionalist sentencing framework is that the two conceptions are too disparate. Here, the making-amends model should be helpful: while it is informal and discursive in ways that conventional criminal justice is not, the model utilizes a *wronging* paradigm – and resembles penal censure in that it is retrospectively oriented, to give recognition to the degree of blameworthiness of the conduct.

Horizontal equity may be better safeguarded. True, the disposition would be based on the parties' views concerning how injurious and culpable the conduct was, and what a fair response should be; and ordinal-proportionality constraints would need to be relaxed to a modest degree to facilitate the parties' reaching accommodation.[f] But these negotiations still would operate within firm proportionality limits, based on the system's assessment of seriousness and appropriate severity.

Imposing such limits on the degree of severity of the response may well facilitate (rather than retard) the negotiating process, by discouraging maximalist demands. In the case of a common assault, for example, the victim would be given to understand that – while he might point to the

[f] See, in this connection, the discussion of a 'modified' desert model in 9.8; and Appendix 2.

extra harm he has suffered – the negotiations will substantially be constrained by public norms concerning by the blameworthiness of this kind of conduct. The victim will not be able to get a severe response, merely by calling attention to his personal situation.

8.6 Conclusions

What conclusions might be drawn from this discussion? At the least, the following points emerge, and on these the three authors of this chapter are in agreement. (1) The conventional multi-purpose stated rationales for RJ have serious problems of coherence, and may serve a largely aspirational role. (2) It is possible to develop a 'making amends' model for RJ that is more coherent, and we have attempted to describe such a model. Such a model could yield certain standards of application, evaluation criteria, and proportionality limits. Such a model does, however, raise concerns about impartiality of the decision-maker, the central role of attitude, and 'privatization' of the response to criminal wrongdoing. (3) An ambitious version of the making-amends model would be a 'free-standing' scheme, designed as the primary response to victimizing crime generally. This, however, would present serious difficulties, concerning the regulation of discretion, the treatment of uncooperative offenders, routinization, and the loss of horizontal equity. (4) The difficulties of this ambitious version could be partially alleviated by giving RJ schemes more limited scope, within certain limits established by a larger sentencing framework emphasizing proportionality.

These four points, however, do not settle the ultimate question of whether a making-amends model is worth implementing, provided it is thus limited in scope and placed within proportionality-based constraints. On that question, the three authors of this chapter are not of one mind. One of us (Shearing) would view such a model with considerable sympathy; the other two (von Hirsch and Ashworth) are more sceptical. The latter authors remain to be persuaded that a discursive, negotiated process between victim and offenders can function well within parameters of law enforcement and criminal law. They remain concerned, also, about the drawbacks noted already – concerning the lack of an impartial decision-maker, the emphasis on attitude, and the 'privatization' of the response.

In certain settings, we do agree, a making-amends model may well become the preferable solution, in view of serious deficiencies in the formal criminal-justice process. In Northern Ireland, for example, the formal process, for substantial segments of the community, appears largely to have lost its legitimacy, having become perceived as part of a hostile occupying regime. Here, RJ proceedings might be much preferable to the existing alternative of local vigilante justice. What we have addressed here, however, is the issue of principle: whether a making-amends model would truly be preferable, when there are reasonable alternatives.

Notes

1. Braithwaite 2003.
2. See, eg, Zehr 1990; Van Ness 1993; Pettit and Braithwaite 1993; Braithwaite 1999; Bazemore 1999; Braithwaite 2003; Walgrave 2003.
3. Christie 1977.
4. See 8.2.6.
5. Ibid.
6. See Christie 1977.
7. For a somewhat similar conception, see Duff 2003.
8. In certain cases, where the victim wishes not to appear, it might be possible to designate a victim representative.
9. A comparable issue arises in desert theory, concerning the extent to which ulterior (say, rehabilitative) goals may be pursued within a system of proportionate sanctions, see 9.7.
10. Contrast, on this issue, Dignan 2003 with Walgrave 2003.
11. Braithwaite 1999.
12. See, eg, Kurki 2003; Daly 2002; Daly 2003.
13. See National Academy of Sciences 1986; von Hirsch and Ashworth 1998, 113–127.
14. Kurki 2003, 298.
15. Morris and Maxwell 2003, 262–64.
16. Daly 2003, 222–27.
17. Pettit and Braithwaite 1993.
18. Braithwaite 2003.
19. Dignan 2003.
20. The case-law jurisprudence of the German Constitutional Court includes such a ban, for example.
21. See von Hirsch 1993, ch. 9.
22. See Chapter 2.
23. See, eg, Walgrave 2003.
24. See 8.1.1.
25. See, eg, Walgrave 2003.
26. For the need of judicial adjudication of guilt, see 8.3.1.
27. See Dignan 2003.
28. Ibid.
29. Braithwaite 1999.
30. von Hirsch 1985, ch. 11; von Hirsch 1993, ch. 10; Dignan 2003.
31. Strang, Barnes *et al.* 1999.

9

Criteria for Proportionality: A Review

9.1 Introduction

The previous chapters in this volume chiefly address the 'borderlands' of desert theory: how the theory can deal with various special cases (eg, juveniles, dangerous offenders, 'equity' factors, the socially deprived), how it relates to other conceptions of punishment (penance theory, restorative justice), and what some of its political dimensions are. It is these issues which have occupied our thinking about sentencing theory during the last decade.

The core of proportionality doctrine – how deserved sentences should be decided in ordinary cases – has not been addressed in these chapters, as it has been dealt with in previous monographs.[1] That doctrine, however, was developed over time, and is not conveniently available to readers in one place. It also needs updating, on a number of issues. We therefore thought it helpful to provide a 'restatement' that sets forth, in systematic form, the criteria for proportionality of sentence and their rationale. That is the aim of the present chapter.

9.2 Why Punish Proportionately?

In a minimal sense, proportionality always had a role in sentencing policy: penalties grossly disproportionate in relation to the gravity of the offence were perceived as unfair. Statutory maximum sentences reflected that understanding, which also had a constitutional dimension: some jurisdictions have adopted a constitutional bar against grossly excessive punishments.[2] This alone, however, gave proportionality of sentence only a peripheral role – for example, of barring draconian sanctions for lesser offences.

What is distinctive about contemporary desert theory is that it moves the notion of proportionality from this peripheral role to a central one in determining sanctions. The primary basis for scaling punishments, the theory holds, should be the principle of proportionality – requiring the severity of the penalty to be proportionate to the seriousness of the criminal conduct of which the defendant has been convicted.

It is worth reviewing the justification for this principle. Why should sentences be proportionate to offences' gravity? A variety of possible justifications have been suggested, some based on crime prevention, and others based instead on fairness grounds related to the censuring features of punishment. In our view, only the latter provide a firm basis for the principle of proportionality.

9.2.1 Beccaria and Bentham's deterrence argument

The first account of the principle of proportionate sanctions was utilitarian, and was provided over two centuries ago by Cesare Beccaria and Jeremy Bentham.[3] These theorists advocated a tariff of graded penalties, based on objectives of crime prevention, especially general deterrence. When people offend, Beccaria and Bentham argued, it is preferable that they commit lesser offences rather than serious crimes. Hence, the state should grade its prescribed sanctions according to the seriousness of offences, so that potential offenders would be induced (to the extent that they decide to offend at all) to prefer petty thefts over burglaries, burglaries over violent crimes and so forth. Failure to observe the principle of proportionality in sentencing would result in a misdirected structure of disincentives: those choosing to offend might as soon commit grave crimes as lesser ones.[a]

This account, however, would leave the proportionality principle weak and prone to exceptions. To avoid sentencing policies' creating perverse incentives, penalties might be scaled *on average* in some approximate relationship to the gravity of crimes. But there could well be extensive exceptions – for example, the imposition of exemplary punishments on selected individuals in order to intimidate others more efficiently. When

[a] A problem with this argument is our limited knowledge regarding deterrent effects. To decide sentencing policy on the basis of deterrence, one needs to be able to gauge how much the rates of various crimes are affected by changes in penalties. We are still far from having reliable information of this sort – and such evidence as exists suggests that crime rates are not much influenced by changes in sentencing policies (see, eg, von Hirsch, Bottoms, Burney *et al.* 1999; Doob and Webster 2003a). There is thus little evidence to support Bentham and Beccaria's claim that if proportionality were not observed, offenders might be induced to shift their offending behaviour toward more harmful kinds of conduct. A possible response to this difficulty would be to treat the Bentham–Beccaria thesis as a *prophylactic* principle. In the absence of empirical data, one might construct scenarios of what could happen if (say) penalties for middle-level offences were raised to approach the severities imposed for serious crimes. Were changes in sanction severity generally to have little impact in crime rates, then there would be no counterproductive effect of increased serious offending. If, however, sentence severity were to matter in deterrence terms, then counterproductive effects – of a switch to more serious offending – might well occur. Since serious offending is so much more damaging, individually and socially, that consequence would be highly undesirable. For a fuller development of this scenario approach, see von Hirsch, Bottoms, Burney *et al.* 1999, 41–43.

the proportionality principle is thus defended on grounds of crime-preventive efficacy and nothing more, it loses its status as an independent ethical requirement and remains subject to whatever dilutions appear to be needed in the name of crime control.

9.2.2 Positive general prevention: The inhibition-reinforcement argument

Continental penologists, even when utilitarian in general outlook, have tended to recognize the limitations of general deterrence as a guide to sentencing policy. As an alternative, they have stressed the role of punishment as a reinforcer of citizens' moral inhibitions against crime. The criminal sanction, Johannes Andenaes asserts, is a 'concrete expression of society's disapproval' of criminal acts, and thereby 'creates conscious and unconscious inhibitions against crime'.[4]

This norm-reinforcing function is sometimes said to provide the basis for the principle of proportionality. The German criminal law scholar Claus Roxin contends, for example, that a penalty structure in which penalties are kept commensurate with the gravity of crimes will be perceived as more just, and being so perceived, will better strengthen citizens' self-restraint and respect for law.[5] Disproportionate sanctions are said to risk weakening the moral influence of the penalty structure.

Plausible as this argument sounds, it does not stand up well to scrutiny. The idea, ultimately, remains one of crime prevention. It involves the assertion that if sentences are made proportionate, the citizenry's moral inhibitions will better be reinforced, which in turn will enable the criminal law to carry out its crime-restraining role more successfully.

The question that naturally comes to mind is: how does one know? There is not much reliable evidence on whether, and to what extent, punishment reinforces law-abiding attitudes,[6] although there are developments in compliance theory which suggest that punishments perceived as fair and legitimate might to some degree influence behaviour.[7] Moreover, even if there were stronger evidence of the supposed 'disappointment' of citizens' expectations of fairness that disproportionate sanctions could evoke, and the possible resulting weakening of their inhibitions against criminal behaviour, it is unlikely that citizens take sufficient notice of the specifics of sentencing doctrine to have their inhibitions against offending much affected.[8]

The more fundamental difficulty with the argument, however, arises from its failure to recognize that proportionality is not just a prudential but an ethical principle. We feel there is something *wrong*, not simply counterproductive in the long run in preventing crime, about inflicting punishments that are not fairly commensurate with the gravity of offences. That sense of wrongfulness cannot be explained merely by arguing that proportionality influences citizens' attitudes in such a way as to reinforce their inclination to law-abidingness (see more fully 2.3.2).

9.2.3 The argument from censure

The principle of proportionality does not, in our judgement, rest primarily on crime prevention considerations. It is grounded, instead, on the blaming character of punishment.

Punishing someone consists of inflicting a deprivation on him, because he has purportedly committed a wrong, under circumstances and in a manner that conveys disapprobation of the offender for his wrong. The visitation of censure, as noted earlier (Chapter 2), is a central justifying feature of punishment. If one asks why penalties ought to be proportioned to the gravity of the criminal conduct, therefore, the answer is not that this would create the optimum deterrent or inhibition-reinforcing influence, for it may or may not do so. The requirement of proportionate punishment is, instead, derived directly from the censuring implications of the criminal sanction. Once one has created an institution with the condemnatory implications that punishment has, then it is a requirement of justice, not merely of efficient crime prevention, to punish offenders according to the degree of reprehensibleness of their conduct. Disproportionate punishments are unjust not because they possibly may be ineffective or counterproductive, but because they purport to condemn the actor for his conduct and yet visit more or less censure on him than the degree of blameworthiness of that conduct would warrant.

A few comments about this censure-based justification for proportionality are in order. It makes clear that the principle of proportionality does not rest on factual claims that commensurability in punishment enhances the crime-preventive utility of the system. Suppose we are able to discover evidence that proportionate punishments were no more effective as a deterrent than (and even possibly somewhat less effective) than disproportionate ones. Suppose, further, that new psychological evidence were to suggest that formal penal sanctions, whether proportionate or not, contribute only to a limited extent to the development of people's moral inhibitions against injurious conduct. Would such evidence mean that one properly could ignore the requirements of proportionality? Certainly not. As long as the state continues to respond to injurious conduct of various kinds through the institution of the criminal sanction, it is treating those whom it punishes as wrongdoers and conveying disapprobation of them for their conduct. If the sanction thus authoritatively visits blame, the severity of the state's response ought to reflect the degree of blameworthiness (that is, the seriousness) of the actor's conduct.

This argument uses a commonly understood concept, employed in everyday discourse: the notion of censure. The idea is that once a condemnatory institution has been established to respond to criminal acts, then its sanctions ought to be allocated in a manner that reflects its logic of blaming – that is, that comports fairly with the degree of reprehensibleness of those acts. The argument does not presuppose the idea of requiting evil for evil, or other arcane notions that have at various times surfaced in the literature of retribution.

Johannes Andenaes has asked whether this censure-based argument for proportionality is circular.[9] Punishment entails blaming, he asserts, only in a system in which the severity of the sentence is tied to judgements about the degree of reprehensibleness of the conduct; were the system's rules for allocating sentencing more utilitarian, the link between punishing and blaming might disappear. We do not agree. The nexus between punishment and blame has deeper roots than the sentencing rules of the particular jurisdiction. Censure is integral to the very concept of punishment – as should be apparent from the censure-based account of the institution of punishment which we have sketched previously (Chapter 2).

9.2.4 The censure argument stated more fully

The argument in favour of the principle of proportionality is, in brief, the following: since punishment does and should convey blame, its amount should reflect the degree of blameworthiness of the conduct. This argument, however, needs to be articulated more fully. Stated schematically, the case for proportionality involves the following three steps:

Step 1: The state's sanctions against specified kinds of injurious conduct should take a punitive form; that is, visit deprivations in a manner that expresses censure or blame.

Step 2: The severity of a sanction expresses the stringency of the blame.

Step 3: Hence, punitive sanctions should be arrayed according to the degree of blameworthiness (ie seriousness) of the conduct.

Let us examine each of these steps. Step 1 reflects the claim made in Chapter 2: that the response to the harmful conduct with which the criminal law centrally deals should convey censure. A 'neutral' sanction embodying no blame would not just be a (possibly) less efficient preventive device; it would be objectionable on the ethical ground that it does not treat the actor as a moral agent answerable for his or her behaviour.

Step 2 has also been touched upon in that chapter: in punishment, deprivation ('hard treatment') is the vehicle for expressing condemnation. When a given type of conduct is visited with comparatively greater severity, that signifies a greater degree of disapprobation.[b]

Step 3 – the conclusion – embodies the claim of fairness. When persons are (and should be) dealt with in a manner that ascribes demerit, their

[b] See discussion of the 'intertwining' of the censuring and preventive function, in 2.5.2 above.

treatment should reflect how unmeritorious their conduct should be judged to be. By punishing one kind of conduct more severely than another, the punisher implies that it is worse – which is appropriate only if the conduct is indeed worse (ie more serious). Were penalties ordered in severity inconsistently with the comparative seriousness of crime, the less reprehensible conduct would, unfairly, receive the greater reprobation.

The foregoing case for proportionality would be straightforward enough were censure the sole warrant for punishment. But the justification for the existence of punishment that we offered in Chapter 2 is a bifurcated one, which relies on notions of prevention as well as censure. Does this account create a Trojan horse? If punishment's existence is justified even in part on crime prevention grounds, might prevention be invoked in deciding comparative severities of punishment? Were that permissible, proportionality would be undermined.[c]

Were the two justifying elements, censure and crime prevention, to operate separably on different features of the criminal law, this would become a problem. Suppose, for example, that it were asserted that the judgement of conviction represents censure of the offender for his conduct, and the penalty then imposed serves only a preventive function. Then, the determination of the sanction's severity could be determined on preventive grounds, and proportionality requirements could be disregarded. Such a model, however, would be unacceptable, because if the penalty were to operate purely preventatively, instead expressing censure for the offender's conduct, then this separate non-condemnatory response would clearly fall outside the proposed justification for punishment sketched previously (Chapter 2).

What is crucial about our suggested 'mixed' rationale for the penal system is the intertwining of punishment's reprobative and hard-treatment features. It is the penal deprivation, not just the judgement of conviction, that expresses the censure of the offender, as well as serving as the prudential disincentive. Imposing a penal deprivation on the offender visits him with censure that is justifiable only if he is at fault – which is why the fault requirements of substantive criminal law should be observed.[10] Varying the amount of penal deprivation will alter the relative degree of censure conveyed, and is warranted only where that reflects the degree of

[c] David Dolinko (1992) makes this objection: if the institution of the criminal sanction has the twin objectives of censure and crime prevention, why not distribute punishments according to the latter aim? He then notes desert theorists' reply: that reprobation is not merely an aim but an essential characteristic of punishment, so that the comparative severity of penalty will convey the degree of reprobation. His response is an odd one: tort liability, he says, in some sense conveys censure, since the prerequisite of liability ordinarily is fault on the part of the actor. Yet the amount of civil recovery depends not on fault but on what is required to compensate the plaintiff. Why, then, need fault be the measure for the quanta of punishments? The answer to Dolinko's argument should be obvious: civil tort remedies are designed to compensate, and do not have blaming as a central defining feature as punishment does.

blameworthiness (ie the seriousness) of the criminal conduct – which is why the requirements of proportionality ought to be observed. Once this crucial feature of intertwining is understood, we need not fear a Trojan horse.

A simple illustration can bring out this last point about intertwining – and suggest why our bifurcated account for the punishment's existence does not permit comparative severities to be decided on crime-preventive grounds. Consider a proposal to increase sanctions for a specified type of criminal conduct (beyond the quantum that would be proportionate) in order to create a better incapacitant (or a stronger deterrent). Could such a step be justified, on grounds that prevention is said to be part of the general justifying aim of the penal system, and that this measure might help achieve prevention more efficiently? No, it could not, for the following reasons:

- Suppose the increase were accomplished simply by raising the sentence for this type of crime. That increase in punishment would express enhanced disapprobation for conduct that, *ex hypothesi*, has become no more reprehensible. The increase thus would be objectionable because it treats the offender as more to blame than his conduct warrants.
- Alternatively, the increase might be accomplished (if its aim is to incapacitate the offender) by visiting the proportionate punishment, and then imposing a separate *non-condemnatory* term of confinement.[11] Since the additional imposition purportedly is not reprobative in character, it would appear to involve no unjustifiable increase in blame. There is, however, another objection: this separate non-condemnatory sanction clearly falls outside our proposed justification for the hard treatment (see Chapter 2). One is no longer speaking of a censure-expressing sanction that, for preventive reasons, also involves material deprivation. Instead, the additional sanction is purely preventive and not reprobative at all. It is of the 'beast control' kind that does not address the actor as a moral agent.

9.3 Scaling Proportionate Sanctions: Ordinal Proportionality

Much of the debate over the idea of penal desert has concerned the degree to which it constrains the choice of sanctions. Retributivists are said to assert that desert should be the primary guide to the fixing of penalties. Others, including Norval Morris, disagree and claim that the concept of desert provides no more than outer limits. Our view is that the proper role of desert is actually more complex than either position would suggest.

Professor Morris's view is one he calls 'limiting retributivism' – a mixed model somewhere between full retributivism and pure penal utilitarianism.[12] Desert, he contends, supplies only the upper (and possibly lower bounds) on the severity of the penalty that can justly be levied; within these bounds, crime prevention aims (eg, deterrent, incapacitative or rehabilitative considerations) should be decisive. Desert thus can serve only as a limiting, not a determining principle. In his words:

> Desert is not a defining principle; it is a limiting principle. The concept of 'just deserts' sets the maximum and minimum of the sentence that may be imposed for any offence and helps to define the punishment relationships between offences; it does not give any more fine-tuning to the appropriate sentences than that. The fine-tuning is to be done on utilitarian principles.[13]

The reason desert is only limiting, he argues, is that none of us have an idea precisely how much punishment is deserved for any offence. We can grasp only what would be manifestly *dis*proportionate in lenience or severity.

Since desert is only a limit, Morris continues, the sentencer is not obligated to impose equally onerous sentences on equally deserving (or rather, undeserving) criminals. Cases that are alike in respect to the blameworthiness of defendants' conduct may be treated *unlike* where necessary for utilitarian ends – provided none of those disparate punishments infringe Morris' 'retributive' limits. We think Morris' view is mistaken. To explain why, we need to sketch an important distinction: between relative scaling of penalties and the fixing of a penalty-structure's anchoring points.

9.3.1 Ordinal v cardinal scaling

When one asks whether desert is limiting or determining, it is necessary to specify: determining or limiting for what purpose? It is essential to distinguish between *ordinal* and *cardinal* scaling of punishment – that is, between (1) the question of how severely crimes should be punished relative to each other, and (2) the question of what overall levels of onerousness should be chosen to anchor the system of penalties. To view desert as significantly determinative of comparative punishments does not commit one to the claim that it is determinative also for deciding the net degree of punitiveness or lenience of the system.[14]

For desert theory, this distinction is crucial. In deciding ordinal ranking of penalties, desert provides considerably more guidance than Norval Morris's thesis suggests. But desert provides a lesser degree of guidance (albeit some, as we argue below) in deciding the system's overall severity levels and anchoring points.

The issue of ordinal proportionality concerns how severely a criminal act should be punished compared to similar acts, and compared to other crimes of greater or lesser seriousness. Its requirements are reasonably specific. Persons convicted of criminal acts of like gravity should receive punishments of like severity. Persons convicted of acts of differing gravity should receive punishments correspondingly graded in their degree of onerousness. These requirements of ordinal proportionality are not mere limits, and they are infringed when persons found guilty of comparably reprehensible conduct receive substantially unequal sanctions on ulterior (eg crime prevention) grounds. The ordinal proportionality requirements are readily explained on the censure-based argument for the principle of proportionality we have outlined previously (see 9.2). Since punishing one offender more severely than another expresses greater censure of the former, it is justified only to the extent that the first offender's crime is more reprehensible.

This conception militates against resolving questions of comparative severities of sentence on grounds other than the degree of blameworthiness of the offender's conduct. It precludes, for example, punishing a particular burglar more severely than other convicted burglars not because his particular criminal conduct is any worse, but because he is more likely to reoffend, or because giving him a higher-than-usual punishment might make a useful example to others.

To disregard ordinal proportionality requirements, and treat desert as providing only limits in the manner Morris proposes, would disregard the censuring implications of punishment. Suppose one were to decide that, for a given type of crime, less than *x* months' imprisonment is undeservedly lenient, and more than *y* months, undeservedly severe. Suppose, following Morris, that one viewed desert as supplying only those limits – that the sentence must fall somewhere between *x* and *y* – and then allow the disposition to be decided within these bounds on crime-prevention grounds. This would permit sentences of differing severity to be imposed on two offenders whose conduct is equally reprehensible but who, say, are considered to present differing degrees of risk of recidivism. One offender may receive a punishment close to the lower limit, *x*, and the other may get a sentence at the upper limit, *y*. Through these different penalties, the two offenders would be visited, unfairly, with different degrees of censure although the reprehensibleness of their conduct is substantially the same. In fact, a defendant who commits a less serious offence may receive comparatively the greater penalty, if he is deemed to represent a higher risk. It may be true that much depends on the width of the limits in limiting retributivism, and on the relative precision of ordinal proportionality, but it seems clear that the Morris approach is vulnerable to this critique.

9.3.2 The three sub-requirements of ordinal proportionality

Ordinal proportionality has three sub-requirements. The first is *parity*: when offenders have been convicted of criminal conduct of similar seriousness, they deserve penalties of comparable severity. This requirement does not necessarily call for the same penalty for all acts within a statutory crime category – as significant variations in seriousness may occur within that crime category, in regard to the conduct's foreseeable degree of harmfulness or degree of culpability. But once such within-category variations in crime-seriousness are controlled for, the resulting penalties should be of substantially the same degree of onerousness.[d]

A second sub-requirement is *rank-ordering*. Punishing crime *Y* more than crime *X* expresses more disapproval for crime *Y*, which is warranted only if it is more serious. Punishments thus should be ordered on the scale of penalties so that their relative severity reflects the seriousness-ranking of the crimes involved.[e]

The third sub-requirement concerns the *spacing* of penalties. Suppose crimes *X*, *Y* and *Z* are of ascending order of seriousness; but that *Y* is considerably more serious than *X* but only slightly less so than *Z*. Then, to reflect the conduct's gravity, there should be a larger space between penalties for *X* and *Y* than those for *Y* and *Z*.

Because of these three ordinal proportionality constraints, proportionality provides considerably more guidance than Norval Morris's view of desert-as-mere-limits suggests. The constraints, however, are not wholly 'determinative': they do not impose a unique set of solutions on comparative penalty scaling. The spacing requirement requires that differences among penalties be sufficient to call attention to significant differences in the degree of gravity of the offences involved. This might be achieved through various possible spacing conventions designed to give reasonable cognizance to such differences. However, there seems to be no uniquely appropriate spacing convention.[f] Thus it would be an overstatement to say that ordinal proportionate requirements are 'determinative'; but they do provide considerably more guidance than the broad desert limits of which Morris speaks.

9.3.3 How much does ordinal proportionality restrict reliance on crime-prevention concerns?

To what extent do ordinal proportionality requirements restrict the pursuit of crime prevention in determining the sentence? That depends largely

[d] This parity requirement has one exception, concerning the role of prior convictions, that will be discussed in 9.6.

[e] If broad statutory offence categories are in use, however, the rank-ordering requirement would still permit a certain degree of overlap of sanctions. If the least serious sub-type of robbery were roughly equivalent in blameworthiness to the most serious sub-type of residential burglary, for example, there would be no objection in having comparable sentences in these types of cases.

[f] The criteria for gauging seriousness (discussed in 9.5) should be able to suggest approximate differences in the reprehensibleness of various crimes involved. However, these criteria are unlikely to be sufficiently precise to provide exact estimates of their degrees of difference in seriousness – which is why there might be a variety of possible spacing conventions. There thus could be more than one way to arrange the spacing among penalties on the scale.

on whether or not the particular crime prevention strategy requires substantial inequalities in the punishments imposed on those whose crimes are comparably serious. The pursuit of certain crime-preventive aims would thus be ruled out – a notable example being that of predictively-based incapacitation, in which convicted defendants predicted to be higher risks would receive longer prison sentences in order to prevent them from recidivating. As predictions of risk of recidivism depend chiefly on factors that do not relate to crime seriousness (eg, those relating to prior arrests and to employment or educational history)[15] utilizing these factors to decide the severity of sentence would infringe the parity requirements of ordinal proportionality.

Not all prevention strategies require such inequalities of sentence, however. Rehabilitation, for example, need not do so. Consider, for example, those convicted of more serious crimes and sent to prison; if, among such persons, those amenable to treatment are selected for enrolment in a rehabilitative programme, this does not substantially alter the degree of onerousness of their punishment and hence involves no breach of parity requirements. Likewise, ordinal proportionality is observed when a choice may be made among comparably severe non-custodial penalties on rehabilitative grounds – as will be discussed more fully below (at 9.7). Crime control may be invoked in deciding the comparative severity of sentence, in other words, when this does not disturb the proportionate ordering of punishments.

9.4 Cardinal Magnitudes and the Fixing of the Penalty Scale's Anchoring Points

Once penalties have been graded according to the comparative seriousness of crimes, the system of penalties as a whole still needs to be anchored. This issue, of anchoring the penalty system by fixing actual (and not just comparative) severity levels for at least some crimes, is the issue of cardinal magnitude. It is here that desert can play only a more limited role.

The intuitive reason why this is so is the greater difficulty of making cardinal desert judgements. Suppose one is trying to find the appropriate, deserved penalty for the offence of residential burglary. If one has already decided the penalties for some other crimes, then one can locate the burglary penalty by making comparative judgements: by much more or less serious a typical burglary (or a standard burglary of a certain subtype)[g] is than those other crimes are. Such judgements require a starting point, however, and the issue of cardinal magnitude deals with finding that

[g] For possibilities of subcategorizing broad-category offences such as robbery for purposes of rating their degree of harmfulness, see Appendix 3.

starting point. There seems to be no crime for which one can readily perceive a specific quantum of punishment as the uniquely deserved one.

This intuition is confirmed when one considers the notion of censure that underlies a proportionalist sentence theory. Assessments of ordinal proportionality rest on judgements of comparative blameworthiness. When judged in absolute rather than comparative terms, the censure expressed through penal deprivation is in part a matter of a convention. Altering the scale's overall punitiveness by making *pro rata* upward or downward changes in all prescribed sanctions would represent a change in that convention.

Does this leave the anchoring of the scale of penalties too wide open? Could it permit a very severe system of penalties, so long as it is not *so* harsh as to impose drastic sanctions on manifestly trivial crimes? We think not. To see why, let us begin with a hypothetical scale of penalties which is ordered internally according to ordinal proportionality requirements, and which approximates in its overall degree of onerousness existing penalty levels in the jurisdiction involved. If the censure expressed through assumed levels of penal deprivation is in the first instance a matter of convention, as just suggested, then a plausible place to begin the analysis is with the existing convention regarding overall severity levels. The issue then becomes whether this convention should be altered – either in the direction of a net increase in penalty levels, or in the direction of net penalty reductions.

We have argued in favour of the latter:[16] that compared to standards of punitiveness prevailing, say, in most Western European countries, penalties' onerousness should not be increased, and should, where feasible, be scaled downward. What kind of arguments could be made in support of this view? One argument draws on a principle that extends beyond desert theory: the principle of sparing use of coercive state interventions. The principle calls for parsimonious use of state intrusions into individuals' lives that causes them substantial suffering.[17] Raising the overall degree of punitiveness of the sentencing system would, according to this principle, be undesirable because of the increased suffering and loss of freedom of choice that it visits on those punished. It would, ordinarily, also involve a greater reliance on imprisonment, particularly long-term imprisonment, with its devastating effects on those incarcerated.

High overall severity levels also would be inconsistent with the moral functions of penal censure discussed earlier (Chapter 2). Through punishment's censuring features, we argued, the criminal sanction offers a normative reason for desistance that can be offered human beings viewed as moral agents: that doing certain harmful acts is wrong and hence should be refrained from. Punishments' material deprivations may then be viewed as providing a supplemental disincentive – as providing citizens (given human fallibility and the temptations of offending) an additional prudential reason for compliance. The harsher a penalty system becomes, however, the less significant would be the normative reasons for desistance supplied by penal censure, and the more predominant would become the system's purely threatening aspects – that is, the more the system becomes, in Hegel's apt words, 'a stick raised to a dog'.[h] This argument points towards keeping penalties at moderate levels.[18] Indeed, it might even be permissible, as far as proportionality is concerned, to scale down the sanctioning system so that lengthy prison terms would be reserved only for the most serious violent offences.[19] There appear to be political and practical reasons why a very large reduction in punitiveness would be unlikely to be implemented in most Western countries. The argument here, however, points toward a direction for desirable change in sanctioning policy: toward restraint in the use of substantial penalties.

How much guidance will our model give? Admittedly, it would provide only a limited degree of guidance on the setting of the penalty system's anchoring points – that is, the system's overall degree of punitiveness. But the model tells one considerably more (albeit not providing unique solutions) about the comparative scaling of penalties: about punishing equally reprehensible conduct approximately equally, and about scaling unequally serious conduct according to conduct's differing degree of seriousness. Desert provides a great deal more structure than Norval Morris's thesis concedes.

9.5 Seriousness, Severity and the Living-Standard

The principle of proportionality requires the *severity* of penalties to be determined by reference to the *seriousness* of crimes. We thus need a way of assessing the two predicates, of crime-seriousness and punishment-severity. Suppose someone proposes that crime *X* be visited by punishment *Y*. In order to tell whether this is a proportionate sanction, one needs to be able to judge how grave *X* is compared to other crimes, and also how onerous *Y* is compared to other penalties.

9.5.1 Gauging crimes' seriousness

How is crime-seriousness to be assessed? Ordinary people, various opinion surveys have suggested, seem capable of reaching a degree of agreement on the comparative seriousness of criminal offences.[i] The rulemaking bodies

[h] For fuller discussion, see von Hirsch 1993, ch. 5.

[i] A number of empirical studies have assessed public perceptions of the seriousness of offences, the classic study being Thorsten Sellin and Marvin Wolfgang's *The Measurement of Delinquency* (1964). These studies provide a sample of members of the public with brief descriptions of various criminal incidents, and ask them to rate on a numerical scale the seriousness of the offences described. The studies suggest that persons from differing walks of life tend to rank common offences similarly.

that have tried to rank crimes in gravity have not run into insuperable practical difficulties, moreover. Several US state sentencing commissions (including those of Minnesota, Washington state and Oregon) were able to rank the seriousness of offences for use in their numerical guidelines.[20] While the grading task proved time consuming, it did not generate much dissension within these rule-making bodies.

Less apparent, however, has been the conceptual basis for notions of seriousness. What criteria should be used for gauging crimes' gravity? The gravity of a crime depends upon the degree of harmfulness of the conduct, and the extent of the actor's culpability. Culpability can be gauged with the aid of clues from substantive criminal law doctrine. The substantive law already distinguishes intentional conduct from reckless conduct and from criminally negligent behaviour. For purposes of sentencing doctrine, more refined distinctions might be made, concerning the degree of purposefulness, indifference to consequences, or carelessness in criminal conduct. The doctrines of excuse in the substantive criminal law could also be drawn upon to develop theories of partial excuse – for example, of partial duress, and diminished capacity.[21] The harm dimension of seriousness is more puzzling, however, because the substantive law provides less assistance here: it does not formally distinguish degree of harm in systematic fashion.[j] How, then, can one compare the harmfulness of acts that invade different interests: say, compare crime *X* that invades property interests with crime *Y* that chiefly affects bodily integrity?

A theory of criminal harm that relies on notions of quality of life may help answer that question, and such a theory was sketched in a 1991 essay by Andrew von Hirsch and Nils Jareborg[22] (a revised and updated version of which is included in this volume as Appendix 3). According to such a theory, victimizing harms are to be ranked in gravity according to how much they typically would reduce a person's *standard of living*. That term is used here in the broad sense suggested by Amartya Sen,[23] which reflects both economic and non-economic interests.

The living standard is one of a family of related notions, including wellbeing, that refer to the quality of persons' lives. Wellbeing, however, can be highly personalized: one's wellbeing depends on one's particular focal aims, so that were one to wish to devote one's life to contemplation and prayer, material comfort and ordinary social amenities might matter little. However, the living standard, in Sen's sense, does not focus on actual life-quality or goal achievement, but on the *means* or *capabilities* for achieving a certain quality of life. Some of these means are material (shelter and financial resources) but others are not (eg, privacy and freedom from humiliation). It is also standardized, referring to the means and

[j] The English prohibition of robbery, for example, defines this offence as consisting of theft involving the use of threat of force; see Theft Act 1968, s. 8. It does not, however, make any explicit reference to the degree of harmfulness of the behaviour.

capabilities that would *ordinarily* promote a good life. Someone has a good standard of living if he has the resources, material and immaterial, that people generally can use to live well.

Using the living standard as a way of gauging harms has a number of advantages. First, it seems to fit the way we usually judge harms. Why is an aggravated assault more harmful than burglary? It is because the overall quality of the person's life has been more adversely affected. Second, the living standard idea permits drawing from a rich array of experience – including experience outside the criminal law. We can ask how the harm in an arson compares with that in an accidental fire. Finally, a living standard analysis would allow for cultural variation. Differing living arrangements in different societies can affect the consequences of criminal acts, and normative differences among cultures can affect the impact of those consequences on the quality of persons' lives. The harmfulness of residential burglary, for example, depends on the degree to which the home is ordinarily the focal point for people's private existences; and on the degree to which privacy is valued in a given culture. A living standard analysis thus could, in another culture, lead to a different rating for burglary – if the home has a different social role and if a different valuation is given to privacy.

The suggested analysis begins with parcelling out the various kinds of interest dimensions that offences typically involve; after these are thus identified, their importance is judged by assessing their significance for the living standard. Most victimizing offences involve one or more of the following interest dimensions: (1) physical integrity, (2) material support and amenity, (3) privacy, and (4) freedom from humiliation. A simple residential burglary, for example, chiefly involves material amenity and privacy. The material loss would consist of what is stolen, plus the inconvenience and expense of repairs. The privacy loss consists of the intrusion of a stranger into one's personal living space. To rate the harmfulness of the conduct, the living standard criterion should be applied to each dimension, successively. In the case of the burglary, the analysis would thus begin with the offence's material-amenity dimension. Here, the impact on the living standard would be rather small: not much is taken in the typical burglary, so that a standard person's material wellbeing would not be much affected. Next, the privacy dimension would be considered. Here, the rating would be somewhat higher, given the importance of privacy to a good existence, and the extent to which an intrusion into the home affects privacy. The attraction of this mode of analysis is that each dimension involved – physical integrity, material support, privacy, or whatever – can ultimately be assessed in terms of a common criterion: that of impact on the living standard. This means that, in the burglary, one can compare the living standard impact of the material loss (rather minor) with that of the privacy intrusion (somewhat greater). One could also compare a burglary with another victimizing offence involving different interests: say, an assault, where physical integrity and freedom-from-humiliation are primarily involved.

To aid in this analysis, the living standard itself can be graded. One might use at least four living standard levels: (1) subsistence, (2) minimal wellbeing, (3) 'adequate' wellbeing, and (4) standard wellbeing.[k] The first, subsistence, refers to survival but with maintenance of no more than elementary human capacities to function – in other words, barely getting by. The remaining levels refer to various degrees of life quality above that of mere subsistence (see further, Appendix 3, section 4). The function of these gradations is to provide a rough measure of the extent to which a typical criminal offence of a certain type intrudes upon the living standard. To take an obvious example, aggravated assault threatens subsistence, and thus risks substantially more harm than the harm involved in a routine theft, that still leaves the person with a basically unchanged level of comfort and dignity.

This analysis is to be used chiefly in gauging the standard harm involved in various categories or subcategories of offence. The point is to assess the injuriousness of typical instances of (say) residential burglary, or residential burglary of a certain kind (we might, say, distinguish simple burglary from ransacking); not to gauge the injury done to a particular individual when his apartment was broken into and his favourite vase was stolen. The living standard relates, as we noted, to the *standardized* means or capabilities for a good life – not to the life quality of particular persons. Deviations from such standardized assessments should be made only in certain kinds of special circumstances, where the differences from the ordinary case are plainly apparent.[l]

This harms analysis is not a formula providing ready answers, because the impact of a crime on the living standard is itself very much a matter of factual and normative judgement. It also is designed mainly to address crimes directly affecting natural persons, rather than crimes involving collective interests.[m] The analysis nevertheless may be helpful as a guide to thinking about rating harms. Some attempts have also been made to apply the analysis in the contexts of Swedish, English, and German sentencing law.[24]

[k] In von Hirsch and Jareborg's original 1991 article, an additional living standard level was suggested, of 'enhanced wellbeing'. Further reflection suggests its elimination, however. Whereas it is possible to speak of an enhanced living standard with respect to material amenity, this notion cannot so readily be applied to other interests, such as those of physical wellbeing.

[l] While assessments of harm are thus to be standardized to a degree, culpability judgements need not be. A desert-based sentencing system may (indeed, should) afford room for pleas of reduced personal culpability on a variety of grounds – such as, for example, that of provocation. (On provocation, see von Hirsch and Jareborg 1987; Narayan and von Hirsch 1996.)

[m] In von Hirsch and Jareborg 1991 an attempt was made to apply the living standard analysis to the latter kind of crimes, but we are now less satisfied with that aspect of the analysis. This issue requires further exploration.

9.5.2 Gauging punishment's severity

Grading sanctions presupposes an ability to assess their comparative severity. While prison sanctions can be compared by their duration, non-custodial sanctions' onerousness is affected also by their varying degrees of intensity: three days of community service may be tougher than three days' probation but not so onerous as three days of home detention.

A number of studies have attempted to measure sanction severity through opinion surveys. A selected group of respondents is shown a list of penalties of various sorts, and asked to rate their severity on a numerical rating scale. The surveys tend to show a degree of consensus.[25] This research, however, generally does not attempt to elucidate what is meant by severity; to elicit respondents' reasons for their rankings; or to assess the plausibility of those reasons. It is necessary to consider what *should* be the basis of comparing penalties – ie, to develop a theory of severity.

A possible account of severity would be that it depends upon how disagreeable the sanction typically is experienced as being. On this view, opinion surveys would be a useful way of assessing penalties, as these would reflect how unpleasant various penalties are perceived as being. Unpleasantness or discomfort is ultimately subjective: a matter of how deprivations typically are experienced. If penalty *x* is experienced as being more onerous than penalty *y*, that simply would make it so.[26]

Such a subjectivist conception of severity has its difficulties, however. It would permit a high degree of variation among offenders. Some convicted persons are tough, others are tender, so that greater deprivations might be visited on the tough ones (irrespective of the seriousness of their offences) because they would feel them less keenly. That would have troublesome social implications, to the extent that the degree of inuredness to deprivation are related to social class and to prior experience of having been punished.

The subjectivist approach is also problematic in principle. What makes punishments more or less onerous is not any identifiable sensation; rather, it is the degree to which those sanctions interfere with people's legitimate interests. The unpleasantness of intensive probation supervision, for example, depends not on its 'feeling bad' in some immediate sense, but on its interfering with such important interests as that of freedom of choice.

It would thus seem helpful to apply an interests analysis comparable to the one just suggested for gauging crime seriousness. The more important the interests intruded upon by a penalty are, on this theory, the severer it is. Penalties would be ranked according to the degree to which they typically affect a punished person's freedom of movement, choice regarding his activities, choice of associates, privacy, and so forth. The importance of those interests could then be gauged according to how they typically impinge on persons' *living standard* – in the sense of that term just discussed. Such an interests analysis seems to fit the way we often discuss punishment's severity. When asked to explain why long-term imprisonment is a severe sanction, for example, one would most naturally answer in terms of how its deprivations typically impinge on the quality of someone's life.

Adopting an interest analysis approach means that the assessment of severity is made less dependent on the preferences of particular individuals. The living standard, as noted earlier, refers to the means and capabilities that *ordinarily* assist persons in achieving a good life. Imprisonment thus qualifies as a severe penalty, because the interests in freedom of movement and privacy it takes away are normally so vital to a good existence. This helps answer an objection that sometimes has been raised to desert theory: namely, that it is impossible to grade penalties' onerousness, because people's subjective perceptions of painfulness may be so varied.[27] There remain, however, certain practical problems of applying an interest analysis approach to gauging the severity of sanctions: the exercise is much easier for terms of imprisonment and for financial penalties than it is for community penalties and other non-custodial measures, which can vary so much in their conditions and in the extent of their restrictions on liberty.[28]

9.6 Desert and Previous Convictions

In traditional discretionary sentencing systems, most judges adjusted the sentence to take account of the offender's previous convictions. The weight to be given to the criminal record was uncertain, however. Should the criminal record be the primary determinant of the sentence? Or should the sentence chiefly reflect the seriousness of the current crime, with perhaps a modest adjustment made for the person's criminal record? Under a discretionary system, different judges answered such questions differently. However, the notion of rule of law requires that such decisions be taken on a principled basis, a point that becomes clear when sentencing guidelines are being considered. But what should the principles be?

The question has no simple answers. It is sometimes asserted, for example, that the criminal record should not be considered at all, because the offender has been 'punished already' for his previous crime. However, this reasoning is circular. If some feature of an offender's having been previously convicted affects the grounds for his present punishment, then adjusting his sentence is not penalizing him twice for his past crime. If, for example, the offender has received a discount in the penalty for his first offence, removing that discount if he subsequently reoffends may not be punishing him twice over.

The significance of the prior record will vary, depending on what rationale for sentencing is assumed. A rationale emphasizing prediction and incapacitation could give the record primary weight. Prediction studies tend to show that the statistical likelihood of someone's reoffending is influenced chiefly by his previous criminal history, rather than by the seriousness of his current criminal act. What predicts recidivism best (or rather, least badly) is the person's previous record of arrests (especially, early arrests), plus certain facts about his social history, such as use of drugs and lack of regular employment.[29]

What should be the role of the criminal record on a desert rationale, according to which punishments are to be proportionate to the seriousness of the criminal conduct? There has been some disagreement on this subject among desert theorists. Some of these theorists hold that the prior record should not be considered at all.[30] Others favour a theory of 'progressive loss of mitigation':[31] that the offender who is convicted for the first time gets a modest discount from his sentence, but that discount diminishes – so that after a certain number of repetitions (say, the third or fourth), it is lost entirely. Thereafter, the criminal record should not matter; the sixth shoplifting would be treated no differently than the fourth. The discount, under this theory, would also be limited in magnitude – so that the seriousness of the current crime, rather than the criminal record would primarily determine the onerousness of the penalty.

This latter view is preferable, in our judgement. The offender should be punished somewhat less when first convicted, but the discount should progressively be reduced. We now examine the reasons for this approach.

9.6.1 Explanations directed to the present act

Could the fact of a prior conviction or convictions alter the seriousness of the current crime? To do so, the prior offence would have to affect the harm or the culpability involved in the current conduct.

The harmfulness of the conduct does not seem affected. Obviously, the conduct's direct consequences or risks are unaltered. Conceivably, it might be argued that there is something akin to 'harm' involved – namely, defiance: the repeater is flouting the law when he reoffends after having been punished already. However, in a liberal society, defiance should not constitute a wrong that justifiably enhances what an offender deserves. Treating defiance in itself as an extra harm presupposes authoritarian assumptions about the state and the criminal law.[n]

What about the offender's culpability for his offence? In a 1976 volume, one of us claimed that culpability is affected.[32] Before the offender has been first convicted, the argument ran, he is simply part of the general

[n] For a fuller discussion of this point, see von Hirsch 2002, 446–47.

audience to whom the legal prohibition is addressed. He may not have paid the prohibition much attention, or understood its scope. The censure embodied in the punishment for the first offence, however, serves as a dramatic way of confronting the actor with the wrongfulness of the conduct. Thereafter, claims to possible ignorance or inattention to the prohibition become progressively less plausible.

Further reflection suggests, however, that this argument is mistaken. Granted, in some instances, a first offender may not have been fully aware of the prohibition or understood its scope or applicability. And even though most jurisdictions restrict the excusing effect of ignorance of law,[33] sentencing theory might give legal ignorance (or partial ignorance) a wider culpability-reducing effect. The difficulty is, however, that many of those convicted for the first time may have been perfectly aware of the prohibition and of the wrongfulness of the conduct, but simply committed it anyway. Ignorance, or failure fully to understand or take notice, does not support a discount that is generally applicable to first offenders.

9.6.2 Explanations directed to the criminal career

Why not look, instead, to the offender's career? There are contexts in everyday life where we address the merit or demerit of a person's career as a whole. A prime example of career-desert is provided by prizes for distinguished research that some learned societies periodically offer. Candidates' names, CVs and writings go to a panel of experts; the panel, after due deliberation, chooses for the award one or more individuals whose scholarly output is thought to show particular distinction.

Such judgements, however, have a different logic from that employed by the criminal law. The prize is not *for* any particular work, but relates to the recipient's whole *oeuvre*. Nominees are not (as they are in essay competitions) required to submit any new product. The candidate's most recent efforts may be given little weight, or even may be discounted entirely by judges, if his earlier contributions are considered more significant.

The criminal law is structured otherwise. The actor is punished *for* a particular crime – that for which he now stands convicted. The substantive criminal law defines, classifies, and prohibits *crimes* (a career-oriented system would classify *persons* according to the frequency and gravity of their offending. It would make habitual offender laws the archetype of the criminal law, rather than its exception.) Existing trial and sentencing procedures are suited mainly to determining the defendant's guilt or innocence for the current crime and to evaluating, extenuating and aggravating circumstances surrounding that crime.

There are both pragmatic and principled reasons against a career-based approach. In practice, the criminal process does not have adequate means to inquire into the degree of demerit of a person's whole criminal career with care and discrimination, and would require major alterations in order to do so.[o] In principle, an important role of criminal and sentencing law is that it focuses on crimes and thereby provides a comprehensible valuation of conduct. What chiefly counts is what was done, not who did it. The penal sanction thus furnishes a reasonably unambiguous public valuation of the degree of blameworthiness of different kinds of criminal conduct (for fuller discussion of this point, see 2.6 above).

A career-based system would make the law's public valuation of conduct much more diffuse. The focus would no longer be on what was done, but rather, on who did it and how frequently he had done it before. It is true that the law's rules or principles would have to rate the gravity of crimes in order to set standards for criminal careers. But the punishment – the public expression of penal censure that is the product of such reckonings – would vary independently of the gravity of the offender's current act, depending on the prior criminal record. As a result, the criminal sanction would no longer so clearly testify to the degree of wrongfulness of the conduct, and to the significance of the rights that had been infringed.

9.6.3 An alternative theory – 'tolerance' and the criminal record

We prefer an alternative theory, first put forward in a 1981 article.[34] The discount for the first offender should not rest on claims of reduced culpability that relate to lack of full knowledge or appreciation of the prohibition. The discount is, rather, a concession made to the fallibility of human nature. The scaled-down response for the first offence serves to accord some respect for the fact that the person's inhibitions functioned before, and to show some sympathy for the all-too-human weakness that can lead to a first offence. The idea is thus one of a limited tolerance for human frailty.

Notice that we have this tolerance only because we have certain expectations, or should have them, about human beings and their nature. If we were angels, we would not have or need it. Were we sufficiently puritanical about humans, we would also deny the discount: frailty, on this view, would be something to be abominated and confronted with vigour. But because humans are not angels, and should not be judged as though they were,[p] a certain tolerance seems appropriate.

But how, precisely, does the fact of human frailty link with notions of censure and desert? And if one wishes to be tolerant of human weakness,

[o] Evaluating a criminal's 'career-desert' would call for *in-depth* information about the past crimes for which he has been convicted. It would be necessary, for example, to have full information about any aggravating or mitigating circumstances that had been found to exist with respect to any such prior crime. Existing sentencing procedures and record-keeping methods are not remotely capable of establishing such facts.

[p] For fuller discussion of this perspective on human frailty, see 2.5.2.

why not continue to make the discount available? It also seems to be a fact of human nature that some people keep on offending, so why not continue to grant discounts on the sentences even of multiple repeaters?

Our everyday moral judgements include the notion of a *lapse*. A transgression (even one of a substantial nature) is judged less stringently when it occurs against a background of prior compliance. The idea is that even an ordinarily well-behaved person can have his moral inhibitions fail in a moment of weakness or wilfulness. Such a loss of self-discipline is the kind of human frailty for which, arguably, some understanding should be shown.

In sentencing, the lapse of which we are speaking is not just any moral failure, but an infringement of the standards of the criminal law. And the prior compliance in question is that of not having committed and been convicted for a criminal offence.[q] It is not the offender's whole moral life that should be the subject of inquiry, but only his criminal record. The logic of the first-offender discount, however, remains that of dealing with a lapse somewhat more tolerantly.

The somewhat muted disapprobation that the actor gets through the scaled-down penalty for the first offence is still censure. It confronts the person with the wrongfulness of the conduct and with disapproval of him for that conduct. That remonstrance should give the person the opportunity to reconsider, reflect on the propriety of his conduct, and decide whether to pursue a different course (see 2.4.1). This is not a matter of giving the actor notice that the conduct was wrong. He ought to have been aware of that already (and probably, has actually been so). His offence may have been the result not of ignorance, but of having at the moment placed his own needs or inclinations above the requirements of respecting others' rights. But fallible humans are capable of acting thus in a moment of unwisdom, and the censure expressed through the first punishment gives the person the opportunity to reflect on his conduct.

Why, then, should we scale down the condemnatory and punitive response initially? It is because it is assumed that humans are both fallible and capable of doing something worthy of respect – namely, attending to

[q] Empirical research does suggest that, for each previous crime for which they were officially apprehended and punished, many offenders admit having committed several unpunished offences; see, eg, Petersilia, Greenwood and Laven 1977, 15–18. The vicissitudes of being discovered, arrested, prosecuted, and convicted are such that the absence of a record of criminal convictions is not a reliable indicator of whether a defendant actually has committed previous crimes. But it would be unjust – and in some cases simply be inaccurate – to impute prior criminality to a defendant facing his first conviction, on the basis of such statistical information about the behaviour of many offenders. To deny a defendant the benefits of first-offender status, the sentencer should have proof that he in fact was guilty of past crimes and that he had been censured for them through having been punished. The one safe proof that he was guilty – safe in the sense of meeting the requirements of proof beyond reasonable doubt – is a conviction for those prior crimes. The one formal mode of censure that the criminal law has available is the imposition of a sentence following conviction.

the censure. The fallibility calls for a limited tolerance of failure, expressed through some diminution of the initial penal response. The respected process, on account of which the discount is also granted, is that by which a person can attend the disapproval visited upon him and alter his course of conduct accordingly. In viewing the person as a moral agent, we initially assume him capable of such a response and thus give him his 'second chance'.

Why, however, give up the discount after a certain number of repetitions? Repetitions can less and less plausibly be characterized as a lapse – an aberrational failure of moral inhibition. Repetition after confrontation with penal censure also suggests a failure on the part of the offender to make the extra effort at self-restraint – the effort which should be the response to being faced with censure.

Might there be special instances where one would be reluctant to treat continued offending as a failure to take the previous condemnation seriously? Arguably, there might, where the continued offending is linked with special indicia of reduced capacity. This might be true of the repeat offender of limited intelligence, whose continued offending might be attributable to an inability to grasp fully the censure that the previous conviction conveys.[35] More debatable are cases of repeat offending that are grounded in a special degree of social deprivation – for example, the homeless petty repeat offender (see Chapter 5, above).

Adopting this 'tolerance thesis' does not involve adopting the career-desert perspective that was criticized earlier in this section. The thesis presupposes that the person is being judged primarily for his present conduct. Career-desert judgements would be different: the seriousness of the present crime would only be one factor to be considered in the sentence, along with the extent and seriousness of the prior record; were the prior record serious enough, the offender now convicted of a lesser offence might now receive quite a severe punishment.

Is this a reinvention of rehabilitation? Giving offenders a 'second chance' might sound like a rehabilitative argument, but it is not. The claim is not that the discount for first offending will in fact 'work' better to induce future compliance than a full dose of punishment would. The first-offender discount reflects, instead, an ethical judgement concerning tolerance for human fallibility, and concerning moral agents' capacity for attending to the censure in punishment.

What has been so troublesome about traditional penal rehabilitationism is that sentences are made to depend not on the degree of blameworthiness of the offender's criminal choices, but on his supposed future amenability to treatment. On that view, the availability of any discount would depend on how responsive the offender is expected to be. If he is deemed the 'amenable' type – who would learn better self-control from a scaled-down dose of punishment and whatever treatment programme seems indicated – he would receive a reduced sentence. If he is deemed the 'unamenable' type, the discount could be denied. On our suggested account, however, no such picking and choosing on the basis of anticipated future behaviour would be permitted. The discount should be available to *every* first offender – and continues (at diminishing levels) until he has accumulated the requisite number of prior convictions to lose it; it does not depend on the particular offender's expected degree of responsiveness. The reason why is, again, suggested by the communicative element in desert: every offender, as a human being, is to be deemed as a moral agent capable of understanding the censure expressed through punishment and responding accordingly. The person forfeits the tolerance, and loses the associated penal discount, only through his actual subsequent criminal choices.

While this account is not a reinvention of the rehabilitative sentence, it embodies something we may feel is legitimate behind the idea of rehabilitation. This is not the conventional positivist idea that sentences should be based of offenders' diagnosed treatability. It is, rather, that people's capacity to take condemnation of their acts seriously is something that has a moral dimension and should be acknowledged in the criminal law.

9.6.4 The number and seriousness of previous convictions

Should the seriousness of the prior convictions count, in making adjustments to the sentence for the criminal record? In everyday judgements of censure, the gravity of the prior misconduct does make a difference. Suppose someone has committed a serious intentional wrong, and wants to claim that the act is uncharacteristic of his past behaviour. Suppose he has previously been censured for other wrongs, but of a much less serious character. He might still plausibly argue that it was uncharacteristic of him to commit wrongs of this magnitude; he might claim, 'Yes, I've committed petty acts of malice before, but this is the first time I've done something like *this*'.

Similar logic should hold for sentencing. Someone convicted of his first serious crime should be entitled to plead that such gravely reprehensible conduct has been uncharacteristic of him, and hence that he deserves to have his penalty scaled down – even when he has a record of lesser infractions. Where the current offence is serious, in other words, the criminal history should take into account the gravity of prior convictions as well as their frequency.[r]

[r] See von Hirsch 1981, 615–16, 620–21. What if the current crime is relatively minor? Then, it becomes more debatable whether the gravity of prior offences should count. When someone has been convicted of a routine property crime, for example, it should not seem to matter whether such prior offences were other such lesser offences, or offences of a more serious character such as burglary or robbery. In any event, the offender's record shows that crimes of at least the present degree of seriousness are not uncharacteristic of him.

How many repetitions must occur before this 'tolerance' plea loses its force entirely? This is a matter of judgement: a possibility would be that the discount should be lost after about three prior convictions, but there are no magic numbers. However, it should be apparent from what has already been said that, after a limited number of repetitions, the plea will have been spent, and the offender will get the 'full measure' of punishment appropriate for a crime of that degree of gravity. If, after that, the actor commits further repetitions, he should not get stepped-up further responses: there simply would no longer be any mitigation due. Were it permissible to continue increasing the punitive response with each subsequent repetition, even relatively minor offences could eventually receive severe penalties.

9.7 Proportionate Non-Custodial Sanctions

Imprisonment – and particularly, imprisonment for significant durations – is a severe penalty. Under a proportionality-oriented sentencing scheme, this sanction should therefore be reserved for crimes of a serious nature. Other, less serious offences should ordinarily be punished by less onerous non-custodial sanctions. A properly constructed penalty system therefore requires norms and principles guiding the use of such sanctions.

How, then, should non-custodial sanctions be arrayed, under a desert rationale? Martin Wasik and Andrew von Hirsch sketched a model.[s] The discussion here addresses some of the issues which the Wasik-von Hirsch scheme raises – issues concerning scaling of non-custodial sanctions, comparability among penalties, back-up sanctions for breach, and related matters.

9.7.1 Scaling non-custodial sanctions: The basic elements of a model

The Wasik-von Hirsch scheme contains the following main elements:

- Non-custodial sanctions would be graded and arranged to reflect the degree of seriousness of the crime of conviction. 'Intermediate sanctions' – that is, non-custodial sanction of the middle range severity – could be employed only for crimes of medium seriousness, and *not* for lesser crimes.

[s] Wasik and von Hirsch 1988, see also von Hirsch 1993, ch. 7. The article makes use of numerical sentencing tariffs, for heuristic purposes, in order to make explicit the relationships between the various elements of the system. However, the model does not presuppose the establishment in law of such numerical standards – since other techniques of guidance, such as statutory sentencing principles, may be preferred as a way of guiding judges' sentencing choices (on this issue of numerical guidelines v statutory sentencing principles, see von Hirsch, Knapp and Tonry 1987, ch. 3; von Hirsch 1987).

- Substitution would be permitted among sanctions of comparable onerousness, but with policy-based limitations (discussed below) on how extensive that substitution may be.
- There would be significant restrictions on the severity of the back-up sanctions that may be used against offenders who violate the conditions of a non-custodial sanction.

Such a scheme has a number of advantages. First, it restricts the use of imprisonment. Incarceration, as a severe punishment, would be prescribed chiefly for crimes of the higher range of gravity. Offences of intermediate or lesser seriousness would generally draw non-custodial sanctions.

Second, the scheme would limit the use of intermediate sanctions (for example, those depriving offenders of significant portions of their incomes or leisure time) to crimes that are of middle-level gravity – and *not* permit their use for low-level offences, merely because the perpetrators might be expected to be co-operative with programme requirements. It is the defendant who commits (say) a house burglary – and not the petty thief – who should be the prime candidate for such sanctions.

The sentencing scale could be reasonably simple, because of the limits on interchangeability discussed below. For each level of sanction severity, one type of sanction might normally be recommended. Substitutions of sanctions of equivalent onerousness would be permitted when there were special reasons – say, the defendant's need for and amenability to treatment. Free substitution would be barred, as would be the piling up of multiple sanctions on particular defendants.

Finally, the breach sanction would be brought under control. Offenders would not end up in prison for significant durations, merely because they had violated the technical conditions of a non-custodial sentence.

Each of these various features merits closer examination. Let us begin with the question of substitution among penalties.

9.7.2 Interchanges: equivalent penal bite

In fashioning guidelines for the use of imprisonment, the question of substitutability of sanctions seldom arose, because imprisonment (at least for lengthier periods) seemed to be so much tougher than other penalties. With non-custodial sanctions, the problem presents itself in earnest: several penalties of comparable onerousness may exist, and it is necessary to decide which should be invoked and under what circumstances.

The criterion for substitutions among penalties should, on a desert model, be that of comparable severity: approximate equivalence in penal bite. The principle of proportionality addresses the *severity* of penalties, not their particular mode. When sanctions are ordered according to the gravity of crimes, replacing a particular type of penalty with another having approximately the same degree of onerousness does not infringe ordinal proportionality: that is, it disturbs neither the parity nor the rank-ordering of penal responses.

Employing this criterion, of approximate equivalence in severity, requires judging the relative onerousness of the various penalties involved: a fine of how many days' earnings, for example, is 'worth', say, a day under home detention? Severity, as suggested earlier in this chapter (9.5.2), is a matter of how much a sanction intrudes upon the interests a person typically needs to live a good life. Gauging comparative severity thus would involve assessing how much the various sanctions typically would intrude on persons' living standard, in the sense discussed.

What of crime prevention concerns? A desert rationale does not permit crime prevention to be relied upon to make substitutions among penalties of substantially differing severity, as that would infringe ordinal proportionality (particularly, the requirement of parity). That is the objection to schemes such as selective incapacitation, wherein prison terms of markedly different lengths are to be imposed on offenders, depending on their estimated likelihoods of recidivism (see 9.3.3). When two kinds of penalties have approximately the same penal bite, however, parity is satisfied – in which event one penalty may be chosen over the other on crime-prevention grounds.

A.E. Bottoms has provided an illustration.[36] Suppose two offenders, *A* and *B*, are convicted of comparable offences of intermediate seriousness. *A* is a first offender, and has a fairly 'stable' background. The other, *B*, has a criminal record. Since a desert model allows the lack of prior convictions to be treated as extenuating to a limited extent (see 9.6), *A* deserves a somewhat (but not much) reduced penalty compared to *B*. The record, however, is also an indicator of risk, and how should this be taken into account? The offender's likelihood of returning to crime would not, on a desert rationale, justify a wider severity differential than the modest one just indicated. However, risk may be used to decide the mode of the penalty: whereas *A* might receive a substantial financial penalty in relation to his income, *B*'s sanction might involve intensive probation supervision, designed to reduce (at least partially) his likelihood of reoffending.

Numerical sentencing guidelines (such as Minnesota's) have tended to have a firm demarcation between custodial and non-custodial sanctions. These guideline schemes prescribe significant periods of custody for conduct above a certain degree of seriousness, and non-custodial sanctions for the lesser conduct.[37] Any such 'hard' demarcation has its drawbacks: it can, for example, mean unnecessarily sharp transitions in severity as one moves from non-custodial measures to custody.

A desert rationale requires no sharp demarcation, since the most demanding community penalties may be assessed as being roughly as equivalent in severity with brief periods of incarceration. Where this equivalence exists, substitutions could be permitted. The penalty scale might, in its high ranges, prescribe various durations of incarceration in excess of say, six months, without permitted substitution. The next most severe range of penalties might consist of fairly onerous community sanctions, such as home detention with electronic supervision. Here, however, short periods of full custody – measured in days or weeks – might be the permitted substitute. The substitute might be invoked, for example, for offenders whose previous records of absconding suggest they would not comply with a home-detention order. The duration of that full custody would be calibrated so as to be comparable in its severity to the normally applicable non-custodial sentence. Any such authority to interchange short prison terms with other sanctions, however, should be limited to crimes in the upper-middle seriousness range. If imprisonment is a permissible option for less serious crimes, the whole scheme of non-custodial sanctions is endangered.

Should there be any policy-based limits on substitutability? A desert rationale could allow varying degrees of substitutability – from none to a wide degree. At one extreme would be a penalty scale with *no* substitutions permitted. The scale would consist of bands of penalties of ascending onerousness, with (say) cautions and small fines at the bottom end, more significant financial penalties in the middle, community-service penalties next, and full custody at the top. Within each band, a single type of sanction could be prescribed: for crimes in the intermediate range of gravity, for example, substantial monetary penalties (relative to income) might be the only sanction prescribed. Such a scheme does grade conduct according to the seriousness of the offence, as proportionality requires. It could also significantly reduce the use of imprisonment, provided that custody is restricted to crimes that are serious. Nevertheless, the scheme's rigidity is a drawback. It would, for example, bar the courts from substituting probation for a normally applicable financial penalty, even for offenders who might benefit from probation supervision. The prescribed sanction in a given band, moreover, may not be capable of being carried out for certain offenders. Financial penalties for crimes in the intermediate seriousness range, for example, could not be collected from offenders lacking in regular earnings.

At the opposite pole would be a 'full-substitution' scheme. Any penalty could be substituted for any other, provided that the resulting severity is not altered. The sentencing standards thus could prescribe, not particular penalties, but 'sanction units' instead – that is, units of comparable severity. A crime of upper-intermediate gravity, for example, would be punishable by a stated number of sanction units. These sanction units then would be translatable into actual penalties, depending on the latter's severity. The appropriate penalty-unit sentence could be carried out through a variety of sentencing options. Different penalties could be combined, so as to achieve the prescribed total number of units.

Such a full-substitution scheme, however, would have significant disadvantages. It presupposes a degree of sophistication in the ability to calibrate and compare the onerousness of different sanctions that is not likely to exist. In a scheme with limited substitutions, one can make a judgement about whether the prescribed sanctions are arrayed properly in ascending order of severity. The more numerous and variable the sanctions are, the more difficult and elusive would become the task of comparing their severity. It is also not clear why full substitutability is needed. There are two main kinds of situations where substitutions would be useful: (1) where the usual sanctions cannot feasibly be enforced and a more easily enforceable substitute is called for, and (2) where a substitute may have some enhanced rehabilitative effect, as in A.E. Bottoms' previously cited example. There might conceivably be some other situations as well, but it is not obvious what purpose would be served by cafeteria-style sentencing with unrestricted substitutions.

What remains is *limited* substitutability: some sanctions preferred over others of equivalent severity, and this is what the Wasik-von Hirsch model proposes. According to that scheme, one type of punishment would be prescribed in each range of sanction severity, and would be the normally recommended type of disposition. However, the substitution of other specified sanctions (of approximately comparable severity) could be invoked for certain reasons. These reasons could be preventive (where, for example, the sentencer had special reasons for believing that the alternative sanction might have some rehabilitative effect), or administrative (where, for example, the standard sentence could not effectively be enforced against this type of defendant).

9.7.3 Back-up sanctions for breach of conditions

Non-custodial sanctions require back-up sanctions. Something needs to be done with the individual who, say, is placed on probation but refuses to comply with the probation routines he is called upon to observe.

In Anglo-American jurisdictions, the ultimate breach sanction has been imprisonment. The form of traditional non-custodial sanctions made that apparent. Probation, for example, is in many jurisdictions a conditional disposition whereby a sentence of imprisonment is put in suspension, provided that the offender abides by specified conditions of supervision in the community. If these conditions are violated, the prison sentence held in reserve may be reimposed.

Relying on incarceration as the breach sanction is problematic, however, especially for intermediate sanctions. Offenders receiving these sanctions often have extensive requirements to fulfil, and their compliance tends to be more closely monitored. Violations of those requirements are thus more likely to be uncovered than would be the case for traditional non-custodial sanctions (such as probation in many countries[t]). Easy resort to imprisonment for breach conditions might well mean that *more* such offenders would end up in prison than would have been had the intermediate sentences not existed at all.

When someone refuses to observe the required routines of a non-custodial sentence, the breach can be seen as involving two components. (1) The offender has not yet completed his original punishment, and still 'owes' the uncompleted portion in some comparable form. (2) The act of breach is, arguably, itself a reprehensible act, calling for some added punishment. With these elements identified, it is evident why a desert rationale should restrict the severity of breach sanctions; thus:

- Element (1) may call for the uncompleted portion of the original penalty to be served in some different, more easily enforced form. It does not, by definition, call for any additional severity.
- Element (2) could call for a modest addition, depending how reprehensible the act of breach itself is deemed to be. The question is, how reprehensible? Victimizing acts can be gauged in part by the extent to which they typically affect a victim's living standard (see 9.5.1); but the act of breach per se lacks a victim. Breach seems hardly comparable, however, with acts (say, of threatened violence) that typically should be deemed serious enough to warrant routine resort to incarceration.

On the basis of such arguments, the Wasik-von Hirsch model proposes only a modest step-up in severity: breach would result in the offender's receiving a sanction that is one band in severity up from the band in which his initial penalty was located.[u] Whether this particular rule should be adopted depends on the character of the penalty structure – and also on the seriousness with which the breach of conditions is regarded. The principle, however, should be apparent: breach should occasion only a modest increase in severity, and imprisonment should be sparingly invoked as the breach sanction.

Thus far, we have been speaking of breaches of those conditions of a non-custodial penalty that prescribe the routines which the offender must undergo as his punishment – say, the requirements of a particular kind of probation or 'community rehabilitation' order. Some kinds of non-custodial sanctions – probation for example – impose the further condition that the offender refrain from committing new crimes. When the latter condition is violated through the offender's committing a further

[t] In many (especially Anglo-American) jurisdictions, probation was routinely resorted to as the non-custodial penalty of choice, with large caseloads and minimal actual supervision.

[u] For heuristic purposes, the Wasik-von Hirsch model sets forth a series of bands of ascending sentence severity, depending on the seriousness-range of the offence. This solution permits moving one band upward as the breach penalty.

crime that should be treated differently: as a case of recidivism. The sanction should thus depend primarily on the degree of seriousness of the new criminal act – with the modest adjustment for reoffending that was suggested earlier in this chapter (9.6). Imprisonment of significant periods would thus be warranted only if the act of reoffending would – taking this adjustment into account – be deemed serious enough to justify such a custodial sentence.

Abiding by restrictions such as these on the back-up sanction would help preserve the proportionality of the response. It would also serve the important practical goal of preventing sanctions for breach becoming a major route into the prison.

9.8 Limited Deviations from Proportionality: A Modified Desert Model?

Desert theory sets priorities among sentencing aims: it holds that it is more important to have proportionately-ordered sanctions than to seek other objectives – say, incapacitating those deemed more likely to return to crime. This understandably evokes discomfort: why cannot one seek proportionality *and* pursue other desired ends, whether they be treatment, incapacitation or deterrence?

To an extent, the desert rationale permits consideration of other aims: namely, to the degree that is consistent with the proportionate ordering of penalties. Thus when there is a choice between two non-custodial sanctions of approximately equivalent severity, proportionality constraints are not offended when one of these is chosen over the other on rehabilitative grounds (see 9.7). Nevertheless, a desert model remains somewhat constraining: ulterior aims may be relied upon only where these do not substantially alter the comparative severity of penalties. Why not, then, relax the model's constraints to allow greater scope to such other aspirations?

A possibility, sometimes referred to as a 'modified' desert model, would be to relax parity constraints to a limited degree.[38] Proportionality would still determine comparative punishment rankings, but limited variations would be permitted (say, in the range of 5–10 per cent) in the severity of sanctions imposed on crimes of comparable seriousness. While departures from parity requirements involve a sacrifice of equity, as explained above, the extent of that sacrifice depends on the degree of the deviation involved. Limited deviations, arguably, would permit the pursuit of ulterior objectives without 'too much' unfairness.[v] This model differs, however, from

[v] This model also differs substantially from the Bottoms–Brownsword model for dangerous offenders, discussed in Chapter 4 above. There, we were speaking of large deviations from the proportionate sentence, for the purpose of confining especially dangerous individuals. Because

Norval Morris's 'Limiting Retributivism' model, in that it requires closer scrutiny of inequalities in punishment.[w] Since parity is regarded as an important requirement of fairness, not just a marginal constraint, it matters how much deviation from parity is involved, and for how strong ulterior reasons. Only modest deviations, to achieve other pressing objectives, would be permissible.

Could such deviations be employed to enhance the crime-preventative effect of the sentence? Large preventative effects cannot be expected, because such a strategy is likely to encounter a fairness/effectiveness dilemma. Consider incapacitative strategies: substantial added incapacitative effects tend to be achievable (if achievable at all) only when the sentence differential between lower and high-risk individuals is large.[39] Large differentials, however, would mean infringing proportionality constraints to a great degree – not to the restricted degree which this limited-deviation model contemplates. Keeping differentials modest, however, would mean restricted or non-existent added preventative benefits.

What other reasons might there be for deviating from parity? One might be to facilitate the scaling of non-custodial penalties. Under a desert model, substitutions among sanctions would be permissible only when the penalties are about equally onerous. Relaxing parity constraints might allow substitutions to be made somewhat more easily, and might also facilitate devising back-up sanctions for offenders who violate the terms of their sentence.[x] This might be accomplished with only rather limited deviations from parity.

This approach still makes the seriousness of the offence the primary determinant for the ordering of penalties, but gives a little extra scope for ulterior purposes. Even such schemes remain constraining, however: some extra leeway might be granted to suit a non-custodial penalty to the offender's apparent treatment needs, but not a great deal.

Could still more scope be given to non-desert considerations? In a mixed rationale, either desert will predominate or something else will. If, in the ordinary case, the seriousness of the crime is the penalty's principal determinant, the system remains desert-dominated. If other (say, crime-preventive aims) are emphasized, however, that creates a system dominated by those aims. That will re-introduce the familiar problems of consequentialist sentencing schemes – for example, those relating to disparate outcomes, and those of insufficient systematic knowledge of preventive effects (see Chapter 1).

of the size of these deviations, exceptionally urgent reasons needed to be cited to justify them. Here, we are speaking of deviations from parity of a much more modest nature.

[w] For further discussion of the 'Limiting Retributivism' model, see Appendix 2 below.

[x] For fuller discussion of such back-up sanctions and their relation to desert requirements, see 9.7.

Notes

1. See particularly, von Hirsch 1981, von Hirsch 1985, von Hirsch 1993, von Hirsch and Ashworth 1996.
2. The German Constitutional Court, for example, has adopted such a ban on grossly disproportionate sentences: see BverfGE 50, 125, 133 m.w.N.
3. See Bentham 1982, 168; Beccaria 1963, ch. 23. For modern variants of these 18th century penologists' theses, see Stigler 1970; Friedman and Sjostrom 1993; for discussion, see Zimring and Hawkins 1997, 169–73; von Hirsch, Bottoms *et al.* 1999, ch. 9.
4. Andenaes 1982, 3–33.
5. Roxin 1979, 304–307; for a similar Scandinavian perspective, Törnudd 1975. For a critique of the evidentiary and ethical basis of this argument, see Schünemann, von Hirsch and Jareborg 1998, 17–28, 83–100, 125–152.
6. Schumann 1998.
7. Bottoms 2003.
8. Frisch 1998.
9. Andenaes 1988, 42; for a response, von Hirsch and Jareborg 1989.
10. See more fully 2.5.4.
11. For a comparable suggestion, see Wood 1988.
12. See Morris 1976; Morris 1982, ch. 5; see further Appendix 2.
13. Morris 1982, 199.
14. This distinction was first systematically set forth in von Hirsch 1985, ch. 4.
15. See von Hirsch 1985, ch. 11; Zimring and Hawkins 1995, ch. 2.
16. Ashworth 1989; Ashworth 2000, ch. 10; von Hirsch 1993, ch. 5.
17. See 1.4; von Hirsch 2003, 65.
18. See more fully, von Hirsch 1993, at 42–46.
19. von Hirsch 1993, at 45–46; von Hirsch 1976, ch. 16 – in which it was recommended that terms of confinement over five years should be limited primarily to aggravated forms of homicide.
20. von Hirsch, Knapp and Tonry 1987, 96–101.
21. von Hirsch 1985, 71–74. For an analysis of how this might be done under German law, see Hörnle 1999, 226–44.
22. von Hirsch and Jareborg 1991.
23. Sen 1987.
24. For an exploration of how the living standard idea might be applied in Swedish sentencing law, see Asp and von Hirsch 1999; for applications under English law, see Ashworth 2000, ch. 4; Ashworth and von Hirsch 1997; for applications under German law, see Hörnle 1999, 226–44.
25. See, eg, Sebba and Nathan 1984.
26. On this approach, an issue might be that of whether the persons surveyed have actually experienced the penalties involved; this might call for a survey of punished offenders as a way of checking the findings of wider opinion surveys.
27. For a statement of this objection, see Walker 1991, 99–100.
28. See the discussion by Bottoms 1998, 56–57 and 62–63.
29. National Academy of Sciences 1986; von Hirsch 1985, ch. 11.
30. Fletcher 1978, 460–466; Singer 1979, ch. 5; Hörnle 1999, 164–66.

31. Wasik 1987; Ashworth 2000, ch. 6.
32. von Hirsch 1976, ch. 10.
33. For an analysis of the doctrine and theory concerning ignorance of law, see Husak and von Hirsch 1993.
34. von Hirsch 1981; and subsequently, von Hirsch 1985, ch. 7, and von Hirsch 1998.
35. Thus under Swedish law, such an offender could claim mitigation under the provisions of Article 29, s. 3 of the Penal Code, on grounds that the conduct was based on a 'manifest lack of development, experience, or capacity for judgment'.
36. Bottoms 1989.
37. For a fuller description of the Minnesota and Oregon schemes, see von Hirsch 1995.
38. See von Hirsch 1993, ch. 6.
39. von Hirsch 1985, 163.

Appendix 1
Equity Factors in Sentencing

1 Introduction

It follows from the desert model that a sentence for a crime may be adjusted to take into account factors that aggravate or mitigate the seriousness of the offence. Where there are features, for example, that make the foreseeable harm substantially less than normal, this renders the offence less serious in the circumstances, and should be reflected through a reduced sentence. Similarly, so should features demonstrating that the offender's culpability was reduced – for example, provocation cases, where the offence was a response to the victim's own gross misconduct.[1]

The question to which we turn in this first Appendix is whether there are other factors, not relating to the crime's seriousness or the penalty's degree of onerousness, that should be permitted to affect the severity of the sentence in special cases. What, if any, are the reasons for reflecting such 'equity factors' in the sentence? To what extent, if at all, are these factors related to, or compatible with, the proportionality principle – or with conceptions of desert in a wider sense?[2] It seems intuitively right that there should be such sentence reductions – for example, that the sentence should be scaled down on account of an offender's advanced age or serious ill health.

What is less clear, however, is why this should be so. The subject of equity factors has scarcely been addressed in the sentencing literature, and only a handful of articles in the philosophical literature exist on the general subject of 'mercy'. We ourselves have not dealt with this topic before, and find that we still have not come up with a systematic analysis, comparable to those that we have offered in earlier chapters. What we can only offer here is some possible themes for further consideration.

2 Equity Reasons for Mitigation: The Swedish Provisions

The most fully elaborated set of provisions on the subject of equity mitigation is contained in Sweden's proportionality-oriented sentencing statute. That statute lists a variety of aggravating and mitigating factors that relate to the 'penal value' (ie, seriousness) of the offence.[a] The statute goes on, however, to list seven additional factors which it terms 'equity factors' (*billighetshänsyn*). These are described in the law as *not* affecting the offence's penal value – but are to be treated nevertheless as reasons for reducing sentence.

The relevant Swedish provisions on equity mitigation are set forth in Chapter 29, section 5 of the Swedish Penal Code – which came into effect, along with the principal provisions on proportionality of sentence, in 1989. The provisions sets out seven discrete matters for the court to consider, once it has determined the 'penal value' (seriousness) of the offence.

1. Whether the accused as a consequence of the crime has suffered serious bodily harm;
2. Whether the accused according to his ability tried to prevent, or repair, or mitigate the harmful consequence of the crime;
3. Whether the accused voluntarily gave himself up;
4. Whether the accused is, to his detriment, expelled from the country in consequence of the crime;
5. Whether the accused as a consequence of his crime has experienced or is likely to experience discharge from employment or other disability or extraordinary difficulty in the performance of his work or trade;
6. Whether a punishment imposed according to the crime's penal value would affect the accused unreasonably, due to advanced age or bad health;
7. Whether, considering the nature of the crime, an unusually long time has elapsed since the commission of the crime . . .

This collection of 'equity factors' provides for departures from normal proportionality criteria when compassion seems appropriate for the offender's predicament, particularly where the offender is specially vulnerable or is experiencing other suffering.[b] A number of these listed factors have considerable intuitive plausibility as grounds for reducing sentence. This is true, for example, of factor 2 [attempts by the defendant to alleviate the harm done]; factor 6 [the defendant's advanced age or ill health]; and factor 7 [lengthy lapse of time since the offence]. Others seem more debatable: where commission of the crime results in an accident in which the offender is injured [factor 1], for example, has he not brought his difficulties on himself? But the Swedish list of factors provides a valuable starting point for discussion.

[a] These are set forth in Swedish Penal Code, Art. 29, ss. 2 and 3. Specified grounds for aggravation are, for example, that the accused showed a 'special degree of indifference to the conduct's adverse consequences'. Mitigating grounds include provocation through the victim's grossly wrongful conduct.

[b] Finland, which also has a proportionality-oriented sentencing system, likewise has a provision authorizing reduction of sentence on account of equity factors. The stated factors are: (1) 'another consequence' to the offender of the offence or the sentence; (2) advanced age, poor health, or 'other personal circumstances' of the offender; (3) a 'considerably long period' has passed since commission of the offence. Finnish Penal Code, ch. 6, s. 7.

What is also important about the Swedish scheme is its analytical framework. The statute generally reflects a desert rationale: sentences are to be proportionate in their severity to the seriousness of the offence.[3] The normal grounds for departing from the sentencing norm are the proportionality requirements themselves: the seriousness of the crime, for example, is altered because the defendant's culpability is reduced. These departures are authorized, as just noted, in the separate sections on aggravation and mitigation. The provision on equity factors makes it clear that its listed factors, which we have set out, are not related to the offence's seriousness. Is it possible, nevertheless, to provide an account of these provisions which reflects some of the values underlying desert theory?[c]

This question of what the relevant values should be is raised by the English judicial practice of mitigating sentence on account of 'worthy social contributions'. The defendant who has been active in public charities, or has behaved heroically in saving a child from drowning, may receive a reduced sentence.[4] The approach appears to be one of placing the offender's crime in the context of his wider personal history. Such an approach would seem to call for a 'social accounting' conception that treats the punishment as concerned in part with a defendant's general personal worthiness or unworthiness. This would have little in common with a proportionalist sentencing model, which (as discussed earlier (see 9.6.2)) is concerned with censure for the offender's *criminal* conduct. Our question here, therefore, should be a more focused one: to what extent should equity factors be recognized, that are *consistent with certain basic values embodied in the proportionalist sentencing model*?

3 Equity Mitigation, Discretion, and the 'Paradox of Mercy'

What are the possible justifications for allowing some or all of these 'equity' factors to reduce sentence? Some philosophers have invoked the concept of mercy. Jean Hampton has described mercy as 'the suspension or mitigation of a punishment that would otherwise be deserved as retribution, and which is granted out of pity and compassion for the wrongdoer'.[5] In ordinary speech one may speak of 'tempering justice with mercy', but this phrase raises an immediate problem of definition.

[c] The provisions of Ch. 29, s. 5 of the Swedish statute were added late to the drafting process, and the statement of purpose that accompanied introduction of law – which in other respects is quite detailed – has provided little explanation here. The Swedish sentencing literature, since adoption of the law – which in other respects is also rather extensive – also has not examined 'equity factors' in much detail. A brief but useful conceptual framework is supplied, however, in Jareborg and Zila 2000, and a descriptive analysis, in Holmqvist 1999.

It suggests that mercy is different from, and even opposed to, justice in punishment. Such an approach could seem to generate the so-called paradox of mercy; in Jeffrie Murphy's words:

> If mercy requires a tempering of justice, then there is a sense in which mercy may require a departure from justice ... Thus to be merciful is perhaps to be unjust. But it is a vice, not a virtue, to manifest injustice. Thus mercy must be, not a virtue, but a vice – a product of morally dangerous sentimentality.[6]

What is actually at issue here is the extensiveness of the concept of justice. When one speaks of the 'just' sentence, this may denote either the sentence that is just according to all the normal criteria (but which may subsequently be altered to take account of exceptional considerations, such as mercy or equity factors); or else it may refer to the sentence that is just, taking account of every factor with a good claim to affect sentencing (which would include mercy or equity factors). The former is a defeasible concept of justice, whereas the latter is a conclusory concept. On this basis, it may not be crucial whether equity factors are regarded as within or outside justice, so long as there is consistency in the analysis. The strength or weakness of the justifications for reflecting equity factors would be unaffected; and, on both views, they operate to modify the sentence that would be appropriate according to normal proportionality considerations. This demonstrates the error of the claim that, when a court determines the just sentence, and then makes a further reduction to reflect equity factors, the sentence that it ultimately imposes must be unjust. This argument involves a confusion between the two senses of justice that are in play. If a court purportedly departs from the just sentence to take account of mercy factors, then 'the just sentence' means the sentence that is just in a defeasible sense – that is, liable to be derogated from, to some extent, by such factors. If a court regards equity factors as part of the process of arriving at a just sentence, then the issue of an unjust sentence does not arise since equity is regarded as an element in determining the just sentence.

However, there is a related question to be borne in mind, that is concerned with the principle of treating like cases alike. It is sometimes assumed that courts have a *discretion* to take account of equity factors, because by their nature they involve compassion in individual cases. Thus in the leading English decision, *Bernard,*[7] the appellant had been convicted of being concerned in the importation of some 27 kilos of cannabis. The trial judge stated that the appropriate sentence would be six years' imprisonment but that, taking account of Bernard's age (64) and his medical condition, a sentence of five years would be imposed. There was medical evidence that he suffered from a narrowing of the oesophagus (which caused difficulty in swallowing), diabetes and hypertension. He was said to be at particular risk of a stroke or heart attack. When he appealed against his sentence, the Court of Appeal received further medical evidence to the effect that prison conditions were exacerbating his condition and increasing the risks of a heart attack or stroke. The court articulated two general principles. First, a medical condition which may at some unspecified future date affect either life expectancy or the prison authorities' ability to treat the person satisfactorily is not a reason for the Court of Appeal to interfere with an otherwise appropriate sentence, although it may be a matter for the Home Secretary to consider in relation to his powers of release.[8] The offender who is HIV positive would fall into this category. Secondly, a serious medical condition, even when it is difficult to treat in prison, does not entitle the offender to a lesser sentence than would otherwise be appropriate, although it might enable a court, as 'an act of mercy in the exceptional circumstances of a particular case, rather than by virtue of any general principle' to reduce the sentence.

Clearly, the Court of Appeal's language when articulating this second principle was intended to negate a duty of mercy. It preserves the possibility that in a case on precisely the same facts as *Bernard* a court may decide not to reduce the sentence. This cannot be supported on the basis that the discretion is necessary to take account of other possible countervailing factors in a case, because the defendant's medical condition creates only *a* reason for sentence reduction, capable of being overridden by other factors. But if there is no such countervailing factor, the reduction of sentence ought to be required. Thus any justification for reducing the sentence in Mr Bernard's case should apply equally in a similar case, and both sentences should be similar. The Court of Appeal's determination to preserve discretion for sentencers in this matter is therefore unsupportable. Ross Harrison has argued persuasively that the exercise of power by state authorities ought to be rational and consistent, and therefore that this purely discretionary approach to mercy cannot be acceptable.[9] More recently John Tasioulas has similarly also warned, that under a discretionary approach:

> how offenders are dealt with in relevantly similar cases will depend on the vagaries of judicial temperament. This will leave some offenders plagued by the excruciating realization that, had their case been tried by the more compassionate judge in the adjoining courtroom, the sentence imposed would have been considerably lighter.[10]

The Court of Appeal's principle in *Bernard* is plainly objectionable because it leaves mitigation of sentence as a discretionary matter rather than seeking to articulate principles for applying equity factors. Part of the difficulty with *Bernard* and similar cases lies in their use of the term 'mercy', which tends to connote a highly exceptional, one-off exercise of a special dispensing power. In order to avoid those connotations, we will refer here to equity factors rather than to 'mercy'.

4 Previous Discussion of Equity Mitigation

Various scholars have explored the grounds for equity mitigation, usually under the title, 'mercy'.[11] At one time the topic was discussed largely in the context of invoking mercy in order to temper the rigidity of legal rules, particularly regarding the death penalty for murder, but many of those doctrines now form a recognized part of sentencing law and practice.

The most notable recent effort is a 2003 essay by John Tasioulas. He discusses 'four paradigm grounds for mercy selectively drawn from legal practice'.[12] His first ground is where an offender's upbringing is such as to erect 'formidable obstacles ... to forming a decent and law-abiding character'. Tasioulas argues that the reason for mitigation in this type of case does not reside in reduced culpability, and must therefore be a form of mercy. This type of case seems to involve the socially deprived offender – a topic which has been addressed already in Chapter 5. His second category is composed of offences committed in circumstances which 'posed unusually severe obstacles to law-abiding behaviour'. His primary example is provocation, but this is now widely recognized as a factor that reduces culpability.[d] An offender's diminished culpability renders his offence less serious, so that this ground for reduction of his sentence can be justified straightforwardly by applying ordinary proportionality principles. Tasioulas takes the view, however, that we should preserve the possibility that there may be some provocation cases that do not qualify for mitigation on normal proportionality grounds but in which it would be proper to show mercy.

More germane is Tasioulas' third category, which ranges from the merciful remission of punishment for those suffering from a terminal illness to taking account of the fact that one or more members of the offender's family died as a result of his offence. Tasioulas is careful to state that this does not refer to cases where the offender has suffered social ostracism as a result of the offence: his principal target seems to be what are sometimes termed 'nearest and dearest' cases, as where an offender causes the death by dangerous driving of a family member or close friend. This takes us back towards factor 1 in the Swedish law, and the idea of 'natural punishment'. However, Tasioulas does not provide a clear explanation of why sentence should be reduced in these cases. One argument is that a person who has suffered personal injury

[d] Indeed, the Swedish sentencing statute expressly recognizes provocation as a culpability-reducing factor, affecting the seriousness of the offence in the particular circumstances; see Swedish Penal Code, ch. 29, s. 3:1. For discussion of provocation as a culpability factor, see, eg, von Hirsch and Jareborg 1987; Narayan and von Hirsch 1996. For further discussion of provocation, see Simester and Sullivan 2004.

while committing the offence or has lost a friend or family member through the offence is likely to be psychologically damaged to such a degree that less punishment is needed in order to inflict the 'normal' amount of hard treatment on him. That would be an application of the principle of equal impact, that is, that the quantum of punishment should be adjusted so as to remove a substantial inequality in the impact of the standard sanction (see 6.1 below). Tasioulas prefers the general affirmation that mercy should be recognized as the ground for reducing sentence, simply out of compassion for the offender's predicament in this type of case. Certainly, this third category has no bearing on culpability, unlike the previous examples, and so it appears that broader 'equity' reasoning is needed if there is to be justification for mitigating sentence.

His fourth category may be regarded as somewhat more controversial – where there is evidence of sincere repentance. Let us quickly remove the unconvincing cases in which offenders state their remorse for the offence without adducing persuasive evidence of it other than a plea of guilty, and also the cases where acts done by the offender since the commission of the offence (such as paying compensation to the victim) only debatably appear to constitute evidence of remorse. Even in those cases where we are satisfied that the offender is genuinely remorseful, is this a justification for mercy at the sentencing stage? It cannot affect the offender's culpability for the offence, since it occurs subsequently, but Tasioulas hints that it affects the punishment decision because that should take account of the changed character of the person who is being sentenced.

In terms of conceptions of the standard criteria for proportionality, it would be difficult to see the relevance of remorse. Why, then, is it thought to be a case calling for compassion? Tasioulas, commenting generally on his four examples, states that the unifying factor is that 'the imposition of the penalty specified by the retributive norm is an excessive hardship'.[13] But why should it be a particular hardship for the remorseful offender? He is not suffering from a terminal illness, nor has he had to cope with the death of a friend or family member. There seems to be no evidence that he would be more frail or vulnerable than any other offender. Tasioulas points to the suffering of the truly remorseful offender and, linking it with the rationale of the third category, claims that 'the process [the offender] has undergone in the aftermath of the offence justifies punishing him less than he deserves'.[14] The reasoning appears to be that the offender's repentance shows that the deserved punishment would be unduly harsh, not in proportionality terms, but more generally because we should show some sympathy towards a person who seems already to have taken the message of punishment to heart and to have started to mend his ways.

5 Equity Mitigation: Possible Principles

If deviations from proportionality are to be justified in the situations discussed earlier in this Appendix, we need a more coherent set of conceptions. There appear to us to be three, partially interlocking, possible reasons why sentences should be mitigated on account of equity factors: an 'equal impact' principle, arguments from compassion, and quasi-retributive conceptions. These reasons are examined in this section, their interrelation discussed; then, they are applied to sentencing practice in the following section.

5.1 An 'equal-impact' principle?

To what extent can equity factors be accounted for by a principle of equal impact? According to this principle, when an offender suffers from certain handicaps that would make his punishment significantly more onerous, the sanction should be adjusted in order to avoid its having an undue differential impact on him. A disabled, wheelchair-bound offender would thus experience a term of imprisonment being more onerous; the penalty, accordingly, would be scaled down to avoid this differential impact.

This 'equal impact' principle is connected with the proportionalist sentencing model, but is not part of it in standard cases. Although that model is not claimed to produce precise calibrations of the relative seriousness of offences and the appropriate severity of punishments, it does aspire to generate workable general criteria for determining seriousness and severity. It does so largely through principles and concepts such as the living standard analysis, which (as applied to the severity of sanctions) requires that the comparative severity of sentences should be gauged by reference to the importance of the interests upon which the sentence typically impinges (see 9.5.2). If there are unusual cases that diverge significantly from the norm, that would speak for attending to those unusual features and, if appropriate, modifying the sentence – so as to ensure there is not an unequal impact (or, as Tasioulas puts it, 'excessive hardship' is avoided). As with the assessments of seriousness and severity themselves, the claim is not that a precise calculation can be produced but rather an approximate norm for dealing with unusual situations.[e]

[e] This is not the same as the analysis that should be used for calculating the amount of financial penalties. In most sentencing systems, the level of fine appropriate to a case will be considered in relation to the financial resources of the offender. In the sentencing systems of many European countries, including those of Sweden and Germany, this has been formalized through a 'unit-fine' system: the fines imposed by the court are measured in units that correspond (with various adjustments) to numbers of days' earnings. A court might thus, for a given offence, impose on the offender a fine of 60 units – which would reflect 60 days' worth of earnings. The actual amount he must pay would then be calibrated, after considering his level of

The equal-impact principle does not actually function as true equity mitigation, because it actually does not call for qualifying defendants to suffer less punishment: it merely is a way of avoiding that such defendants be made to suffer *more*. Suppose the standard sentence for a given species of offence is three years' imprisonment. If this sanction is applied to a defendant in a wheelchair, he actually – under an interest analysis[f] – has his interests set back to a greater degree. Reducing the sentence under an equal-impact theory would be designed merely to eliminate this increment in severity. However, there may be cases where – for compassion or other reasons we discuss below – it would seem desirable actually to reduce the degree of onerousness of the penal imposition he must suffer. The very old or ill defendant, arguably, should not go to prison at all – and not just get a scaled-down prison sentence designed to produce equal impact.

The equal-impact principle is also too narrow in its potential application, however, to serve as a part of a general account of equity mitigation. It would apply only when the degree of onerousness of the sanction in the defendant's particular circumstances is at issue. It would work for old, ill, or disabled defendants, where the sanction appears to be altered in its impact by the person's disability, but not for other equity mitigation cases such as that of delay since commission of the offence [Swedish factor 6, above] where onerousness of the sanction does not seem to be altered. Even for the old or sick, however, the scope of the equal-impact principle would be narrow. It would apply to punishments having demanding routines, such as imprisonment, community service, or intensive probation – which may become considerably more onerous for persons with these disabilities.

We shall suggest below (at 6.1) that there may be some remaining applicability for the equal-impact principle in certain kinds of cases. However, we will not treat this principle as accounting for equity mitigation generally – which thus requires us to ask what other principles would need to be fashioned.

5.2 Arguments from compassion

Jean Hampton, as noted earlier, describes mercy as involving the mitigation of punishment that otherwise would be deserved, on grounds of

daily earnings. The aim here is not to accommodate non-standard cases, but rather to achieve a modicum of standardization in the *normal* assessment of fines. The drawback of assessing fines directly in monetary amounts is that earnings are so unevenly distributed: a fine measured as so-and-so many Kronor or Marks would have a greatly variable impact on offenders' living standards, depending on their earnings. When fines are assessed on the basis of daily earnings, however, it becomes more feasible to assess how much a given number of fine units could affect an offender's 'living standard' in the sense discussed in 9.5.2 above.

[f] Our interest analysis for gauging severity of punishments dealt with the living standard impact of various types of sanctions on standard offenders; see 9.5.2. Certain kinds of non-standard cases, however, can themselves be analysed in terms of typical impacts for the

compassion for the offender. Whether this would suffice to define mercy is debatable, but notions of compassion seem to play an important role in judgements about equity factors. This appears to be the case for the very elderly or seriously ill defendant, where there seem to be obvious reasons for sympathy – for their having to both endure the discomforts of their disability and the deprivations of punishment. This is a normative as well as emotive proposition – that we *ought* to show sympathy for the offender in such situations.

Invoking compassion raises the further issue – compassion for what? Something else should be needed, beyond sympathy for a person's suffering, in order to justify mitigation. Where the person goes bankrupt through no fault of his own, or loses his only child, this also warrants sympathy for his plight, but it is doubtful that his punishment for an offence should be reduced on that account. Some further link needs to be established between the offender's misfortune and the punishment he must undergo. What should that link be? It should, we think, concern 'quasi-retributive' grounds for penalty reduction.

5.3 Quasi-retributive grounds

Quasi-retributive grounds do not form part of the general principles of proportionality in punishment, since they are not directly related either to the seriousness of offences (in terms of harm and culpability), the severity of punishments (in terms of the standard impact on people's interests), or to the permissible role of prior convictions (in terms of notions of limited tolerance for lapses).[g] Instead, they relate to the wider underlying conceptions of penal censure as a response to criminal offending.

Censure for an offence provides reason for the offender to reflect on the wrongdoing and to consider the reasons for his conduct. Quasi-retributive grounds may address special situations which relate to this reflective process. Where an offender makes voluntary reparation, for example, it may be argued as grounds for equity mitigation that he has already given evidence that he has reflected on the wrongfulness of his behaviour and has acted to express that recognition through attempting a remedial action (see 6.3 below). Similarly, when the offence for which he is being sentenced was committed several years earlier, the process of eliciting a reflective response may become more problematic after such a long delay (see 6.4 below).

Recognizing equity claims for such reasons would not involve adopting Antony Duff's perspective that the primary purpose of sentence should be

members of that group. One thus could analyse how imprisonment typically becomes more burdensome for those with specified physical disabilities. For further discussion of such 'standardized special cases', see Narayan 1990.

[g] See 9.5 and 9.6.

to elicit penitence (for our critique of that view, see Chapter 7 above). The sentence would still normally be viewed as conveying authoritative censure, and it would not be tailored to elicit specified repentance in offenders. Our point is, rather, that the rationale underlying the censuring response has something to do with the capacity of an offender, as a moral agent, to engage in certain kinds of moral reflection.

5.4 The link between suffering and quasi-retributive grounds

We have just suggested that equity mitigation should have something to do with (1) compassion for the defendant's suffering, arising from (2) quasi-retributive grounds. But what of the relation between these two elements? Must there be some independent source of misery, or may the suffering inflicted by the punishment itself suffice for equity mitigation? If an independent source of misery is required, mitigation could be granted only for very old or ill defendants. In the case of the defendant facing sentence for a long-past offence, or his having made timely reparation for his crime, there is no additional suffering other than his undergoing the penalty.

To deal with these latter kinds of cases, we should concede that the compassion may relate to the suffering the offender undergoes through his punishment. What the quasi-retributive ground does is to explain why we should have extra sympathy for the defendant's having to experience that suffering. So the formulation should be something like this: *Equity mitigation is appropriate in certain types of special cases, where needed (i) to reflect* ***compassion or sympathy*** *for the suffering undergone by the defendant in virtue of his punishment, provided that (ii) this compassion or sympathy rests on* ***quasi-retributive grounds****, related to the values underlying the desert rationale.*

Notice two features of this formulation. First, it makes it clear that the only suffering involved may be that inflicted by the penalty: no extra source of misery is required. Second, it makes it clear that the sympathy/compassion should be based on quasi-retributive grounds, such as those just discussed. If it is not based on these grounds, it is far from clear that we should alter the person's *punishment* (rather than doing something else); or that the reduction in punishment has anything to do with equity mitigation.

6 Applying the Principles: The Four Cases

To test out the principles of equity mitigation we have just suggested, we might try to apply them to the four main types of cases cited in the Swedish statute.

6.1 Offender's advanced age or serious illness

The compassion or sympathy for the defendant would not relate just to the fact of being old or ill. Illness or old age will happen to us all, and our suggested conception is not designed to provide mitigation in punishment for all of life's misfortunes. The compassion concerns *being punished* when one is very old or seriously ill – in view of the morally demanding character of the penal censure in punishment, and the greater difficulty meeting such moral demands when one is debilitated through age or illness. There are several points involved here. The first concerns the morally demanding character of penal censure: it calls upon the actor to accept criticism, to take a self-critical stance concerning his past conduct; and to make efforts at desistance in future (see Chapter 2). (Granted our theory is not Duff's, so the penalty only invites the offender to take such a stance: but that invitation is for a morally demanding course.) The second point is that a certain resiliency would be helpful in responding to such demands. The actor needs to be able to accept criticism without undue loss of self-esteem, and yet be able to respond constructively to it. The third point – and this is the one about compassion or sympathy – is that we understand how difficult it could be to deal with such demands, when one's resiliency and vitality are sapped by serious illness or debilitating old age. Notice the two elements in this argument; first, it concerns a special compassion for the offender in his more difficult situation; and second, it relates to values underlying the desert rationale.

This ground for mitigation should hold, by the logic of the argument just set forth, only for cases where the offender is seriously affected by advanced age or illness. In that event, a substantial reduction of sentence may be appropriate – for example, a full remission of a term of imprisonment. The question thus arises about an offender who suffers from a disability, but not one of this degree – for example, he has a modicum of physical and mental vigour, but still has a physical handicap that impedes his movement sufficiently to make the routines of being imprisoned more onerous.

In such cases, the 'equal-impact' principle (5.1 above) might still apply. This would involve adjusting the penalty so as to take into account its more onerous character in the particular circumstances. The duration of a prison sentence might thus be reduced to some degree. The aim would not be equity mitigation based on compassion and quasi-retributive reasons, but rather making adjustments in sentence to deal with certain foreseeable differential impacts (see 5.1 above).

6.2 Forms of 'natural' punishment

We saw above (section 2) that Swedish law regards as mitigating factors the fact that the offender suffered injury as a result of the crime [Swedish factor 1]; and the fact that the offender's employment prospects have been damaged as a result of conviction [factor 5]. In our view, the fact that the offender is already suffering for other reasons does not increase the severity of the punishment arising from the sentence itself. The notion of 'natural punishment' is not attractive, since it lumps together the hardships flowing from the sentence with other hardships that have entirely different origins. We also doubt whether there are strong grounds for compassion in cases where the offender has brought the injury or difficulties upon himself, particularly if such consequences were foreseeable risks of the criminal enterprise. One might argue, for example, that an offender who mounts the roof of a building in order to break into it must realize the risk of injury. In many of these types of cases, falling within categories (1) or (5) on the Swedish list, it will be possible to identify this kind of foreseeability.

It might be argued, however, that the equal-impact principle would still apply (see 5.1). Suppose, for example, that our insufficiently agile burglar falls off the roof and becomes physically handicapped as a result. Were the circumstances such as to indicate that a prison sentence would be called for in burglaries of this type, it might be argued that a prison sentence becomes significantly more onerous for mobility-restricted persons, and that this defendant's sentence should be scaled down to some extent, accordingly. Since equal-impact rather than compassion is at issue here, it should matter less whether the defendant assumed the risk through his conduct.

6.3 Voluntary reparation or surrender

Voluntary reparation [Swedish factor 2] is a case where the only suffering the defendant may face is that of being punished. But it nevertheless fits in our conception of equity mitigation. It is appropriate to have some compassion for the offender's suffering the punishment, for a reason that is related to the values underlying the desert rationale.

One of those underlying values is to give a punished defendant the opportunity of providing recognition of how he has wrongfully injured the victim (see Chapter 2). Efforts at reparation are a form of such recognition.[h] Whether voluntary surrender to the authorities [Swedish factor 3] is comparable is less certain, however, because there are so many possible reasons for doing this.

[h] An important feature of this kind of situation is that the offender has not merely reflected on and recognized the wrongfulness of the action himself, but has taken action to convey that recognition to the person wronged, in a manner that is closely linked with the wrongful conduct itself. The case for equity mitigation may well become considerably weaker where the offender merely feels or expresses remorse but takes no such action – although that would warrant further discussion. (Conceivably, a penance-based theory such as Duff's might permit greater scope for mitigation in the latter kinds of cases, although Duff himself has questioned such a result; see, Duff 2001, 120–21.)

6.4 Time delay since the offence

Should long time delay since the offence [Swedish factor 7] be grounds for equity mitigation? Here again, the only suffering the defendant experiences is from the punishment. There appears, nevertheless, to be a basis for compassion that concerns quasi-retributive reasons related to the desert rationale – because a moral function of penal censure is to confront the person with disapprobation, which should give them the opportunity to reflect on the conduct and recognize its wrongfulness. Normally, this is appropriate because the conduct is recent enough so that it does reflect badly on the actor. But with the lapse of time, the possibility increases that the actor may have changed significantly – so that his long past act does not reflect badly on the person he now is.

7 Conclusions

The purpose of this Appendix has been to examine the role of equity factors in sentencing. We have argued that simply to rely on a broad concept of mercy is unsatisfactory, especially when it is treated as providing a discretion that may be exercised or withheld at will. The focus of our analysis has been on a number of mitigating factors that have been utilized in the one statutory framework that specifically addresses this subject – the equity-factors provision of the Swedish sentencing statute. We have acknowledged the role of compassion in supplying part of the justification for some grounds of mitigation, but we have also addressed the role of quasi-retributive ideas in providing a rationale for equity mitigation. We believe that our account provides somewhat more in the way of principled guidance than others previously produced by the few writers who have addressed this subject previously. However, our analysis of equity factors is still a very tentative one, as we have not fully spelled out the justification for equity mitigation or adequately limited its scope. At best, we have provided some ideas for further discussion of this important but elusive question.

Notes

1. In Swedish sentencing law, provocation is treated in this fashion – as a generally applicable grounds for sentence mitigation; see Swedish Penal Code, ch. 29, s. 3:1.
2. See discussion of the rationale for the existence of punishment, in Ch. 2.
3. See von Hirsch 2001b, ch. 9; Lappi-Seppälä 2001.
4. See Ashworth 2000, ch. 5.
5. Hampton, in Murphy and Hampton 1988, 158.

6. Murphy, in Murphy and Hampton 1988, 167.
7. [1997] 1 Cr App R (S) 135. The case is discussed in Ashworth and Player 1998, and in Walker 1999, ch. 13.
8. The Home Secretary has power to release a prisoner 'in exceptional circumstances' or 'on compassionate grounds'; Criminal Justice Act 1991, s. 36.
9. Harrison 1992.
10. Tasioulas 2003, 129.
11. See, eg, the much-cited essay, Smart 1969.
12. Tasioulas 2003.
13. Tasioulas (in n 10 above) also discusses (at 119) the reluctance of Antony Duff to accept remorse (other than immediate repentance) as grounds for mitigating sentence; see Duff 2001, 120–121.
14. Tasiolas (n 10 above) at 119, where he points to the relevance of 'the impact of a proposed punishment on the offender's well-being' and argues that mercy is appropriate where it may be said to be 'cruel' to impose the full, normal sentence.

Appendix 2

Limiting Retributivism and 'Modified' Desert

In developing a rationale for sentencing, an important problem (as we have seen in the preceding chapters, particularly Chapter 9) is to decide upon the relative weight to be given to proportionality and to other (eg, crime-preventive aims) in determining sentence. A desert rationale would place the pre-eminent weight on proportionality; a utilitarian sentencing rationale would emphasize the crime preventive factors, such as incapacitation. Certain conceptions, however, would make use of mixed models. In this Appendix, we compare two mixed models. One of these is 'limiting retributivism', first developed by Norval Morris in the mid '70s.[1] According to Morris's theory, crime-seriousness sets upper (and, less unequivocally, lower) limits on the severity of the sentence. Within those limits, the sentence may be decided on ulterior grounds. The other rationale is the 'modified' desert model, discussed briefly in an earlier chapter (see 9.8). This latter scheme would determine comparative punishment rankings on the basis of desert, but permit limited variations in the sanctions imposed on crimes of comparable seriousness.

A number of sentencing schemes have placed explicit reliance on a proportionalist sentencing rationale, as we have noted earlier (see Chapter 1). Now, the American Law Institute, in its work on a revised Model Penal Code, is considering recommending use of 'limiting retributivism' as the basis for a system of sentencing guidelines.[2] As these two conceptions appear to have certain important similarities, it is worth subjecting them to a comparative analysis – a task which we will undertake here.

1 A 'New' Limiting Retributivism?

As limiting retributivism was initially formulated by Norval Morris, the differences between it and desert-based conceptions were quite apparent. Limiting retributivism, on his account, would make use of the seriousness of the current offence only to set broad limits on the permissible sanction, within which the sentence in the individual case would be set on other (including crime-preventive[a]) grounds. However, there have been significant changes in the limiting retributivism approach more recently – ones that would lead to results that are somewhat more congruent to those yielded by desert principles.

Morris, in his initial formulations, treated his broad desert limits as being based in community sentiment: sentences are not to exceed *what is seen by current popular mores* as excessive.[3] The difficulty with such a formulation, however, is that it provides scant restraint: draconian sanctions (as well as very wide sentence ranges) could become permissible, were community sentiment to support them.[4] Later, however, other advocates of limiting retributivism (notably, Michael Tonry[5] and Richard Frase[6] have been moving away from the community mores perspective, and have come to favour desert-based upper limits on sentence ranges – ones that would be derived from desert-oriented notions of penal censure.

This change in approach constitutes a considerable improvement, but raises the question how the *lower* limits on permissible punishments be determined. Proponents of limiting retributivism seem also to be reconsidering their position here. Although Morris sometimes spoke of there being lower (as well as upper) desert limits on permissible punishments, he did not articulate how these might be set. Tonry, in a 1994 essay,[7] asserted that there should be no lower limits based on desert; yet in the absence of such lower desert limits, it becomes difficult to sustain any kind of graded sanctions at all. In a 1997 National Institute of Justice publication on sentencing guidelines,[8] Tonry seemingly changes position and, as a practical matter, opts for lower offence-based limits. A sentencing guidelines system, he suggests, might have about six severity bands (in his terminology, 'zones of discretion'), based on the seriousness of the offences involved. Substitutions among unequally severe penalties may be made within a given band, but not outside of it. This approach would ensure that serious crimes ordinarily received significant sentences, and that there would be an approximate ordering of penalties according to offence gravity. It seems, however, to involve acceptance of the idea of desert-based lower bounds on penalties. More recently, Richard Frase, another advocate of limiting retributivism, explicitly accepts the idea of desert-based lower bounds, which would be ordinally scaled in the same manner

[a] In an essay with Marc Miller (Morris and Miller 1985), Morris suggested that these ulterior grounds could include incapacitation: predictions of likelihood of recidivism could be employed to fix the sentence anywhere within the applicable desert limits. Given the breadth of those limits on his formulation, this could have made predictive judgements a major (indeed, the primary) determinant of the sentence. In a seemingly technical qualification, however, he asserted that permissible predictive judgements must rely on factors other than the seriousness of crime or the offender's criminal record (Morris and Miller 1985, 37). But since the latter factor, the criminal record, is ordinarily the main basis for predictive judgements, this would sharply restrict the scope of those judgements. Morris does not explain his reasons for adding this qualification, but it seems to reflect a sense of discomfort at a sentencing system resting chiefly on risk predictions.

of the upper desert limits; he speaks of 'a . . . series of proportioned lower limits (at least for those offenses deemed serious enough to require minimum desert standards)'.[9]

The upshot would be a scheme of 'limiting retributivism' that has considerably greater similarities to a desert-based approach than Morris's early formulations. Crime seriousness (at least, in ordinary cases) would have a key role in determining the penalty. Yet there still might be significant differences from desert theory. Greater freedom might still exist to make interchanges among unequally severe penalties. The lower desert limits might be more permeable – to allow consideration, for example, of mitigating factors that do not directly relate to offence gravity but nevertheless suggest merit on the part of the defendant.[b] In assessing how much greater freedom this model allows, however, the possibilities of limited modifications of the desert model also need to be considered. These could, for example, permit modest deviations from the parity requirements of desert – as the 'modified' desert model contemplates (see 9.8).

2 Rationalizing Narrowed Sentencing Ranges?

With a 'modified' desert model, the link between relatively narrow sentencing ranges and the underlying desert rationale is easy enough to explain: it is provided by ordinal proportionality requirements. Those requirements – particularly, the parity requirement – call for comparably severe punishments for comparably reprehensible behaviour, so that it is recognized that variations in penalties (to the extent not accounted for by crime seriousness in the offence's particular circumstances) entail some sacrifice of fairness. However, the extent of that sacrifice of fairness would depend on how much inequality in penalizing comparably blameworthy behaviour is allowed. The idea behind the 'modified' desert model is to permit *limited* inequalities, in order to permit preventive or other consequentialist considerations a modest degree of additional scope in deciding sentence. But since the degree of unfairness would increase as inequalities become more substantial, larger variations in punishment would not be permitted.[10]

If the advocates of limiting retributivism now also support narrowed sentencing ranges, how much support does their suggested rationale give to such an approach? Not a great deal, we think. The reason is that limiting retributivism has offered no clearly articulated ordinal proportionality requirements. Parity is not put forward, even as a prima facie constraint, because the whole idea of limiting retributivism is that desert

[b] See Tonry 1994; he gives the example of the offender from a deprived social background who has succeeded in obtaining steady employment; but see, von Hirsch 1993, 109–10.

provides only upper and lower limits on permissible punishments. If parity has any role at all, these theorists assert, it is only as a much weaker 'guiding principle' not strongly linked with any basic requirements of desert.[11] In the absence of this keystone constraint of ordinal proportionality, it becomes difficult to explain why narrower sentencing ranges would be preferable, as a matter of justice, to Morris's previously suggested wide punishment ranges. It is therefore our conclusion that limiting retributivism, as a theory, provides for scant support for the kind of scheme, with limited punishment ranges, that Tonry and Frase have been suggesting. To account for such a scheme, it would be necessary to begin by relying on the salient principles of desert theory, especially those regarding ordinal scaling of penalties, and then make limited modification as the 'modified desert' model contemplates.

3 Limiting Retributivism as Practical Guidance for Formulating Sentencing Guidelines

Even if limiting retributivism does not serve well as a free-standing sentencing theory, might it nevertheless serve a useful purpose as a practical guide for the development of sentencing guidelines, or the formulation of other forms of practical guidance for sentencers? Consider the American Law Institute's recent proposal to call upon state sentencing commissions to take a limiting retributivism model into account in drafting their sentencing guidelines.[12] Could this serve a useful practical purpose, in helping the commission to formulate their standards?

The directive to utilize a limiting retributivism model could be read as requiring the commission to take proportionality constraints significantly into account in its guidelines. If the commission consults the more recent literature on this model, they may also take note that moderate sentence ranges could be preferable to wide ones (see section 1 above). However, the limiting retributivism model does not provide the analytical tools to explain why this result would be preferable; for that purpose, the commission would need to consult the literature on the desert or modified desert (see section 2).

What of the determination of sentence *within* the applicable ranges? Here, writers on limiting retributivism cite three themes.

(1) The 'starting point' in determining a sentence should be at the bottom of the applicable sentencing range; in Frase's words, 'judges should start at the bottom of the range and increase severity only to the extent needed to meet all appropriate utilitarian and case-specific needs'.[13] Parsimony is cited as the reason for this principle: it would help ensure lower starting points.[14]

(2) The lower desert limits of sentencing range should be quite flexible and permeable (much more than the upper limits) – again, to permit more parsimonious dispositions.[15]

(3) The fixing of the individual sentence within the upper and lower retributive limits should in large part be left to the court in the individual case: the court should have authority both to determine the aim to be achieved (the 'purpose at sentencing'), and what disposition would help achieve that purpose.[16]

Would these three suggested norms be helpful? We doubt it, because each of these norms is problematic, and they also potentially conflict with one another: the second and third of them could suggest results that would be at variance with the first; thus –

- If the lower limit of the sentence range is utilized as the starting point, it would need to be reasonably clearly identifiable. However, we have already noted (in section 2) the difficulty of deriving definite lower limits from a limiting retributivism rationale. The more flexible, variable and permeable those lower limits are, the harder it will be to specify them sufficiently to make use of them as starting points for determining sentence.
- If the bottom of a sentencing range is to serve as a workable starting point, then there would need to be a presumption against exceeding it, except when there are strong countervailing reasons. Insisting on such reasons, however, militates against permitting courts in individual cases to determine the 'purpose at sentencing' – that is, select the aim of the particular sentence and exercise discretion to decide whether and to what extent a sentence above the starting point can achieve that aim. It would be problematical, for example, to permit judges to impose a higher sentence within the applicable desert limits, for deterrence purposes – when there is scant evidence that such a sentence would have enhanced preventive effectiveness.[17]

Were the commission to utilize a desert model – or else, a modified desert model – in fashioning its sentencing guidelines, these difficulties would be avoided. A desert model furnishes ordinal proportionality requirements that would help determine comparative sentence levels. A modified desert model would utilize such requirements – particularly, those of parity in the punishment of comparably severe offences – for deciding the starting points within the sentencing ranges (see section 2). Departures from the starting points, upward or downward, would be permitted to a limited extent: in previous writings, we have spoken of possible deviations from parity of up to 10 or 15 per cent, but certainly not much larger derogations.[18] Where the grounds for departure are crime preventive, the commission should be entitled to assess the relevant state of knowledge – and authorize departures (up to the relevant retributive limits) only where there was reason to believe that those departures might be effective. If the available research does not show, for example, that sentence increases for deterrence in individual cases could have much effect, they simply should not be authorized.

The ultimate drawback of the American Law Institute's proposal, therefore, is to opt for a particular (and in our view, problematical) conceptual model to guide the commission's choices. Assuming, as we have suggested, that it is desirable for the sentencing commission to take proportionality constraints significantly into account in developing its sentencing standards, this could be best achieved by a statutory injunction to do just that. Within those constraints, the choice of which particular conceptual model would be most helpful for the construction of the guidelines (for example, whether a desert model or a 'modified' desert model) would then be left to the commission. The commission would not be required to conceal arguments about ordinal proportionality constraints behind a facade of 'limiting retributivism', were it unconvinced (as we are) that the latter conception is not very illuminating.[c]

Notes

1. Morris 1976; Morris 1982, ch. 5.
2. American Law Institute 2003.
3. Morris 1974, 74–76.
4. See more fully, Zimring and Hawkins 1995, 64–67.
5. Tonry 1994.
6. Frase 2003.
7. Tonry 1994.
8. Tonry 1997.
9. Frase 2003.
10. See 9.8, and, more fully, von Hirsch 1993, 54–56.
11. See, eg, Morris 1982, 202–5.
12. See text at n. 2.
13. Frase 2003, 105.
14. Ibid.
15. Frase 2003.
16. Morris and Tonry 1990.
17. For the limited empirical support for the deterrent effects of increased sentences, see Nagin 1998; von Hirsch, Bottoms *et al.* 1999; Doob and Webster 2003a. For the practical difficulties of using deterrence as a basis for setting individual sentences, see von Hirsch and Roberts 2004, 642–44.
18. von Hirsch 1993, 55.

[c] Were the commission to disagree with the arguments set forth here, and conclude that limiting retributivism were indeed the conceptual preferable model, this statutory injunction would still permit them to take this course and rely on limiting retributivism explicitly.

Appendix 3

Gauging Crime Seriousness: A 'Living Standard' Conception of Criminal Harm

(*Co-author: Nils Jareborg*)

1 Introduction: Harm and Crime Seriousness

The present topic, of gauging criminal harm, is part of the larger topic of assessing the seriousness of crimes. The question of how to judge crime seriousness has gained importance, with the increased influence of desert-oriented conceptions of sentencing – conceptions which make the severity of punishment depend in large part on the gravity of the offence.

Nevertheless, the jurisprudence of crime seriousness has received comparatively little attention. To someone unfamiliar with the criminal law, this will seem surprising. The gravity of the crime has such obvious relevance to the sanction, he would think, that judges and legal scholars surely must have been theorizing about it for years. Yet that has not been the case. Apart from a number of empirical studies on popular perceptions of the seriousness of various crimes (of which, more later), there has not been much discussion of the subject either in the Anglo-American or the Continental penological literature.

Seriousness of crime has two dimensions: harm and culpability. Harm refers to the injury done or risked by the act; culpability, to the factors of intent, motive and circumstance that determine the extent to which the offender should be held accountable (and censured through the criminal law) for the consequences of his act. Both dimensions affect crime seriousness; to use familiar examples, murder is more serious than aggravated assault because the injury is greater, and it is more serious than negligent homicide because the actor's culpability is greater. The problem is to develop criteria for harmfulness and culpability that are more illuminating than simple intuition.

With respect to culpability, there is some theory and doctrine that can be drawn upon, and it comes from the substantive criminal law. The substantive law already distinguishes intentional (ie, purposive, knowing, or reckless) conduct from criminally negligent behaviour. For sentencing doctrine, more refined distinctions could be developed, concerning the degree of purposefulness, indifference to consequences, or carelessness involved in a sentenced offender's conduct. The doctrines of excuse in the substantive law could also be drawn upon in order to develop theories of partial excuse – for example, of partial duress and diminished capacity.[1]

With regard to harm, however, matters are otherwise. Few legal doctrines have been developed on how the gravity of harms can be compared. The substantive law does not provide much guidance, because the occurrence of harm is not explicitly made a general condition of criminal liability. The legal offence definitions simply describe various kinds of prohibited conduct – which the legislature is assumed to have considered harmful enough to be criminalized. This Appendix is devoted to the subject of gauging harm, because we think it is particularly in need of exploration.

2 Scope of the Analysis

We have limited the scope of our analysis of criminal harm in various respects, and should explain at the outset what those limitations are.

2.1 Victimizing criminal conduct

The present chapter addresses only the harmfulness of *criminal* conduct, which injures or threatens to injure *identifiable victims*. We are restricting ourselves to conduct already declared criminal, because our interest in harm arises in the context of sentencing policy. We wish to assess harm, in order to see how serious the offence is; and we wish to determine the offence's seriousness for the purpose of determining the severity of the punishment. There is, of course, another context for considering harm – namely, when deciding whether conduct should be declared criminal at all. Whether conduct is harmful, and how harmful it is, should be an important factor in the legislative consideration about its proscription. However, it is not the only factor: the legislature should also consider how much countervailing social value the conduct has, the extent to which prohibition could be intrusive upon privacy or personal autonomy, the practical feasibility of enforcement, and so forth.[2] Thus the fact that a given species of conduct might meet our suggested criteria for harmfulness, and even for grave harmfulness, does not necessarily settle whether it should be proscribed. We will be speaking of conduct that has been prohibited already.

Our focus is also on victimizing behaviour, that is, behaviour the primary apparent evil of which consists in that it sets back the interests of identifiable natural persons. We will thus be speaking chiefly of the traditional offences such as theft, burglary or assault in which an individual is the primary sufferer, and the concern is with how much he has been harmed. It is these crimes that are most obviously injurious and constitute a logical starting place for the analysis. In thus focusing on victimizing conduct, we are fully aware of the existence of other forms of criminal harm. Some crimes (eg, certain environmental offences) have harm that is primarily collective or aggregative: no identifiable person has his interest set back by activity of an identifiable actor; but if a sufficiently large number of persons engage in the conduct, the public's interests are adversely affected. In focusing on individual victimizing crimes, we do not wish to suggest these other crimes are necessarily less important: only that their harmfulness is a more complicated matter to analyse. Having a theory that addresses victimizing harms should be a useful first step.

2.2 Standardization

We will be concerned chiefly with the *standard harm* involved in a given category or subcategory of crime. How hurtful a given intrusion is depends on the situation of the victim, and particular victims' situations may vary greatly. The theft of a car from a rich person may be no more than a temporary inconvenience; a car theft from a poor person in a rural area may leave him bereft of any means of transportation. We shall assume, in rating the standard case of a given species of crime, that injury occurs to someone who is neither especially vulnerable nor resilient.

Why this emphasis on standard harm? Particular criminal acts are too diverse to be rated on an individualized basis. The analysis is aided when one (1) rates the standard case of an offence, and then (2) addresses unusual cases through supplemental principles (eg, of aggravation and mitigation). The first of these tasks will keep us amply occupied here. The second, on aggravation and mitigation, is complex enough to call for separate treatment.

In sentencing doctrine, one judges harm in order to determine how blameworthy the actor is in committing the conduct, not in order to compensate the victim for his loss. This actor-perspective requires one to consider how much, and within what limits, the act's harmful consequences may justly be attributed to the actor. Conceptions of culpability require that, in assessing the seriousness of conduct, unforeseeable consequences should not be taken into account.[a] The standard harm in

[a] In crimes of intent, the defining elements of the crime must actually be known to the actor. What, however, of the further harmful consequences? How much, for example, need the defendant have known of the humiliating character of an assault in order for humiliation to be considered in gauging a crime's seriousness? A full answer would require an excursus into

any given type of criminal conduct is, ordinarily, foreseeable. However, when one is talking about atypical harms, foreseeability diminishes. The burglar may be expected to understand the typical consequences of a burglary, but not, ordinarily, Jane Doe's particular situation – for example, the extraordinary personal value the vase taken from her apartment had for her as a gift from a deceased friend. A final point about standardization: we should be aware from the outset of the limits of particularizing ratings of seriousness. One can rate the harm category – and also take certain features of the harmfulness of the particular event into account through the aggravation/mitigation principles. But one cannot reasonably expect to approximate, in legal judgements of seriousness, the particularity of everyday judgements. Precisely how much Ms Doe is injured by the loss of her particular vase would require a delving into her personal situation to a degree which the law cannot possibly undertake, and should not try to undertake. The rehabilitative penal ethic lost its credibility in part because of unrealistic claims it made about the individualization of sentence. A proportionalist penal ethic should not make the same mistake. The criminal law reflects a system of public standards, not an arena for personalized judgements. What the law realistically can accomplish is to assess crime seriousness in standard cases, and then permit deviations from that assessment for specified types of special circumstances.

2.3 Normative focus and the question of cultural variability

Our analysis of harm is normative: we are offering a theory on how harms *should* be rated. The reason for this normative emphasis is that our account is part of a broader penal theory: one that claims that the severity of punishment should be proportionate to the gravity of the criminal conduct. The grounds for the proportionality principle are those of fairness: that punishment, as a censuring response to criminal behaviour, should reflect the degree of blameworthiness of the criminal conduct (see Chapters 2 and 9). Such an argument stands only if the judgements of blameworthiness of conduct (including those of harm) reflect how much the offender and his conduct *ought* to be blamed.

Since Thorsten Sellin's and Marvin Wolfgang's 1964 research,[3] a number of studies have surveyed popular perceptions of seriousness. The studies provide the persons surveyed with brief descriptions of a variety of crimes, and ask them to rate those crimes' seriousness on a numerical rating scale. Some consensus has been found: people from different walks of life tend, for example, to give similar rank-orderings to crimes.

culpability theory, which we will not undertake here. However, it should be clear that those ulterior consequences should at least be foreseeable: unforeseeable consequences have no place in the assessment of the gravity of the conduct.

Interesting as such research is, it does not address our question – for it only deals with how various segments of the public in fact rate crimes. Popular ratings do not settle the harmfulness of conduct, for two reasons. One concerns the possibility of factual misjudgement. Respondents have not studied the actual consequences of the crimes which they are asked to assess, and their assessments may be based on erroneous beliefs about those consequences. People may believe that burglary typically involves greater risk of violence than the available empirical evidence suggests it does, or may underestimate the injurious effect of some white-collar crimes. The other reason is that the criteria for judging the known facts have not been reflected on. In judging assaultive crimes, for example, is it only the physical risks that count, or also the impact on the victim's personal dignity? If the latter is considered, *why* so? Just asking people about their assessments of the harmfulness of assault does not support reasoned judgements about such questions. The advantage of a normative theory of harm is that it addresses the 'why' questions.

We are not, however, seeking ratings that are invariant worldwide. How harmful burglary is, for example, depends on its typical impact, and that impact may vary across cultures – depending on both factual and normative differences. The factual differences concern the underlying social arrangements. In our culture, a burglary is an intrusion into someone's home and the home is ordinarily the focus of much of the person's personal life. Were people to sleep in tents, and perform most activities in communal facilities, the impact of a burglary could be much less. Normative differences also matter. Part of the assessment of the harmfulness of burglary depends on the importance accorded to privacy; in a culture where privacy is less valued, the conduct would have less significance. One thus needs to examine the consequences of the offence, given certain assumed social living arrangements, and then evaluate those consequences in the light of certain assumed values (eg, concerning privacy). The role of our proposed theory of harm is to aid in that evaluation. That the theory could yield different harm-ratings in another place, where living arrangements and values are different, is a strength, not a weakness.

3 Harm and the 'Living Standard'

In gauging criminal harms, the difficult task is that of comparing the harmfulness of crimes which involve different interests. How is car theft to be compared with burglary, when the former involves a significant property loss, and the latter a smaller financial setback but an invasion of privacy as well? Making such comparisons calls for common criteria, or at least common guiding ideas, for assessing the interests involved.

The guiding idea, which we have come to find most natural, is one concerned with the quality of a person's life. The most important interests are those central to personal wellbeing; and, accordingly, the most grievous harms are those which drastically diminish one's standard of wellbeing. Mayhem is so serious because it makes its victims live in misery; burglary seems less serious because it does not create such misery, although it still has a significant impact on the quality of life in its intrusion on the person's privacy.

We required a term for this idea, and came upon Amartya Sen's useful essay, *The Standard of Living*.[4] Economists traditionally have used 'living standard' to refer only to degrees of economic affluence or want. Sen, however, suggests a richer use for this term, one that includes not only economic means but other, non-economic capabilities that affect personal wellbeing. We decided to adopt the term 'living standard', understood in this broader sense.

3.1 Inadequacies of the 'welfare-interest' criterion

Our interest in the living standard grew out of dissatisfaction with the 'welfare-interest' criterion which Joel Feinberg proposed in his 1984 book, *Harm to Others*.[5] Previously, one of us (von Hirsch) had relied upon Feinberg's criterion, for the purpose of grading crime seriousness for sentencing.[6] Feinberg suggests that the importance of interests infringed by criminal conduct can be gauged according to the degree to which those interests characteristically affect choice.

The most important interests, according to Feinberg, are so-called welfare interests, and hence the most grievous harms are those that intrude substantially upon such interests. Welfare interests are defined by him as the interests a person needs satisfied in order to have any significant capacity to choose and order his way of living. They provide, in his words, 'the generalised means to the advancement of [the person's] ulterior interests'.[7] When those interests are intruded upon or destroyed, the person is foreclosed from a wide variety of other choices. Physical safety, for example, is a welfare interest because the person is impeded from pursuing almost any aims of his choice, when physically incapacitated. Next in importance come so-called security interests, which Feinberg defines as those needed to provide a certain safety margin to the welfare interests. Lowest-ranked would be all other interests, which he entitles 'accumulative interests.'

How plausible is it to define the importance of interests in the way Feinberg does? There are two ways of interpreting his theory. One is that it describes the logic of assessing interests: people actually judge interests to be of fundamental importance when they provide the generalized means to the advancement of more particular concerns. Sometimes, such an account would seem plausible. Most of us would consider it a basic interest to possess a certain modicum of financial resources. Why so? Because that is necessary to pursue our particular life plans, whatever they may be. But counter-examples readily come to mind, where such an account would seem strained. Consider the interest (which almost all of us would deem very important) in avoiding intense and protracted physical pain. Such pain would doubtless interfere with the pursuit of various specific life plans, but does that really account for why we think the interest so important? Is it not, instead, that the avoidance of pain is *in itself* essential to the quality of a person's life; that a life of physical suffering is an awful life?

Alternately, Feinberg's welfare-interest criterion could be explained more modestly, as a theory of state action. Interests are being ranked in importance to help guide the coercive action of the criminal law. The law's criteria for harm should make allowances for differences in how people value life's goods, and should not elevate one set of focal aims above another because that is for persons themselves to choose. The attraction of the welfare-interest theory is that it helps assure that the criminal law, in its criteria for harm, gives due recognition and scope to individual choice: welfare interests are valued highly because they are a prerequisite to whatever ways of life individuals themselves might choose. The welfare-interest idea thus appears to rest on the tenets of philosophical liberalism.[8]

Relying thus on notions of choice can produce odd results, however. Much as one may value choice, its diminution is not necessarily the worst thing that can happen to one who is victimized. The person who has been maimed or made destitute obviously suffers grievous harm. But is this so merely because his freedom of choice has been restricted? It would seem more straightforward to say the maimed or destitute person might survive but only barely so, with loss of the most basic human satisfactions. As long as one regards the fate of individual humans to be important, one would consider such harms to be serious, without need for invoking further assumptions about the importance of choice.

The idea of liberalism also seems somewhat misapplied. Liberal notions of autonomy are chiefly concerned with limiting the state's power to compel an actor to adopt one or another set of aims for his *own* life. It is thought better that a person be permitted to pursue his chosen manner of existence (however unconventional or seemingly irregular) than that he be required to live as state authorities deem wise or virtuous. In the present context, however, we are speaking of harm to others; the standards of criminal harm do not concern the actor's own way of life, and he remains free to make his self-regarding choices. Instead, the actor has chosen to interfere with the interests of others; and the harm criteria are supposed to measure the degree of that intrusion. That harm may not merely be to other persons' capacities to choose, but to whatever vital interests they may have – and those other vital interests are not necessarily reducible to a capacity to choose.

Granted, the potential victims of harm have a variety of life aims, and that variety should be recognized. Harm should thus be defined broadly enough so that it is not just the interests of a conventional person that are protected. This means that the harm-criteria need to be scrutinized to see if they give sufficient leeway to differences in life style and life aims of potential victims. We will argue later that a living standard criterion provides this leeway.

Besides these conceptual difficulties, the welfare-interest classification fails also to supply sufficient distinctions among harms. Thus:

(1) The highest category, of welfare-interests, would consist of those concerns essential to a minimum of choice. Basic physical health would qualify, as a person will almost always need that to go about his chosen business. A minimum of economic support would be included, for similar reasons. Perhaps, a few more interests would also qualify. Feinberg notes, however, that his choice criterion does not supply a ranking among the welfare interests, because they are interdependent and each is essential for choice.[9] (Good health but destitution debilitates, just as bad health but affluence does.) This is not a problem for his purposes, since he is addressing the decision to criminalize conduct, and is asking whether the conduct is sufficiently injurious to be worth proscribing. It is troublesome for our purposes, however, as for sentencing purposes we require rankings even among the most serious crimes.

(2) The intermediate category – 'security interests' – are defined as those needed to 'cushion' or provide a safety margin to welfare interests. This conception seems deficient in several ways:

- It is so imprecise as to be virtually unworkable. How does one tell, even in principle, whether a given interest is or is not needed to 'cushion' welfare interests?
- It gives middle-level interests, inappropriately, a purely instrumental role. Consider the interest in living with a modicum of comfort. We would regard this interest as having inherent value, because it is so important to personal wellbeing. Its importance does not lie merely in the fact that such comfort provides a margin of security against destitution.
- It allows no distinction in importance among middle-level interests. Some intrusions would put the victim near the subsistence level. Others would merely put him just below a level of wellbeing that seems normal or adequate.

(3) The lowest level of interests in Feinberg's classification – 'accumulative interests' – strikes us as a catchall. Some of these still would play a significant role in the person's overall wellbeing; others would

be purely accumulative in the literal sense. Such cases need to be distinguished.

3.2 The idea of the living standard

The term 'living standard' has a narrow economic meaning, referring to affluence. It has, however, a broader meaning – the one which Sen emphasizes,[10] and which is used also in quality of life studies such as the Stockholm Metropolitan Project.[11] This refers to the quality of persons' existence in a sense that includes not only material support and amenity but other non-economic capabilities that affect the quality of a person's life.

The living standard is one of a family of related notions, including wellbeing, that refer to the extent of human flourishing. Wellbeing, however, can be highly personalized. The quality of my life depends upon my particular focal aims. To the person who wants to devote his life to contemplation and prayer, material comfort and social amenities may matter little. Thus to determine a particular person's wellbeing, one ordinarily needs to know much about his life goals and his reasons for adopting them.

The living standard, however, does not focus on actual life quality or goal-achievement, but on the *means* or *capabilities* for achieving a certain quality of life.[12] It is also standardized, referring to the means and capabilities that would *ordinarily* help one achieve a good life. Consider the person who is in good health, affluent, and with a wide social network from which to draw friends and acquaintances. If his chief goal in life is to write great novels and he lacks the requisite talent he may still be frustrated and unhappy. Nevertheless, it would be appropriate to say that he has a good standard of living: not merely because of his wealth but because he has the other means that people ordinarily can use to live well – whether or not he chooses to make full use of those means or actually enjoys their fruits. These features are important for our present purpose because, as noted in the previous chapter, we are primarily concerned with standard harms.

A given capability or resource can support achievement of a variety of ends of a person's choosing. One thus can make living standard judgements without having either to know a particular person's focal aims or to specify in detail what the standard person's aims are or ought to be. The judgements, in other words, assume a certain degree of pluralism. One may judge, for example, that a person's undisturbed possession of his home has a certain degree of importance to his living standard. The judgement can hold, notwithstanding the varying uses of the home in people's lives: that one individual may use his home chiefly as the locus of family life, another as a place for study, another as a place for entertaining numerous guests. One does not need to assume which of these ends are preferable, or even to assume that a person *should* choose personal goals that involve spending much time at home. The judgement is merely that the home plays a significant role in a variety of lives people choose to live in our society. This pluralism is important for our purposes, for it will permit us to make living standard judgements without an ambitious specification of what people's ultimate focal aims are or ought to be.

The living standard differs, nevertheless, from welfare interests in that choice is not the criterion: the means for achieving a certain quality of life is. Many of the interests important to people's living standard afford, as we just noted, a considerable range of choice. Still, the ultimate focus is not on the extent of choice but on the life quality which those interests help support.[b]

While the living standard, thus conceived, includes non-material capabilities, it is restricted to those capabilities that are self-regarding: those that are involved in the quality of a person's *own* life. Altruistic satisfactions and dissatisfactions would not be taken into account. In Sen's words, 'one's misery at the sorrow of another . . . is not a reduction in . . . the person's living standard'.[13]

3.3 Why the living standard?

Why rely on the living standard in order to gauge harms? A simple answer is that it appears to fit the way in which we ordinarily judge harms. Why is mayhem more harmful than burglary? It is not merely because the maimed person's choices have been narrowed more; but rather, because the overall quality of his life has been so much more adversely affected.

In adopting a living standard criterion, we are not claiming that goodness or badness of conduct depends, as a general matter, on the conduct's effect on the quality of people's lives.[c] Our claim is more

[b] The distinction between (1) wellbeing understood as possessing certain means and capabilities that permit a degree of freedom of choice, and (2) freedom of choice in itself, is usefully elucidated in Amartya Sen's 1984 Dewey Lectures (Sen 1984, 206–8). He supplies the example of the person eating his sandwich on the riverbank, who sees a man drowning in the river. The event adds to the person's choices – because now he has the extra option of saving the victim or not – but those do not add (and may actually detract) from his wellbeing. As Sen notes: 'The additional opportunity of saving the drowning person did not give you a better (or even as good a) way of pursuing your own wellbeing. You were no longer free to eat your sandwich without anxiety, and . . . there was a genuine loss of opportunity to pursue your own wellbeing.' (at 207).

[c] Harm consists of being made worse off. One can gauge how much one is harmed (ie how much worse off one is made), by the impact of the conduct on the quality of one's life. Other evils, however, do not necessarily involve harm as part of their defining characteristics. A possible example is offence. According to the view of one of the authors (von Hirsch), being treated offensively does not necessarily involve being made worse off in the sense of having one's personal resources diminished; its evil resides simply in being dealt with without consideration or respect. To gauge the gravity of the offensive conduct, one thus may require a standard other than one that refers to reduction in the offended person's living standard. For an analysis of offence, and how it differs from harm, see Simester and von Hirsch 2002.

modest: that the living standard provides, not a generalized ethical norm, but a useful standard which the law can use in gauging the harmfulness of criminal acts. We think this is so for several reasons.

Victimizing harms involve intrusion into various personal resources or interests people have. If one asks why the state should seek to protect such interests through the criminal law, the most plausible answer would be that people require those resources to live decent lives. Robbery and theft are prohibited because people need safety and certain possessions to live tolerably. It thus makes sense to gauge the gravity of criminal harms by the importance that the relevant interests have for a person's standard of living.

Much of a modern state's protective concerns for its citizens is aimed at safeguarding interests of theirs that constitute the generalized means for pursuing a satisfactory life. Social welfare programmes concern the provision of a minimum of economic support to enable people to live decently. Health and safety regulations serve to ensure the physical condition people require to have a comfortable existence, and so forth. Our conception sees the criminal law as having a comparable primary role (see 2.6.2).

The living standard approach also has the advantage of a certain modesty; no 'deep' theory of preferred life aims or appropriate social roles is presupposed. It recognizes, as noted earlier, a considerable degree of pluralism in the uses and ends to which people put their various interests.

An alternative to the living standard analysis could be the more ambitious one, of specifying certain focal aims or social roles as pre-eminently important or valuable; then, harms could be assessed by their degree of interference with the achievement of these life aims or the performance of these roles. David Braybrooke takes this view in his analysis of needs. The definition and importance of needs, he asserts, should depend upon their function in carrying out certain central social roles, viz., the role of parent, householder, worker, and citizen.[14]

We find such an approach troublesome for a number of reasons. First, there is a problem of justification: why these particular life-ends or social roles and not others? Braybrooke asserts that his list of social roles is self-evident. In his words, 'having a life of minimum normal scope consists just in having an opportunity to perform those roles and tasks'.[15] The list is not self-evident to us, however. If the claim is that Braybrooke's four roles are normatively of overriding importance, it needs to be explained why so. If the claim is descriptive (that most people do primarily direct their lives to the four social functions he lists) it would need to be supported by empirical evidence. Such evidence would not be so easy to supply – given the various and overlapping character of people's goals. Braybrooke lists 'householder' as one of his four functions. Most people in our society establish households, but is this because they see householdership as something valuable in itself, or because (as we think more plausible) a household may serve various ulterior ends people have? If so, why not consider these ulterior ends as pre-eminent?

Second, there is the problem of achieving sufficient specificity. A broad enumeration of pre-eminent focal aims or social roles such as Braybrooke's would not take us far in rating criminal harms, especially intermediate or lesser harms. Homicide or mayhem obviously interferes with the social roles of which he speaks, but how much does a purse-snatching interfere with the victim's role as parent, householder, worker, or citizen? Braybrooke could reply that he need not address such questions since he is only trying to define basic needs. But the problem would become acute if one tried to extend his approach, of defining needs in terms of specified social roles, to the assessment of the wide range of interests protected by the criminal law.

Finally, we wonder about the appropriateness of the preferred social roles approach. Criminal harms are being rated to help decide upon the severity of state sanctions. We doubt whether a theory of state sanctions, in a plural society, should attempt to specify the ways of living that merit special respect. Consider Braybrooke's category of parenthood. Much as many persons value family life, others in our society legitimately have different life priorities. Granted, moral paternalism is not the issue here: no one is being compelled to raise a family, since the standards of criminal harm (as noted already) do not seek to regulate the actor's own lifestyle. Still, pluralism is a matter of concern. The standards of harm affect the extent to which the state protects different interests people have, through the sanctions of the criminal law. In a society that respects diversity, those standards should to the maximum feasible extent acknowledge the variability of people's personal aims and purposes. This it cannot do if those standards rest on assumptions that certain life aims or social roles have pre-eminent worth. If a person wishes to devote his life to contemplation, how are his preferences respected if legally protected interests are valued solely by reference to aims (such as child-rearing) not his own?

The living standard criterion is not so vulnerable to such objections. The security of the home is judged to contribute to the living standard to a certain degree, not because householding is deemed an intrinsically valuable social role or one that contributes to another preferred role such as child-rearing, but because the home contributes to various ways a person may choose to live his life (from study through child-rearing to valetudinarianism); that potential contribution makes the home a resource having a certain role in the standard of living. Since the living standard is concerned with standard cases – with the means or capabilities ordinarily needed to achieve a good life – certain non-standard modes of life concededly will receive less attention. The valuation given the home does not do much good to the person who opts to live as a travelling mendicant. But the grounds for this treatment of non-standard cases are less troubling. It is not that mendicancy is deemed less worthy than (say) child-rearing. It is, rather, a recognition that the criminal law, with its general rules and its emphasis on foreseeable harms, is mainly equipped to deal with standard cases.

In thus emphasizing the pluralism of the living standard criterion, have we re-embraced the earlier-rejected theory of welfare interests? (After all, the supposed *raison d'être* of that theory was choice.) We think not. A distinction should be drawn between the harm standard itself and the reasons supporting it. One reason, among others, why we favour the living standard criterion is that it recognizes a certain pluralism of legitimate life-ends and social roles. Nevertheless, pluralism should not be the harm criterion's principal basis. In assessing how burglary affects the living standard, one certainly should be mindful of the variety of legitimate uses to which people put their homes. But to account for the injuriousness of burglary, it does not suffice to call attention to the extent to which the occupant's choices have been narrowed; one needs to consider the impact the conduct also has on his comfort and peace.

The living standard idea is a rich one. It rests on something we consider in everyday existence and various arenas of social policy: the elements of a good life. It will be possible to make comparisons: if a typical person's standard of living is at issue, the interests protected by the criminal law can be compared with other interests. We can ask how a beating compares with a minor accident, or how an arson compares with an accidental fire in one's apartment. We can compare these harms by reference to various generic interest dimensions that may be involved: for example, the beating may compare in physical injuriousness with a minor accident, but has an additional component of humiliation that the accident lacks. It will be possible also to make the factual and value judgements more explicit: to separate out (1) the factual question of the various typical consequences of a given type of crime, from (2) the value judgement about how significant those consequences are in reducing a person's standard of living.

The living standard is also rich in another sense, of leaving room for ancillary moral judgements. Freedom, privacy, and a variety of other values may (indeed, should, as we will see shortly) be considered in applying living standard judgements. What the living standard thus provides is not a single, essential standard but a *perspective* through which a variety of ethical and practical judgements can be made about the impact of criminal acts on the quality of people's lives.

Finally, the living standard analysis would explicitly allow for cultural variation. Different social living arrangements can affect the consequences of a criminal act; and normative differences among cultures can affect the impact of those consequences on how well a victim lives. This sensitivity is an advantage of the living standard approach: as noted earlier, we need criteria capable of taking cultural variation into account.

3.4 Factual v normative elements of living standard judgements

How, and from whose perspective, are living standard judgements to be made? The kind of analysis we are proposing presupposes certain social practices of our society and certain assumed values; but, given those practices and values, calls for a *reasoned* application of the living standard criteria to particular species of criminal harm. Let us explain.

When one examines how much a given species of criminal harm typically intrudes upon someone's living standard, certain factual, but also certain normative judgements are involved. The mix of fact and norm varies as the analysis proceeds. Consider burglary again. This is an intrusion into the home, requiring one to assess the importance of the home in a person's living standard. The assessment might begin with the interest in health and safety. The home has certain functions in providing shelter, warmth and rest that are critical to basic physical well-being. It is fact that in cooler climates people's health deteriorates when they are homeless and not offered substitute shelter (a fact too sadly evident on the streets of many English and American cities). This interest, however, is not ordinarily involved in burglary, as the offence intrudes upon but does not deprive the person of his dwelling-place. Another kind of concern, that of privacy, brings normative judgements more to the fore. A breaking-and-entering of a dwelling invades the privacy of the home, but the significance assigned to privacy is ultimately a moral judgement. That judgement, too, may be rooted in certain ethical and cultural traditions.[d] How, then, should the evaluator (that is, the agency responsible for gauging the conduct's harmfulness) make and justify these various judgements?

An ambitious approach would be for the evaluator to try to justify the underlying values: for example, to give an account of privacy and derive therefrom the judgement of its importance to the living standard. Such an account – if possible at all – would have to be grounded in a more fully articulated moral theory than we can supply here. The account is also not needed, for reasons that should be evident already: we are not trying to develop an invariant harm-analysis, but instead to derive ratings

[d] A philosopher might ask whether such norms are rooted in the ethical traditions of our own culture, or have more universal applicability. We do not have to address the question, however, as we are not at the moment attempting to apply our living standard criteria in other cultural settings. Our own view would be that respect for other persons' interests is essential to any valid system of ethics, but that particular moral principles through which that respect is expressed – eg principles regarding privacy – may legitimately reflect a culture's ethical traditions. For a somewhat comparable view, see Hampshire 1989, ch. 2.

applicable *in our society*, given certain prevailing social practices and also certain ethical traditions. Nor do we even need to try to describe those practices and values in full, which would be a formidable task in itself. Instead, we need merely incorporate certain assumptions into the analysis: for example, about the role of the home in everyday living, and about the importance of personal privacy. Granted, the making of such assumptions involves the exercise of judgement. The analysis, however, requires merely that such judgements be explicitly spelled out. Other evaluators, who disagree, can simply make their own, adjusted assumptions. Our aim, as noted earlier, is not to settle such differences of opinion, but to pinpoint their location, and thus permit conditional conclusions: if privacy is accorded such-and-such a degree of importance, these are the consequences that follow.

What, however, of the next step, of applying the living standard principles to the valuation of particular species or subspecies of harm? Suppose, for example, we are asking how much a typical home burglary – involving a breaking-and-entering, theft of a TV, but no ransacking – reduces the living standard, considering certain assumptions about the importance of privacy and other interest-dimensions to wellbeing. *That* judgement has to be made in the analysis itself, by reasoned application of our suggested principles. It cannot be made simply by reference to prevailing opinion. Why so, should be evident already: ours is a normative analysis that begins with certain factual judgements about the consequences of the crime, and then applies certain stated valuation principles to those facts. The value of the exercise – the reason we have opted for the living standard approach rather than simply asking members of the public for their ratings of harm – lies precisely in the opportunity (1) to check the factual basis of such judgements, and (2) to scrutinize how well-reasoned is the application of the assumed valuation principles to those facts.

3.5 Why our conception is not utilitarian

Is reliance on the living standard a reversion to a utilitarian doctrine of punishment? After all, a deterrence theorist might employ the idea of living standards to estimate the social harm wrought by (say) the offence of burglary; and then set a penalty designed to reduce the crime's incidence and hence its social injuriousness.

The answer is (obviously) negative. A utilitarian penal theory is aggregative and consequentialist; it seeks to estimate how much the totality of future harms may be reduced through this or that penal strategy. Our theory of harms, and the use to which we propose to put it, is neither of these things. We are not aggregating. Because a burglar is responsible only for his own conduct, it is the harm that his conduct typically causes or risks that determines the gravity of the offence – and not the totality of harm caused by the acts of all burglars, over whom he has no control.

Moreover, we are assuming a desert-oriented criterion for how much to punish burglary, not a consequentialist and preventive one. We look to the living standard to decide the degree of harmfulness of a standard act of burglary; and look to that assessment, in order to determine the seriousness of the crime of conviction. The sanction – according to desert assumptions that have been detailed earlier in this volume (Chapters 2 and 9) – should be proportionate in severity with the gravity of the offence, thus determined. This is wholly different from designing a sanctioning system in order to optimize citizens' *future* aggregate living standards; such a system, to have the desired preventive effects, might have to have sanctions that are disproportionate to the gravity of the offence.

4 Elements of a Living Standard Analysis

Having sketched our rationale, we need to explain how criminal harms may be graded through a living standard analysis. Let us, then, sketch the main elements of that analysis.

4.1 The standard person

Estimating the impact of a given intrusion on someone's living standard requires assumptions to be made on what other resources he possesses. The more slender those resources, the more devastating the intrusion. How, then, should one determine the standard impact?

Our living standard analysis is designed to gauge harms affecting a variety of interests, from the most to the least important. It is thus helpful to imagine someone who has various interests, and then ask how deprivation or intrusion into *this* particular interest would affect that person's quality of life. The hypothetical victim would thus be assumed to have the interests needed for the various living standard levels: certain interests or resources required to subsist; and others required to raise his wellbeing to higher levels. These assumptions provide a perspective for judging the importance of a particular intrusion: it enables one to judge how important the particular interest or resource intruded upon ordinarily is to a good life, compared to the various other interests and resources a person may have.

4.2 Temporal perspective

What temporal perspective should one adopt when judging the impact of a crime on someone's wellbeing? The perspective makes a difference. Consider having one's pocket picked. If the question is 'How was your day?' it makes perfect sense to answer that it was awful, because one has lost one's wallet with all of one's IDs. However, if the question is how one's year has been, it would be odd to say that it has been awful, merely because one's pocket was picked four months ago.

Living standard judgements are addressed to the quality of someone's life, and this suggests a considerably longer temporal perspective than the highly variable quality of experience from day to day. The appropriate perspective is a middle-term one – something approximating 'How has your year been?' or perhaps even a slightly longer duration. An extremely long temporal duration, however, would be too reductive: even awful experiences diminish in importance if the question were: 'How was your last decade?' – and indeed, such questions are seldom asked in ordinary life.[e]

Our suggested temporal perspective is addressed, however, not to the actual duration of the crime and its visible after-effects, but to the importance of the experience from the overall viewpoint of a given time-frame. A physical assault, and its immediate trauma, may soon be over; yet if the experience was painful or humiliating enough, it may still loom large in the evaluation of, say, the quality of a whole year's experience.

4.3 Rating the living standard: The four levels

If harms are to be gauged according to the extent to which they affect someone's living standard, then the living standard needs to be graded. Any grading scheme is bound to be arbitrary, but one should be able to make rough distinctions: for example, between a person's suffering an intrusion that makes him somewhat less comfortable, and one that affects the person's subsistence interests. We propose four living standard levels, which may be formulated as follows:

Level	Category	General Description
1°	Subsistence	Survival, but with maintenance of no more than elementary human capacities to function. No satisfactions presupposed at this level.
2°	Minimal wellbeing	Maintenance of a minimal level of comfort and dignity.
3°	'Adequate' wellbeing	Maintenance of an 'adequate' level (but no more) of comfort and dignity.
4°	Standard wellbeing	Maintenance of full life quality.

This scale is designed to gauge the degree to which a given intrusion affects the person's living standard. If, for example, Crime X affects interests

[e] Of course, the very worst intrusions would remain significant even from such a long-term perspective – a serious assault being an example.

required for subsistence (living standard level 1°), it qualifies as gravely harmful. If Crime Y affects only interests needed to maintain the quality of the person's life at the 'adequate' level (level 3°); this renders the harm less grave but still substantial.

Having four grades is by no means inevitable. Since we are dealing with a continuum, a larger or fewer number of notches could have been cut. We propose these four gradations because the differences among them seem reasonably apparent. Having a larger number of living standard gradations would make it easier to rate harms once the gradation affected by the criminal conduct is determined; but it would make the latter determination more difficult, as the differences among the grades would be less easy to discern.

There will also be variations in wellbeing *within* the four grades. Subsistence, for example, ranges from bare survival to survival but with significant debilitation: both mayhem and aggravated assault affect subsistence, albeit to different degrees. Again, this should not be surprising, if one keeps in mind that we are dealing with a continuum, not neatly demarcated steps.

The function of these four gradations is to measure the extent to which a criminal act typically intrudes into a person's living standard. The (numerically) lower level that is involved, the greater the intrusion. To take an obvious example: an aggravated assault threatens subsistence (1°) and thus is substantially more harmful than a petty theft affecting only level 4°. This explains why we are using a 'positive' conception (the living standard) to rate harm (something negative, involving a taking-away). Criminal harm consists in the intrusion into legally protected interests, and its seriousness depends on the importance of the interests involved. We are gauging those interests' importance in terms of their significance for a person's living standard.

Let us consider the four living standard levels more closely, then, and give a gloss on their meaning.

Subsistence (1°). We have defined subsistence as 'survival, but with maintenance of no more than elementary human capacities to function.' This means barely getting by. Included would be preservation of one's major physical and cognitive functions, and preservation of a minimal capacity for social functioning. Being killed obviously destroys subsistence, but being maimed or made destitute would intrude upon subsistence also.

Critical to our definition of subsistence is that no significant satisfactions are presupposed at this level. Comfort thus is not part of subsistence – although avoidance of intense pain would be. Neither is privacy or self-respect included: one can survive or get by without privacy and despite repeated humiliations.

Minimal wellbeing (2°). This level we have defined as 'a minimum level of comfort and dignity.' It means having more than barely getting by. In addition to surviving, certain elementary human satisfactions are assumed: some comfort, a minimum opportunity for self-respect.

Part of minimal wellbeing is thus a certain level of material support: shelter from inclement weather, nutritious food, etc. Another part is some degree of privacy and personal autonomy. One can subsist without the slightest privacy, but one hardly can be said to have even a barely satisfactory life. Protection against grossly demeaning or insulting treatment falls in this category also: one can subsist despite such treatment, but it impedes the maintenance of any degree of self-respect. Nevertheless, we are speaking only of bare minima of comfort, privacy, etc.: an existence at this level would still be having a substandard quality of life.

'Adequate' wellbeing (3°). We have defined this level as 'maintenance of an adequate level (but no more) of comfort and dignity.' The term 'adequate' is used here not in the sense of being satisfactory, but in the more restricted sense of being not plainly inadequate. Included would be a level of material amenity needed for a minimally comfortable existence, but no more than that. It also includes a degree of privacy and avoidance of demeaning treatment needed to avoid a substantially deprived existence.

Standard wellbeing (4°). This we have defined as 'maintenance of full life quality.' It includes those concerns that improve someone's quality of life to the point where no substantial grounds for complaint exist. Included would be some modest luxuries, and being treated by others with reasonable civility.

Marginal impact. Some criminal harms have only a marginal impact on the quality of a person's life. Paradigmatic of harms in this category are petty thefts. The conduct may cause brief inconvenience, but typically has no significant lasting impact on the person's wellbeing.

4.4 The generic interest dimensions

A criminal act can intrude upon a variety of different kinds of interest dimensions.[f] To cite previously mentioned examples, assault affects both the person's safety and his self-respect; a burglary, a person's material

[f] Are the interest dimensions themselves interests? That one would depend on how broadly one defines 'interest'. Were interests defined as resources, then some of the listed

comfort and privacy. The crime can affect these various dimensions in different degrees, and with differential impacts on the living standard: the privacy intrusion in a burglary, for example, may affect the standard of living more than the comfort intrusion does. Our analysis thus needs to distinguish various generic interest dimensions. We suggest three main dimensions, namely:

- Physical integrity
- Material support and amenity
- Privacy/freedom from humiliation

We do not claim this list is complete, and have used no deep theory to derive it. Instead, we rely on our impressions of the main kinds of concerns that seem typically involved in victimizing crimes. Adding supplemental interest dimensions would not alter the mode of analysis.

How are these interest dimensions to be used? One would first identify and separate out the interest dimensions involved in an offence. Next, one would apply the living standard criteria to each dimension successively. To illustrate, consider simple residential burglary: the offender, during the residents' absence, breaks into an apartment and steals a television set. First, one identifies the interest dimensions. Here, those chiefly involved appear to be (1) material amenity, and (2) privacy. The material loss consists in the loss of a useful home appliance (a TV), the expense of having locks repaired, etc. The loss of privacy derives from the intrusion into the victim's personal space. Second, one applies the rating criteria to each dimension, successively. With respect to the material amenity dimension, the impact on the living standard is usually quite limited: a workable replacement TV, for example, can be obtained at limited cost. However, the rating may well be higher when the privacy/autonomy dimension is taken into account, as we will see shortly.

Let us examine the three interest dimensions more closely.

Physical integrity. This embraces concerns about health, safety, and avoidance of physical pain. An intrusion into physical integrity can, depending upon its extent, affect any of the living standard gradations: from a homicide that destroys subsistence (living standard level 1°) to a

dimensions – for example, physical integrity and material support and amenity would be interests; but other dimensions, such as privacy, would not necessarily be – as one might have privacy concerns that would extend beyond one's resources; see Simester and von Hirsch 2002. In that event, however, privacy would still be helpful as a way of evaluating the harmfulness of intrusions into one's resources. One's living space is a resource, for example. When that resource is intruded upon through a burglary, one of the harmful aspects of that intrusion is the invasion of privacy involved. That privacy intrusion can be treated as an interest dimension in evaluating the harm, even if one does not consider privacy in itself to be an interest.

jostling causing only momentary discomfort that scarcely disturbs the quality of one's life.

Material support and amenity. This embraces someone's material concerns. These range from the most basic ones needed for subsistence (eg, food, drink and a minimum of shelter); to the various material amenities needed for a life of tolerable comfort; to various luxuries. An intrusion into a person's material interests may thus range from those that are very serious (affecting living standard level 1°) to those that are quite trivial and do not affect the living standard at all.

Privacy/freedom from humiliation. Privacy is important to wellbeing not only because it helps promote self-respect, but also because it helps the person pursue preferences of various kinds. It is affected by various offences, from burglary to illegal wiretapping. They are concerns that are culture specific to a degree: in our culture they affect wellbeing considerably, but another social setting with different moral assumptions may give privacy less weight.

The other interest included in this dimension concerns avoidance of certain kinds of disrespectful treatment.[g] We considered various broad terms for this interest, such as 'self-respect' or 'dignity'. These terms, however, seemed overbroad – as one's self-respect and dignity depend on one's own self-conceptions as well as on what harm befalls one. The narrower term – 'freedom from humiliation' – seems more apt, because it refers to those setbacks to self-respect that derive from degrading treatment. That this is a dimension of quality of life should be evident: one is worse off when the intrusion of one's interests also involve being treated in a degrading fashion. This interest is affected by a variety of criminal acts, especially physical assaults.

The two elements of this dimension – privacy and freedom from humiliation – are conceptually distinct. However, there is in practice enough overlap between these concerns to warrant their being treated as a single interest dimension. If one's apartment is burglarized and ransacked, one suffers both from an invasion of privacy and from having been treated in a degrading fashion.

A corollary of this discussion is that some of the interest dimensions do not run through the entire living standard scale. Physical integrity relates to all four living standard levels, depending on the degree of the intrusion.

[g] This dimension creates a degree of overlap between harm and culpability. Humiliation normally presupposes intent (or, at least, apparent intent). I am being humiliated by being beaten – but not normally, by being injured through someone's criminally negligent handling of a vehicle.

Material support and amenity does also. However, the third dimension (privacy/freedom from humiliation) relates to concerns that arise only at living standard level 2° (minimum wellbeing) or higher. The reason is that level 1° (subsistence) concerns merely 'getting by', and no satisfactions are assumed at that level.

4.5 Replacement

What of replaceable items? Something may be important to the quality of one's life and yet readily replaced. Consider the theft of an umbrella in rainy Bergen, Norway. Isn't that serious? After all, the victim will constantly be drenched, cold, and ill without it. Obviously not: the person can obtain a new umbrella cheaply enough so that it makes little difference, ordinarily, to the quality of his existence.

The principle can be stated generally, as follows. Suppose an offence damages or destroys an interest, *X*. Suppose that *X* can be replaced for a certain replacement cost, *Y*. If, in the standard case, making the outlay *Y* would have significantly less impact on the living standard than the loss of the item *X* itself, then the harm should be measured by the impact on the living standard of incurring the cost, *Y*.

In dealing with replacement in this fashion, however, we should keep the generic interest dimensions in mind: an item may be readily replaceable from the perspective of one dimension but not another. Consider our case of burglary and the theft of a television. From a material amenity perspective, the loss is readily replaced. However, the intrusion into privacy is not something which is replaced or made whole by the acquisition of an ersatz TV.

Is this analysis class-biased? After all, some impoverished persons will have great difficulty affording a replacement that most people easily could afford. We are, however, speaking of the hypothetical standard case – so that replaceability should be judged by how affordable the replacement item ordinarily is. One can expect deviations from that norm in both directions: persons who can easily pay even for the most costly replacements, and others who for whom even the most inexpensive could represent a financial sacrifice. These are cases of special resiliency or vulnerability, a matter which principles of aggravation and mitigation may need to address.

4.6 Psychological harm

We have not included 'psychological harm' as a distinct dimension in our analysis. The omission is intentional, because the term is too much of a catchall to be of help.

Emotions, like beliefs and attitudes, are capable of being supported by valid reasons, or not. When I lose a tennis match I may be furious at my opponent, but have no reason for being so. However, if I lose because the opponent has cheated, then my anger becomes warranted: I am entitled to resent the injury.

A variety of emotional states justifiably flow from being criminally victimized. Attacks on one's safety (quite properly) elicit fear; debasements elicit shame and a sense of humiliation, and so forth. Such distress, however, can be considered part of the intrusion into the interest dimension involved. In assessing conduct that involves threat to personal safety, for example, the fear justifiably elicited as well as the actual injury would be considered in assessing the living standard impact. When examining conduct that involves humiliating treatment – as several of the offences discussed below do – the sense of abasement is integral to what reduces the living standard. In this fashion, we can analyse the various forms of warranted distress that various intrusions produce.[h]

Other emotional states may flow from criminal victimization, but with less good reason. A routine burglary may make someone fear serious physical harm, without regard to the conduct's actual effects or risks. Some crimes may specially cause anxiety because of aversions felt against those thought to be typical offenders – for example, against their assumed ethnicity or lifestyle. Such responses would be disregarded in our analysis, as they cannot be were all forms of psychological impact lumped together as 'psychological harm.'

4.7 Some illustrations

Having outlined the elements of a living standard analysis, it might be illuminating to try it out on some hypothetical cases. Here then are some brief offence descriptions. The acts described are meant to be typical instances of various genera of robberies, burglaries, thefts, etc. (The descriptions are not necessarily co-extensive with statutory offence descriptions.)[i] To control for culpability, we shall assume for the moment that each crime is purposely committed, and that the offender is aware of its usual

[h] A comparable issue is that of offensive conduct. Should its offensiveness be assessed by the degree of subjective distress the conduct causes, or by how much the conduct violates norms of respectful and considerate treatment of others? One of the present authors would favour the latter view; see Simester and von Hirsch 2002.

[i] Many jurisdictions have broad statutory offence descriptions. The American Law Institute's Model Penal Code (Art. 221), for example, defines burglary as any entry into a building with intent to commit a crime; and has special provisions only for nighttime residential burglary. Such broad definitions are insufficient for rating the harmfulness of the conduct, as they disregard critical factors typically affecting the living standard impact – in burglary, the amount of vandalization, if any, wrought to the burglarized premises. Hence, in the above hypothetical cases, we may consider separate subspecies of a statutory crime category, viz.: residential burglary with ransacking, and ordinary residential burglary.

consequences. That way, the differences in ratings will be due to the degree of harmfulness of the conduct involved.

Homicide Our standard case is: A (unlawfully and purposely) kills B. The analysis is simple enough. The conduct destroys subsistence, which is rated as 1°. Hence the conduct has the highest harm rating.

Common assaults The assumed standard case is: A beats up B, but produces no lasting injury. Suppose the beating is quite painful, and results in substantial bruises and some lacerations – but not enough to require hospitalization.

Consider, first, the interest dimension of physical integrity. Let us suppose that the harm involved is no worse than accidentally walking into a solid glass door. It hurts badly when it happens, one has a black eye and a headache for a few days, and then it is over. How serious is that?

- Is the living standard level involved level 1° (subsistence)? Obviously not. There is no loss of functioning. It is merely uncomfortable, and comfort, physical or material, is not presupposed at this level.
- Is it level 2° (minimal wellbeing), or 3° (merely 'adequate' wellbeing)? Again, no. We hardly think that the person who walks into a glass door and gets a black eye has his overall living standard reduced to or below such levels of adequacy.
- Is it level 4° (standard wellbeing)? For a certain period, yes. One's quality of existence has definitely gone down while one is still sore and black-eyed. But the period involved may be too brief to qualify from the middle-term time perspective of which we are speaking.

Let us, however, consider another interest dimension: that of *freedom from humiliation*. Here, the intrusion into the living standard is potentially more significant: being beaten up is demeaning. This link between being beaten and being humiliated probably holds in most cultures, and may have deeper roots: even a dog cringes if it is beaten and cannot defend itself. In our culture, at any rate, a beating is ordinarily deeply humiliating. What makes it so is not just the physical intrusion and pain, but the being put at someone else's mercy. The person beaten is literally abased – knocked down, abused – and the beater establishes direct physical dominion over him.

So the question becomes – at which level is this deprivation? It is definitely not as high as level 1°, because subsistence does not presuppose self-respect, in our taxonomy. Is the intrusion at least at 3°? We would say so. A reasonable degree of self-respect is surely a part of this level. And the humiliation of a beating strikes us as grave enough to compromise self-respect at the 'adequate' level.

Is the intrusion still more serious, that is, at 2°? We would think not. There are humiliations that are so grave as to compromise even a minimal level of wellbeing – as we will see when we discuss rape. But we remain unconvinced, for the moment, that the humiliation of such a beating, substantial though it is, would be so devastating to a normal person's self-respect, that it would place the quality of his life at minimal wellbeing, that is, barely above the subsistence level.

Petty assaults Consider the case: A slaps B's face. Here, the material discomfort is trivial. So the question is again one of humiliation. Having one's face slapped is humiliating. But one is not being made helpless, as in the case of beating. One can extricate oneself with dignity – remonstrate, move away, call the authorities, etc. We thus doubt it qualifies as involving level 3°. A reasonable person would not regard himself as having suffered a major deprivation, sufficient to reduce his whole quality of life for an appreciable period to below the 'adequate' level. Conceivably, the humiliation involves level 4°, on grounds that there has been some diminution of overall wellbeing. However, even this conclusion is debatable, given a middle-term time perspective.

Armed robbery The assumed standard case is: A robs B at knifepoint, takes his wallet and the small amount of cash in it. The property loss here is quite minor – ordinarily, too small to have more than marginal impact on the living standard. The major element is the threatened bodily intrusion: namely, the threat to kill or gravely to injure someone. This is a threatened intrusion into a level 1° interest: subsistence.[j] However, we need a discount to reflect that the intrusion is merely threatened and contingent. We therefore say there is a *discounted* 1°. How such discounts might be made will be discussed later.

Forcible rape The standard case is the classic stranger rape: A rapes B at gunpoint or knifepoint. One interest dimension involved is bodily safety. Here, the analysis would be similar to the preceding case: since a threat to survival is involved, this is a discounted 1°. The other interest dimension is that of freedom from humiliation. We hardly need belabour that forced sex is about the most demeaning imposition that can be imagined – far more humiliating than a beating. Because of the strength, in our culture, of the norm that sexual favours may be granted only with consent, forced sexual intercourse is an extreme form of being subjected to another's dominion. Thus we would rate this at the highest level of intrusions to self-respect, namely, at 2°. This analysis explains why we consider rape at knifepoint worse than the just-cited armed robbery. It supplements the discounted 1° for menace to bodily safety, with the actual 2° for humiliation.

'Date rape' A typical case might run something like this. A female student induced to drink to excess at a male student club and then, with

[j] There may also be an element of humiliation in robbery, but for the sake of simplicity we do not address this.

her capacity of physical resistance reduced, is made to have sexual intercourse without her consent. The difference between this and the preceding case is that the threat to bodily safety is eliminated: the victim is not threatened with serious injury (although, that conclusion may change, with increasing prevalence of AIDS). However, the interest in sexual integrity is intruded upon much as in the preceding case – with its attendant grave humiliation. For reasons explained already, therefore, this would seem to involve a 2°.

Burglary with ransacking The scenario is all too familiar: a burglar enters a home and, after stealing some of the contents, defaces the walls and pictures, smashes furniture and china, etc.

Let us first consider the interest dimension of material support and amenity. In its extreme forms, destruction of a person's living space can be very serious. If the person is left literally homeless, and cannot afford alternative accommodation, he joins the ranks of the homeless who – at least in our social environments and climates – live at the subsistence level.

The kind of intrusion involved here, however, is less drastic. A ransacking is, in its material consequences, about comparable to having a kitchen fire in one's flat – in which smoke damage and firemen's efforts result in substantial damage to furnishings, clothing, etc. How much are one's interests set back by such an event?

- Certainly, one is not reduced to the subsistence level (1°). One is not rendered homeless, and still has warmth and shelter.
- One also is not reduced to the minimum wellbeing level (2°). By obtaining some temporary replacement furnishings and a few items of replacement clothing, one can continue to live in minimal comfort.
- Would the intrusion involve 'adequate' wellbeing (ie, level 3°)? A home furnished with basic amenities does appear to be part of our conception of adequate wellbeing. Here, however, the issue of replacement costs arises. The standard person may well be able to afford to replace those basic amenities without a major impact on his standard of living.
- In any event, the intrusion would involve level 4° – reduction in a full life quality for a significant period.

Let us turn, then, to the interest dimension of *privacy*. An important part of privacy is having a home of one's own, in which one may spend a substantial portion of leisure time and which may be the focus of personal, family, and social life. The home may be arranged to suit the taste of the occupant, and may be entered only by invitees. Any residential burglary, therefore, intrudes on this interest.

Being deprived altogether of a home of one's own would be a very serious intrusion. Suppose someone were involuntarily removed from his home to collective living quarters with strangers. Even if board, shelter and amenities were adequate, the loss of privacy and autonomy would seem a large enough setback to wellbeing to affect level 2° – a minimal living standard. (Being institutionalized has this quality.) Ransacking of a home in a burglary is not so great an intrusion, for one still keeps a home of one's own. However, the forced entry of a stranger – coupled with the damage to the occupant's chosen physical environment – would seem to compromise an adequate living standard. Thus, from the privacy/autonomy standpoint, the living standard level involved probably should be rated as 3°.

Simple residential burglary Here, the dwelling is entered, and a common item of property is removed. No ransacking occurs.

(a) *Material amenity* The intrusion on material comfort is relatively minor. A readily replaceable item of property is lost. Otherwise, the liveability of the dwelling is not affected. In material terms the living standard would scarcely be affected.

(b) *Privacy/autonomy* Here, the entry constitutes a significant intrusion into privacy. However, the occupant's preferred arrangements of his/her home are not significantly disturbed. Our judgement is that this would involve level 4°.

Car theft In car theft, only material amenity is at issue. The car is not a zone of privacy akin to the home, ordinarily. For many people, use of a car is important to leisure or even to livelihood. However, cars are insurable against theft, and a stolen car can be replaced by a functioning vehicle. Provided that theft insurance premiums and/or replacement costs are modest, there would be short-term inconvenience but the standard impact on a person's wellbeing would be limited.[k]

4.8 Constructing a harm scale

Constructing and applying the living standard ratings helps, but does not suffice to grade harms. First, for reasons to be explained shortly, there need to be more (at least, two more) harm gradations than the four living standard levels. Second, discounts need to be made for

[k] Thefts become more difficult to analyse, however, when they involve sums of money, rather than standard possessions such as TVs or cars. The difficulty relates to the fungibility of money, and the uneven distribution of financial resources. How a theft of *x* Pounds Sterling affects someone's living standard depends critically on what other financial resources he is assumed to have. Whether our usual suggested techniques suffices – of judging the impact by a hypothetical standard case, and dealing with deviating cases through aggravation/mitigation – is a question deserving of further discussion.

risked or threatened harm. A robbery at knifepoint, for example, risks subsistence, so we described it as a 'discounted' 1°. But it makes little sense to discount directly onto the living standard scale: if one reduced the armed robbery rating to 2°, for example, that would not be saying the offence risks subsistence, but rather that it actually affects the living standard level of minimal wellbeing – which may well not be an accurate characterization. Third, an offence may give rise to multiple living standard ratings in different dimensions. A routine assault, as just noted, has a relatively low rating in the physical integrity dimension, but a higher one in the freedom from humiliation dimension. We thus need a way of combining these diverse assessments into a net harmfulness grade.

Creating the scale. A variety of techniques for constructing the penalty scale might be imagined. Let us suggest a relatively simple structure, for the sake of illustration.

The harm scale would have six gradations. The highest gradation should be for crimes that do not just intrude upon, but terminate the living standard: when the victim is killed. The lowest gradation should be for crimes that do not significantly affect the living standard at all. The simplest harm scale thus would have six gradations, as follows. Each gradation could be set forth as a band, so as to allow differentiations within the band. The gradations would be the following:

Harm gradation	**Living standard level affected**
I – very grave	Living standard terminates (death)
II – grave	Subsistence (living standard level 1°)
III – serious	Minimal wellbeing (level 2°)
IV – upper-intermediate	'Adequate' wellbeing (level 3°)
V – lower-intermediate	Standard wellbeing (level 4°)
VI – lesser	Living standard not affected or only marginally so

Notice this mapping rule, elementary as it is, involves value judgements, for we are characterizing the gravity of various levels of intrusions into the living standard. We are, for example, asserting that injuries affecting subsistence involve grave harms, etc. However, these judgements seem straightforward enough (given our preceding discussion) to require no further elaboration.

In this scale, within-category variations can be denoted simply by the location within a given band: no numbers are necessary. For example, the difference between serious wounding and mayhem (permanent disfigurement) – both of which affect subsistence, but to different degrees – by locating both crimes within the 'II-grave' band, but placing the latter crime above the former within the band. Alternatively, one might be more ambitious – for example, by dividing each of these six categories into an upper and lower range, and thus having 12 gradations of harm.

Discounts for threatened or risked harms. Many crimes only create a threat or risk to an interest, so what matters is not only the importance of the interest but the degree to which it is threatened. The more remote the risk, the greater should be the discount – and hence, the lower the harm rating.

Consider these four offences: aggravated assault, attempted aggravated assault,[1] armed robbery, and drink-driving. All affect the interest in subsistence, but in different degrees. An aggravated assault directly intrudes upon physical integrity; an attempt involves a significant risk to that interest; robbery threatens that interest, but the threat is contingent (the robber might use the gun only if the victim resists). In drink-driving, the risk is more remote, depending on how much alcohol the offender has consumed and how crowded the highways are.

To deal with these situations, a two-step process seems appropriate. The first is to make a living standard valuation of the completed harm. In aggravated assault, we have done that already: the harm directly affects subsistence and hence is in the 'grave' range. The second step is to make an appropriate discount for threat or risk.[16] We might, for example, treat certain attempts as constituting a sufficiently high risk to keep the conduct in the 'grave' range – albeit at a point in that range below the completed harm. Next, we give the threat that is present in armed robbery a somewhat larger discount: perhaps, one would place that offence in the next ('serious') harm category – because (while no assault actually takes place) the risk of grievous injury occurring is still high. As we descend to more contingent risks to physical safety (eg, those typically involved in drink-driving), the discount would be larger, so that the conduct would be placed in a lower harm category.

Combinations. The combination problem arises when an offence (eg, assault, as we just saw) affects two or more interest dimensions. Here, a first step could be to identify the dimension that yields the highest harm rating, and identify that as the 'primary harm'. Suppose that offence *X* affects both physical integrity and self-respect, but in different degrees. Suppose the physical integrity intrusion is a substantial threat to subsistence, that is, a *discounted* 1°. We might, according to the discount

[1] We are assuming here that attempts should be treated as less serious than completed crimes, see Duff 1996; but see Ashworth 1993.

principles just outlined, rate this harm in the third ('serious') category. Suppose the intrusion on self-respect involves an actual (not just risked) humiliation – but only such as to affect living standard level 3° – 'adequate' wellbeing. This, according to our just-described mapping principles, would qualify the intrusion at the fourth harm category, of 'upper-intermediate'. On this analysis, the physical integrity intrusion would have the higher rating, and thus constitute the primary harm.

The next step would be to consider the secondary harms – those in other interest dimensions – as possible exacerbating features. It makes offence X somewhat worse that – besides the primary harm to physical integrity – it also humiliates. How much the exacerbation is depends on how high a rating the secondary harm has. The higher that rating, the more weight it should be given as an exacerbating factor.[17]

5 Applying the Analysis

Could our proposed analysis be helpful in actual sentencing law? Our answer is that it could be helpful, provided that a number of other steps are also taken. One step is completion of the tasks discussed here. We have only begun, by describing the living standard analysis. The additional tasks, of constructing a harm scale and devising rules for discounts for risk and for combinations, have only been sketched here. A second condition is that culpability be dealt with. Ultimately, we are seeking a jurisprudence of crime *seriousness*, which calls not only for an assessment of the conduct's degree of harmfulness but also of the actor's degree of culpability. Failing a full theory for gauging culpability, we at least need a way of controlling for the more obvious differences in culpability among crimes, so that we can assess how much such crimes' gravity is affected by variations in their harmfulness (see below).

Suppose, however, that these conditions have been satisfied. In what way could our approach be useful in making sentencing decisions? The answer to this question will depend on the sentencing structure of the jurisdiction. Let us take a look at two structures: sentencing guidelines such as Minnesota's, and statutory sentencing principles such as those embodied in Sweden's law. Both schemes emphasize the gravity of the offence, but use different decision-makers.

Numerical sentencing guidelines such as Minnesota's rely upon a special rule-making agency (the sentencing commission) to devise the sentencing guidelines.[18] The commission's guidelines are embodied in a sentencing grid. The vertical axis of the grid constitutes a crime-seriousness score; the horizontal, a criminal history score. The cells within the grid set forth the presumptive sentences or sentence ranges, which the courts are expected to apply except where aggravating or mitigating circumstances are found present.

Such a scheme requires the sentencing commission to take each statutory offence category and assign it a numerical seriousness grade, say from '1' (least serious) to '10' (most serious). Where the offence category is broad and embraces heterogeneous conduct (eg, a category such as 'burglary') the commission may establish subcategories and assign these different seriousness grades.

To date, when sentencing commissions undertook this rating task, they relied largely on their members' intuitions. In Minnesota, for example, each commission member was given a list of offences and asked to assign each offence a seriousness rating. When the members agreed, this rating was adopted; when they disagreed, discussion ensued until agreement was reached. This meant that no identifiable theory supported the seriousness judgements; indeed, when there was agreement, no reasons were elicited at all.

Here, a theory for gauging harm would have obvious utility, in providing commission members with a method of reasoning. A simple procedure might be as follows:

(1) The commission would rank the various offence categories in seriousness, using the members' sense of these offences' gravity – as Minnesota did.

(2) The commission would select, from the list of offence categories, a shorter list comprising intentional, victimizing crimes: victimizing, because that is what the present analysis is about; intentional, to try in a simple fashion to control for variations in culpability.

(3) To this subset of offences, the members of the commission or its staff would be invited to apply the analysis we have suggested in this Appendix: make a living standard analysis of the harms involved, and actually rank the harmfulness on a simple scale.

(4) With this harm analysis in mind, the members would be asked to re-rank the offence categories in seriousness. They also would be asked whether the analysis suggests a new or altered subcategorization: to distinguish, for example, between ordinary residential burglary and burglary with ransacking, on grounds that those acts' impact on the living standard are different. Where disagreements arose, members also would be asked to argue their ratings in terms of this theory – that is, to try and identify whether and how their disagreements are based on divergences of view about the conduct's effect on the living standard. The commission could thus determine whether the analysis helps resolve disagreements, and whether and to what extent their initial (intuitive) ratings require change as a result of the analysis.

A procedure of this kind would use our theory the way it should be used: as a guide for judgement, not a formula. Ultimately, the commission would still have to rely upon its best judgement in making the ratings; only now, that judgement would be guided by identifiable, coherent principles.

The theory, of course, would aid the commission only in its first seriousness assessment task: rating the gravity of categories or subcategories of crime. The commission would also need to address aggravation or mitigation: that is, specify what types of special circumstances affect the harmfulness of the conduct or the culpability of the actor, and thus justify a departure from guideline ranges.

The Swedish law takes a somewhat different tack. There is no sentencing commission, and no numerical seriousness score. What the statute prescribes is that the choice of sentence should depend principally on the 'penal value' (ie, seriousness) of the conduct, and that penal value ordinarily depends on the harm or risk of harm of the conduct and the culpability of the actor.[19]

Swedish sentencing doctrine distinguishes between 'abstract' and 'concrete' penal value. The abstract penal value reflects the general harmfulness and culpability of the type or subtype of offence involved. Against the background of the abstract penal value, the concrete penal value of the particular case is then considered – taking into account the particular injuriousness and culpability of the actor's conduct. To aid in the determination of the concrete penal value, the statute sets out a list of aggravating and mitigating factors that increase or diminish the gravity of the conduct in the particular case.[20]

In assessing the abstract penal value, the courts are supposed to consult the statutory penalty scales, that is, the maximum and minimum penalties for various offences prescribed in the Swedish Penal Code. Parliament is expected, in setting penalty scales, to consider the gravity of the conduct compared to that of other crimes. This means that two kinds of agencies are involved in the assessment of seriousness: the Parliament and the courts.

This makes the procedure seem more cumbersome than that of a sentencing commission. How can the legislature and the courts, with their large, diverse memberships and numerous other duties, possibly apply a theory of harm such as ours? Two features of Swedish practice, however, may help facilitate matters. First, major law changes – such as those involved in altering penalty scales – are seldom undertaken at Parliament's sole initiative. Ordinarily, a government-appointed study commission, aided by an advisory panel of experts, drafts the legislation. Such a commission or its advisory panel could deliberate on harm in much the same manner as a sentencing commission. Second, sentencing doctrine (as other major legal doctrines) is developed by the Supreme

Court and the six regional Courts of Appeal. These are more compact bodies, capable of developing doctrines of criminal harm based on the general idea of the living standard, or of utilizing scholarly advice on such doctrines.

Let us emphasize, however: the present discussion is not a recipe for how a sentencing commission, or a Swedish-style panel of experts, should proceed. We are only suggesting that our theory can have practical utility. Our aim has been to suggest a way to think about victimizing criminal harms. The practical applications come later.

Although there remain important topics to discuss (eg, relevant empirical research),[m] we will conclude our discussion here. We have put forward a general approach – one that would gauge criminal harm through the notion of the living standard. What we are proposing is a way of thinking about criminal harm, not a formula. The living standard categories we sketch are far from precise, and their application to criminal harms leave much to judgement. However, we do supply a systematic conceptual framework for making such judgements – and believe that superior to untutored intuition and guesswork.

[m] To date, two kinds of empirical research are available, neither especially helpful. One is survey research on public perceptions of crime seriousness, such as Sellin and Wolfgang's (1964). The limitations of such research have been suggested already; see 2.3 of this Appendix. The other kind of research has been living standard surveys such as Stockholm's (Erikson and Åberg 1987). The researchers construct an index that measures area residents' living standard in terms of various conditions assumed to bear on their wellbeing. Housing conditions, for example, are assessed in terms of number of rooms of the person's residence relative to family size. While such surveys are helpful for their intended purpose, of measuring changes in a population's living conditions over time, the measures used (eg, housing space) were based on researchers' common-sense judgements about the amenities important to a good life, rather than on any general theoretical perspective of how such amenities relate to levels of wellbeing.

Two kinds of research, however, might prove more profitable. One was proposed by the late Richard F. Sparks: empirical study of the type of injury resulting from various offences; see von Hirsch 1985, 65–6. Sparks proposed that the assessment of the harm element should rely not on opinion surveys such as Sellin's and Wolfgang's, but on empirical enquiry into the type of injury actually involved in various types of offences. (Traditional victimization studies have been more concerned with measuring frequency and distribution of criminal acts, than with detailing injurious consequences.) Sparks suggested kind of research would inquire systematically into the short- and long-term consequences of various criminal acts. It could provide a better factual basis for judgements about various crimes' typical consequences – which could then be used when applying our suggested living standard rating categories.

Another species of research would be simulated application of our proposed rating criteria. The researcher might, for example, organize a small group as a simulated sentencing commission, and ask it to rate various crimes. The first step might be to ask the members to rate crimes' gravity intuitively, in the manner that Minnesota did. Next, the members would be asked to rate crimes using the reasoning process suggested in this Appendix. The researcher would identify the extent to which this process produced ratings differing from the original 'intuitive' ones. The group would then be asked to what extent it wished to abide by those original ratings, and to what extent it preferred the revised, theory-based ratings – and why. Such research might suggest how helpful the proposed rating living standard approach is in decision-making situations.

Notes

1. See further Asp & von Hirsch 1999, 171–3.
2. Feinberg 1984, 190–3.
3. Sellin and Wolfgang 1964.
4. Sen 1987.
5. Feinberg 1984.
6. Von Hirsch 1985, 66–74.
7. Feinberg 1984, 42.
8. von Hirsch 1986, 702–706.
9. Feinberg 1984, 57–8.
10. Sen 1987.
11. Erikson and Åberg 1987, ch. 1.
12. Sen 1987, 30–1, 36–7.
13. Sen 1987, 27.
14. Braybrooke 1987, 48.
15. Id., 49.
16. See also Robinson 1987b, 44–45.
17. These steps have been outlined more fully in von Hirsch and Jareborg 1991, 28–32.
18. For an analysis of these guidelines' aims and structure, see von Hirsch, Knapp and Tonry 1987, ch. 5; von Hirsch 1995.
19. Swedish Penal Code, ch. 29, s. 1.
20. Swedish Penal Code, ch. 29, ss. 2 and 3.

Bibliography

American Friends Service Committee (1971) *Struggle for Justice*, New York: Hill and Wang.

American Law Institute (1962) *Model Penal Code*, Philadelphia, PA: American Law Institute.

American Law Institute (2003) *Model Penal Code*, Report 12.9, Philadelphia, PA: American Law Institute.

Andenaes, J. (1982) *Punishment and Deterrence*, Ann Arbor, MI: University of Michigan Press.

——(1988) 'Nyklassicisme, proporsjonalitet og prevensjon', *Nordisk Tljdsskrift for Kriminalvidenskab*, 75: 41.

Ashworth, A. (1989) 'Criminal Justice and Deserved Sentences', *Criminal Law Review* [1989]: 340–355.

——(1993) 'Taking the Consequences', in S. Shute, J. Gardner and J. Horder (eds), *Action and Value in the Criminal Law*. Oxford: Oxford University Press.

——(2000) *Sentencing and Criminal Justice* (3rd edn), London: Butterworths.

——(2003) *Principles of Criminal Law* (4th edn), Oxford: Oxford University Press.

——and Player, E. (1998) 'Sentencing, Equal Treatment and the Impact of Sanctions', in A. Ashworth and M. Wasik (eds), *Fundamentals of Sentencing Theory: Essays in Honour of Andrew von Hirsch*, Oxford: Clarendon Press.

——and von Hirsch, A. (1997) 'Recognising Elephants: The Problem of the Custody Threshold', *Criminal Law Review* [1997]: 187–200.

——and Wasik, M. (eds) (1998) *Fundamentals of Sentencing Theory: Essays in Honour of Andrew von Hirsch*, Oxford: Clarendon Press.

Asp, P. and von Hirsch, A. (1999) 'Straffvärde', *Svensk Juristtidning*, 84: 151–176.

Ball, C., McCormac, K., and Stone, N. (1995) *Young Offenders: Law, Policy and Practice*, London: Sweet & Maxwell.

Barclay, G. and Tavares, C. (1999) *Information on the Criminal Justice System in England and Wales: Digest 4*. London: Home Office.

Baurmann, M. (1998) 'Vorüberlegungen zu einer empirischen Theorie der Positiven Generalprävention', in B. Schünemann, A. von Hirsch and N. Jareborg (eds), *Positive Generalprävention: Kritische Perspecktive im deutsch-englischen Dialog*, Heidelberg: C.F. Müller.

Bazemore, G. (1999) 'After Shaming, Whither Reintegration: Restorative Justice and Relational Rehabilitation', in G. Bazemore and L. Walgrave (eds), *Restorative Juvenile Justice: Repairing the Harm of Youth Crime*, Monsey NY: Criminal Justice Press.

Beccaria, C. (1963) *Of Crimes and Punishments*. Translated by Henry Paolucci. Indianapolis, IN: Bobbs-Merrill. (Original 1764).

Beckett, K. and Western, B. (2001) 'Governing Marginality: Welfare, Incarceration and the Transformation of State Policy', *Punishment and Society*, 3: 43–59.

Bentham, J. (1982) *An Introduction to the Principles of Morals and Legislation*. Edited by J.H. Byrne and H.L.A. Hart. London: Methuen. (Original 1789).
Blunkett, D. (2003) 'I Can't Back Down On Asylum', *Guardian*, 14 December: 29.
Bottoms, A.E. (1989) 'The Concept of Intermediate Sanctions and its Relevance for the Probation Service', in E. Shaw and K. Haines (eds), *The Criminal Justice System: A Central Role for the Probation Service*, Cambridge: Institute of Criminology.
——(1998) 'Five Puzzles in von Hirsch's Theory', in A. Ashworth and M. Wasik (eds), *Fundamentals of Sentencing Theory: Essays in Honour of Andrew von Hirsch*, Oxford: Clarendon Press.
——(2003) 'Some Sociological Reflections on Restorative Justice', in A. von Hirsch, J. Roberts, A.E. Bottoms, *et al.* (eds), *Restorative Justice and Criminal Justice: Competing or Reconcilable Paradigms?* Oxford: Hart Publishing.
——and Brownsword, R. (1982) 'The Dangerousness Debate After the Floud Report', *British Journal of Criminology*, 22: 229–254.
——and ——(1983) 'Dangerousness and Rights', in J.W. Hinton (ed), *Dangerousness: Problems of Assessment and Prediction*, London: George Allen & Unwin.
——and Dignan, J. (1994) 'Youth Justice in Great Britain' in M. Tonry and A. Doob (eds), *Youth Crime and Youth Justice. Crime and Justice: A Review of Research*, 31: 21–184, Chicago: University of Chicago Press.
Braithwaite, J. (1989) *Crime, Shame and Reintegration*, Cambridge: Cambridge University Press.
——(1999) 'Restorative Justice: Assessing Optimistic and Pessimistic Accounts', in M. Tonry (ed), *Crime and Justice: A Review of Research*, 25: 1–127, Chicago: Chicago University Press.
——(2003) 'Principles of Restorative Justice', in A. von Hirsch, J. Roberts, A.E. Bottoms, *et al.* (eds), *Restorative Justice and Criminal Justice: Competing or Reconcilable Paradigms?* Oxford: Hart Publishing.
——and Pettit, P. (1990) *Not Just Deserts: A Republican Theory of Justice*, Oxford: Oxford University Press.
Braybrooke, D. (1987) *Meeting Needs*, Princeton: Princeton University Press.
Brottsförebyggande Rådet (1977) *Nytt straffsystem: Idéer och förslag*, Stockholm: Brottsförebyggande rådet.
Canadian Sentencing Commission (1987) *Sentencing Reform: A Canadian Approach*, Ottawa: Canadian Government Publishing Centre.
Christie, N. (1977) 'Conflicts as Property', *British Journal of Criminology*, 17: 1–26.
——(1980) *Limits to Pain*, Oslo: Universiteitsforlaget.
——(2000) *Crime Control as Industry: Towards Gulags, Western Style* (3rd edn), London: Routledge.
Clarkson, C.M.V. and Morgan, R. (eds) (1995) *The Politics of Sentencing Reform*, Oxford: Oxford University Press.
Council of Europe (1992) *Consistency in Sentencing*. Strasbourg: Council of Europe.
Daly, K. (2002) 'Restorative Justice: The Real Story', *Punishment and Society*, 4: 55–79.
——(2003) 'Mind the Gap, Restorative Justice in Theory and Practice', in A. von Hirsch, J. Roberts, A.E. Bottoms, *et al.* (eds), *Restorative Justice and Criminal Justice: Competing or Reconcilable Paradigms?* Oxford: Hart Publishing.

Dignan, J. (2003) 'Toward a Systematic Model of Restorative Justice', in A. von Hirsch, J. Roberts, A.E. Bottoms, *et al.* (eds), *Restorative Justice and Criminal Justice: Competing or Reconcilable Paradigms?* Oxford: Hart Publishing.

Dolinko, D. (1992) 'Three Mistakes about Retributivism', *UCLA Law Review*, 39: 1623–1657.

Doob, A. (1995) 'The United States Sentencing Commission Guidelines', in C.M.V. Clarkson and R. Morgan (eds), *The Politics of Sentencing Reform*, Oxford: Oxford University Press.

——and Sprott, J. (2004) 'Youth Justice in Canada' in M. Tonry and A. Doob (eds), *Youth Crime and Youth Justice. Crime and Justice: A Review of Research*, 31: 184–242, Chicago: University of Chicago Press.

——and Webster, C. (2003a) 'Sentence Severity and Crime: Accepting the Null Hypothesis', in M. Tonry (ed), *Crime and Justice: A Review of Research*, 30: 143–195, Chicago, University of Chicago Press.

——and ——(2003b) 'Model Penal Code: Sentencing: Looking at the Model Penal Code Sentencing Provisions through Canadian Lenses', *Buffalo Criminal Law Review*, 7: 139–170.

Duff, R.A. (1986) *Trials and Punishments*, Cambridge: Cambridge University Press.

——(1996) *Criminal Attempts*. Oxford: Oxford University Press.

——(1998) 'Dangerousness and Citizenship' in A. Ashworth and M. Wasik (eds), *Fundamentals of Sentencing Theory*, Oxford: Oxford University Press.

——(1999a) 'Punishment, Communication, and Community', in M. Matravers (ed), *Punishment and Political Theory*, Oxford: Hart Publishing.

——(1999b) 'Response to von Hirsch', in M. Matravers (ed), *Punishment and Political Theory*, Oxford: Hart Publishing.

——(2001) *Punishment, Communication and Community*, Oxford: Oxford University Press.

——(2003) 'Restoration and Retribution', in A. von Hirsch, J. Roberts, A.E. Bottoms, *et al.* (eds), *Restorative Justice and Criminal Justice: Competing or Reconcilable Paradigms?* Oxford: Hart Publishing.

——and von Hirsch, A. (1997) 'Responsibility, Retribution and the "Voluntary": A Response to Williams', *Cambridge Law Journal*, 56: 103–113.

——, Marshall, S., Dobash, R.E., and Dobash, R. (eds) (1994) *Penal Theory and Penal Practice: Tradition and Innovation in Criminal Justice*, Manchester: Manchester University Press.

Dworkin, R. (1977) *Taking Rights Seriously*, Cambridge, MA: Harvard University Press.

Erikson, R. and Åberg, R. (1987) *Welfare in Transition: A Survey of Living Conditions in Sweden 1968–1981*. Oxford: Oxford University Press.

Feinberg, J. (1970) 'The Expressive Function of Punishment', in J. Feinberg, *Doing and Deserving: Essays in the Theory of Responsibility*, Princeton, NJ: Princeton University Press.

——(1984) *Harm to Others*. Oxford: Oxford University Press.

Feld, B. (1998) 'Juvenile and Criminal Justice Systems' Reponses to Youth Violence', in M. Tonry and M. Moore (eds), *Youth Violence. Crime and Justice: A Review of Research*, 24: 189–261.

——(1999) *Bad Kids: Race and the Transformation of the Juvenile Court*, New York: Oxford University Press.

Finnis, J. (1980) *Natural Law and Natural Rights*, Oxford: Oxford University Press.

Fletcher, G. (1978) *Rethinking Criminal Law*, Boston, MA: Little-Brown.

Frase, R. (2003) 'Limiting Retributivism', in M. Tonry and R. Frase (eds), *The Future of Imprisonment*, New York: Oxford University Press.

Freiberg, A. (2001) 'Three Strikes and You're Out – It's Not Cricket: Colonisation and Resistance in Australian Sentencing', in M. Tonry and M. Frase (eds), *Sentencing and Sanctions in Western Countries*, New York: Oxford University Press.

Friedman, D. and Sjöström, W. (1993) 'Hanged for a Sheep: The Economics of Marginal Deterrence', *Journal of Legal Studies* 22: 345–366.

Frisch, W. (1993) 'Straftat und Strafzumessung: Zugleich ein Beitrag zur Struktur der Strafzumessungsentscheidung', in J. Wolter (ed), *140 Jahre Goltdammers Archiv für Strafrecht*, Heidelberg: R. von Deckers Verlag.

——(1998) 'Schwächen und berechtigte Aspekte der Theorie der positiven Generalprävention', in B. Schünemann, A. von Hirsch and N. Jareborg (eds), *Positive Generalprävention: Kritische Perspektive in deutsch-englischen Dialog*. Heidelberg: C.F. Müller.

Gardner, J. (1998a) 'The Gist of Excuses', *Buffalo Criminal Law Review*, 1: 575–598.

——(1998b) 'Crime: In Proportion and In Perspective', in A. Ashworth and M. Wasik (eds), *Fundamentals of Sentencing Theory: Essays in Honour of Andrew von Hirsch*, Oxford: Clarendon Press.

Garland, D. (2001) *The Culture of Control: Crime and Social Order in Contemporary Society*, Oxford: Oxford University Press.

Habermas, J. (1971) 'Vorbereitende Bermerkungen zu einer Theorie der Kommunikativen Kompetenz' in J. Habermas and N. Luhmann, *Theorie der Gesellschaft oder Sozialtechnologie*, Frankfurt: Suhrkamp.

Hampshire, S. (1989) *Innocence and Experience*. Cambridge, MA: Harvard University Press.

Harrison, R. (1992) 'The Equality of Mercy' in H. Gross and R. Harrison (eds), *Jurisprudence: Cambridge Essays*, Oxford: Clarendon Press.

Hart, H.L.A. (1968) *Punishment and Responsibility*, Oxford: Oxford University Press.

Hassemer, W. (1981) *Einführung in die Grundlagen des Strafrechts*, Munich: Beck.

Heckscher, S., Snare, A., Takala, H., and Vestergaard, J. (1980) *Straff och rättfärdighet: Ny nordisk debatt*, Stockholm: Norstedts.

Heffernan, W. and Kleinig, J. (eds) (2000) *From Social Justice to Criminal Justice: Poverty and the Administration of Criminal Law*, New York: Oxford University Press.

Holmqvist, L. (1999) 'Billighetshänsyn', *Svensk Juristtidning*, 84: 188–199.

Home Office (1990) *Crime, Justice and Protecting the Public*, London: HM Stationery Office.

——(1996) *Protecting the Public: The Government's Strategy on Crime in England and Wales*, London: HM Stationery Office.

——(2001a) *Criminal Justice: The Way Ahead*, London: HM Stationery Office.

——(2001b) *Making Punishments Work: Report of a Review of the Sentencing Framework for England and Wales*, London: HM Stationery Office.

——(2002) *Justice for All*. London: HM Stationery Office.

Hörnle, T. (1999) *Tatproportionale Strafzumessung*, Berlin: Duncker und Humblot.
——and von Hirsch, A. (1998) 'Positive Generalprävention und Tadel', in Schünemann, B., von Hirsch, A. and Jareborg, N. (eds) (1998) *Positive Generalprävention: Kritische Perspektive in deutsch-englischen Dialog*, Heidelberg: C.F. Müller.
Hudson, B. (1995) 'Beyond Proportionate Punishment: Difficult Cases and the 1991 Criminal Justice Act', *Crime, Law and Social Change*, 22: 59–78.
——(1998) 'Doing Justice to Difference', in A. Ashworth and M. Wasik (eds), *Fundamentals of Sentencing Theory: Essays in Honour of Andrew von Hirsch*, Oxford: Clarendon Press.
Husak, D. (1992) *Drugs and Rights*, Cambridge: Cambridge University Press.
——and von Hirsch, A. (1993) 'Culpability and Mistake of Law', in S. Shute, J. Gardner and J. Horder (eds), *Action and Value in the Criminal Law*, Oxford: Oxford University Press.
Jareborg, N. (1991) 'The Role of Aggravating and Mitigating Factors in Sentencing: the New Swedish Sentencing Law', in U. Goranson (ed), *Modern Legal Issues: an Anglo-Swedish Perspective*. Uppsala: Iustus Förlag.
——(1995) 'The Swedish Sentencing Reform', in C.M.V. Clarkson and R. Morgan (eds), *The Politics of Sentencing Reform*, Oxford: Oxford University Press.
——(1998) 'Why Bulk Discounts in Multiple Offence Sentencing' in A. Ashworth and M. Wasik (eds), *Fundamentals of Sentencing Theory: Essays in Honour of Andrew von Hirsch*, Oxford: Clarendon Press.
——and Zila, J. (2000) *Straffrättens Påföljdslära*, Stocknolm: Norstedts.
Jescheck, H.H. and Weigend, T. (1996) *Lehrbuch des Strafrechts: Allgemeiner Teil* (5th edn), Berlin: Duncker & Humblot.
Kahan, D. (1996) 'What do Alternative Sanctions Mean?' *University of Chicago Law Review*, 63: 591.
Kleinig, J. (1973) *Punishment and Desert*, The Hague: Nijhoff.
——(1992) 'Punishment and Moral Seriousness', *Israel Law Review*, 25: 401–421.
Kurki, L. (2003) 'Evaluating Restorative Justice Practices', in A. von Hirsch, J. Roberts, A.E. Bottoms, *et al.* (eds), *Restorative Justice and Criminal Justice: Competing or Reconcilable Paradigms?* Oxford: Hart Publishing.
Lappi-Seppälä (2001) 'The Principle of Proportionality in the Finnish Sentencing System', in P. Asp, C.E. Herlitz and S.L. Holmqvist (eds), *Flores Juris et Legum*, Uppsala: Iustus Förlag.
Lockyer, A. and Stone, F. (1998) *Juvenile Justice in Scotland*, Edinburgh: T & T Clarke.
Logan, W.S. (1998) 'Proportionality and Punishment: Imposing Life without Parole on Juveniles', *Wake Forest Law Review*, 33: 681–725.
Maxwell, G. and Morris, A. (1993) *Family, Victims and Culture: Youth Justice in New Zealand*, Wellington: Social Policy Agency.
McEvoy, K. and Mika, H. (2002) 'Restorative Justice and the Critique of Informalism in Northern Ireland', *British Journal of Criminology*, 42: 534–562.
Monahan, J. (1981) *Predicting Violent Behaviour: An Assessment of Clinical Techniques*. Beverly Hills, Sage Publications.
——(1982) 'The Case for Prediction in the Modified Desert Model for Criminal Sentencing', *International Journal of Law and Psychology*, 5: 103–113.

——(2004a) 'The Future of Violence Risk Management', in M. Tonry (ed) *The Future of Imprisonment*, New York: Oxford University Press.
——(2004b) *Risk and Race: An Essay on Violence Forecasting and the Civil/ Criminal Distinction*. Manuscript.
Moore, M. (1987) 'The Moral Worth of Retribution', in F. Schoeman (ed), *Responsibility: Character and the Emotions*, Cambridge: Cambridge University Press.
Morse, S.J. (2000) 'Deprivation and Desert', in W. Heffernan and J. Kleinig (eds), *From Social Justice to Criminal Justice: Poverty and the Administration of Criminal Law*, New York: Oxford University Press.
Morris, A. and Maxwell, G. (2003) 'Restorative Justice in New Zealand', in A. von Hirsch, J. Roberts and A.E. Bottoms (eds), *Restorative Justice and Criminal Justice: Competing or Reconcilable Paradigms?* Oxford: Hart Publishing.
Morris, N. (1974) *The Future of Imprisonment*, Chicago Il: University of Chicago Press.
——(1976) *Punishment, Desert, and Rehabilitation*, Washington, D.C.: US Government Printing Office.
——(1982) *Madness and the Criminal Law*, Chicago, Il: Chicago University Press.
——and Miller, M. (1985) 'Predictions of Dangerousness', in M. Tonry and N. Morris (eds), *Crime and Justice: An Annual Review of Research*, 6: 1–50, Chicago: University of Chicago Press.
——and Tonry, M. (1990) *Between Prison and Probation: Intermediate Punishments in a Rational Sentencing System*, New York: Oxford University Press.
Murphy, J. (1973) 'Marxism and Retribution', *Philosophy and Public Affairs*, 2: 217–43.
——and Hampton, J. (1988) *Forgiveness and Mercy*, Cambridge: Cambridge University Press.
Murray, C. (1997) *Does Prison Work?* London: Institute of Economic Affairs.
——(2004) 'Simple Justice', *Sunday Times, News Review*, 25 January: 1.
Nagin, D. (1998) 'Criminal Deterrence at the Outset of the Twenty-first Century', in M. Tonry (ed), *Crime and Justice: A Review of Research*, 23: 1–42, Chicago: University of Chicago Press.
Narayan, N. (1990) *Offensive Conduct: What It Is and When We May Legally Regulate It*, Unpublished Ph.D. Thesis, Philosophy Department, Rutgers University, N.J.
——(1993) 'Adequate Responses and Preventive Benefits: Justifying Censure and Hard Treatment in Legal Punishment', *Oxford Journal of Legal Studies*, 13: 166–182.
——and von Hirsch, A. (1996) 'Three Conceptions of Provocation', *Criminal Justice Ethics*, 15(1): 15–25.
National Academy of Sciences, Panel on Research on Criminal Careers (1986) *Criminal Careers and 'Career Criminals'*, Washington: National Academy of Sciences.
Petersilia, J., Greenwood, P., and Laven, M. (1977) *Criminal Careers of Habitual Felons*, Santa Monica, CA: Rand Corporation.

Pettit, P. and Braithwaite, J. (1993) 'Not Just Deserts, Not Even in Sentencing', *Current Issues in Criminal Justice*, 4: 222–39. Reprinted as 'Republicanism in Sentencing: Recognition, Recompense and Reassurance', in A. von Hirsch and A. Ashworth (eds) (1998) *Principled Sentencing: Readings on Theory and Policy*, Oxford: Hart Publishing.

Rawls, J. (1971) *A Theory of Justice*, Cambridge, MA: Belknap Press.

Rex, S. (1998) 'A New Form of Rehabilitationism?' in A. von Hirsch and A. Ashworth (eds), *Principled Sentencing: Readings on Theory and Policy*, Oxford: Hart Publishing.

Roberts, J.V. (2002) 'Alchemy in Sentencing: An Analysis of Sentencing Reform Proposals in England and Wales', *Punishment and Society*, 4: 425–442.

Roberts, J.V. (2003) 'An Analysis of the Statutory Statement of Purposes and Principles of Sentencing in New Zealand', *Australia and New Zealand Journal of Criminology*, 36(3): 249.

—— and von Hirsch, A. (1999) 'Legislating the Purpose and Principles of Sentencing' in J.V. Roberts and G.D. Cole (eds), *Making Sense of Sentencing*, Toronto: University of Toronto Press.

Robinson, P. (1987a) 'Hybrid Principles for the Distribution of Criminal Sanctions', *Northwestern Law Review*, 82: 19–42.

Robinson, P. (1987b) 'A Sentencing System for the 21st Century?' *Texas Law Review*, 66: 1.

Roche, D. (2001) *Restorative Justice and Deliberative Accountability*, Ph.D. dissertation, Canberra: Australian National University.

Rothman, D. (2003) 'The Crime of Punishment', in S. Cohen and T. Blomberg (eds), *Punishment and Social Control*, New York: Aldine de Gruyter.

Roxin, C. (1979) 'Zur jüngsten Diskussion über Schuld, Prävention und Verantwortlichkeit im Strafrecht', in A. Kaufmann, G. Bemman, D. Krauss and K. Volk (eds), *Festschrift für Paul Bockelmann*, Munich: C.H. Beck.

—— (1997) *Strafrecht: Allgemeiner Teil* (3rd edn), Munich: C.H. Beck.

Scheid, D. (1997) 'Constructing a Theory of Punishment: Desert and the Distribution of Punishments', *Canadian Journal of Law & Jurisprudence*, 10: 441–506.

Schumann, K. (1998) 'Empirische Beweisbarkeit der Grundanahmen von positiven Generalprävention', in B. Schünemann, A. von Hirsch and N. Jareborg (eds), *Positive Generalprävention: Kritische Perspektive in deutsch-englischen Dialog*, Heidelberg: C.F. Müller.

Schünemann, B. (1998) 'Zum Stellenwert der positiven Generalprävention in einer dualitischen Straftheorie', in B. Schünemann, A. von Hirsch and N. Jareborg (eds), *Positive Generalprävention: Kritische Perspektive in deutsch-englischen Dialog*, Heidelberg: C.F. Müller.

——, von Hirsch, A., and Jareborg, N. (eds) (1998) *Positive Generalprävention: Kritische Perspektive in deutsch-englischen Dialog*, Heidelberg: C.F. Müller.

Sebba, L. and Nathan, G. (1984) 'Further Exploration of the Scaling of Penalties', *British Journal of Criminology*, 24(3): 221–249.

Sellin, T. and Wolfgang, M. (1964) *The Measurement of Delinquency*, New York: John Wiley.

Sen, A. (1984) 'Wellbeing, Agency and Freedom: The Dewey Lectures', *Journal of Philosophy*, 82: 169.

——(1987) *The Standard of Living*, Cambridge: Cambridge University Press.
Simester, A.P. and Sullivan, G.R. (2004) *Criminal Law: Theory and Doctrine*, 2nd edn, Oxford: Hart Publishing.
——and von Hirsch, A. (2002) 'Rethinking the Offense Principle', *Legal Theory*, 8: 269–295.
Singer, R.G. (1979) *Just Deserts: Sentencing Based on Equality and Desert*, Cambridge, MA: Ballinger.
Smart, A. (1969) 'Mercy', in H.B. Acton (ed), *The Philosophy of Punishment: A Collection of Papers*, London: Macmillan.
South African Law Commission (2000), *Sentencing: A New Sentencing Framework*. Pretoria: South African Law Commission (Project 82, Discussion Paper 91).
Stigler, G. (1970) 'The Optimum Enforcement of Laws', *Journal of Political Economy*, 78(3): 526–536.
Strang, H., Barnes, G. *et al.* (1999) *Experiments in Restorative Policing: A Progress Report on the Canberra Reintegrative Shaming Experiments (RISE)*, Canberra: Australian National University.
Symposium – Sentencing: Model Penal Code (2003), *Buffalo Criminal Law Review*, 7: 1–306.
Tasioulas, J. (2003) 'Mercy', *Proceedings of the Aristotelian Society*, CIII: 101–132.
Tonry, M. (1982) 'Criminal Law: The Missing Element in Sentencing Reform', *Vanderbilt Law Review*, 35: 607.
——(1994) 'Proportionality, Interchangeability, and Intermediate Punishments', in R. Dobash, R. Dobash, R.A. Duff and S. Marshall (eds), *Penal Theory and Penal Practice*, Manchester: Manchester University Press.
——(1995) *Malign Neglect – Race, Crime, and Punishment in America*, New York: Oxford University Press.
——(1996) *Sentencing Matters*, New York: Oxford University Press.
——(1997) *Intermediate Sanctions in Sentencing Guidelines*. Washington D.C.: National Institute of Justice.
——(1998) 'Interchangeability, Desert Limits and Equivalence of Function', in A. von Hirsch and A. Ashworth (eds), *Principled Sentencing: Readings on Theory and Policy*, Oxford: Hart Publishing.
Törnudd, P. (1975) 'Deterrence Research and the Needs for Legislative Planning', *General Deterrence*, Stockholm: Brottsförebyggande Rådet.
Van Den Haag, E. (1975) *Punishing Criminals: Concerning a Very Old and Painful Question*, New York: Basic Books.
——(1981) 'Punishment as a Device for Controlling the Crime Rate' *Hofstra Law Review*, 33: 706–720.
——(1987) 'Punishment: Desert and Control', *Michigan Law Review*, 85: 1250–1266.
Van Ness, D. (1993) 'New Wine and Old Wineskins: Four Challenges of Restorative Justice', *Criminal Law Review*, [1993]: 251–76.
von Hirsch, A. (1976) *Doing Justice: The Choice of Punishments*, New York: Hill and Wang. Reprinted 1986, Boston: Northeastern University Press.
——(1981) 'Desert and Previous Convictions in Sentencing', *Minnesota Law Review*, 65: 591–634.
——(1983) 'Recent Trends in American Criminal Sentencing Theory', *Maryland Law Review*, 42: 6–36.

——(1985) *Past or Future Crimes: Deservedness and Dangerousness in the Sentencing of Criminals*, New Brunswick, NJ: Rutgers University Press. UK edn, Manchester: Manchester University Press 1986.
——(1986) 'Injury and Exasperation', *Michigan Law Review*, 84: 700.
——(1987) 'Sentencing by Numbers or Words', in M. Wasik and K. Pease (eds), *Sentencing Reform: Guidance or Guidelines?* Manchester: Manchester University Press.
von Hirsch, A. (1989) 'Federal Sentencing Guidelines: Do They Provide Principled Guidance?' *American Criminal Law Review*, 27: 367–390.
——(1990) 'Proportionality in the Philosophy of Punishment: From "Why Punish?" to "How Much?"' *Criminal Law Forum*, 1: 259–90.
——(1993) *Censure and Sanctions*, Oxford: Oxford University Press.
——(1995) 'Proportionality and Parsimony in American Sentencing Guidelines: The Minnesota and Oregon Standards', in C.M.V. Clarkson and R. Morgan (eds), *The Politics of Sentencing Reform*, Oxford: Oxford University Press.
——(1998) 'Desert and Previous Convictions', in A. von Hirsch and A. Ashworth (eds), *Principled Sentencing* (2nd edn), Oxford: Hart Publishing.
——(1999) 'Punishment, Penance, and the State: A Reply to Duff', in M. Matravers (ed), *Punishment and Political Theory*, Oxford: Hart Publishing.
——(2000) 'The Offence Principle in Criminal Law', *King's College Law Journal*, 11: 78.
——(2001a) 'The Project of Sentencing Reform', in M. Tonry and R. Frase (eds), *Sentencing and Sanctions in Western Countries*, New York: Oxford University Press.
——(2001b) *Proportionalitet och Straffbestämning*, Uppsala: Iustus Förlag.
——(2001c) 'Proportionate Sentences for Juveniles: How Different than for Adults?' *Punishment and Society*, 3: 221–236.
——(2002) 'Record Enhanced Sentencing in England and Wales: Reflections on the Halliday Report's Proposed Treatment of Prior Convictions', *Punishment and Society*, 4: 443–457.
——(2003) 'Begründung und Bestimmung tatproportionaler Strafen' in W. Frisch, A. von Hirsch and H.S. Albrecht (eds), *Tatproportionalität: Normative und empirische Aspekte einer tatproportionalen Strafzumessung*, Baden-Baden: C.F. Müller.
——and Ashworth, A. (1992) 'Not Not Just Deserts: A Response to Braithwaite and Pettit', *Oxford Journal of Legal Studies*, 12: 83–98.
——and Ashworth, A. (1996) 'Protective Sentencing under Section 2(2)(b): The Criteria for Dangerousness', *Criminal Law Review*, [1996]: 175–183.
——and Ashworth, A. (eds) (1998) *Principled Sentencing: Readings on Theory and Policy* (2nd edn), Oxford: Hart Publishing.
——and Jareborg, N. (1987) 'Provocation and Culpability', in F. Schoeman (ed), *Responsibility, Character and the Emotions: New Essays in Moral Psychology*, Cambridge: Cambridge University Press.
——and Jareborg, N. (1989) 'Sweden's Sentencing Statute Enacted', *Criminal Law Review*, [1989]: 275–281.
——and Jareborg, N. (1989) 'Straff och proportionalitet-replik', *Nordisk Tidssrift for Kriminalvidesnskab*, 76: 56–63.

——and Jareborg, N. (1991a) 'Gauging Criminal Harm: A Living-Standard Analysis', *Oxford Journal of Legal Studies*, 11: 1–38.
——and Jareborg, N. (1991b) *Strafmass und Strafgerechtigkeit: Die deutsche Strafzumessungslehre und das Prinzip der Tatproportionalität*, Bonn: Forum Verlag Godesberg.
——and Roberts, J. (2004) 'Legislating Sentencing Principles: The Provisions of the Criminal Justice Act 2003 Relating to Sentencing Purposes and the Role of Previous Convictions', *Criminal Law Review*, [2004]: 649–652.
——and Simester, A.P. (2005) 'Punishing Offensive Behaviour: Constitutive and Mediating Principles', in A. von Hirsch and A.P. Simester (eds), *Incivilities: Regulating Offensive Behaviour*, Oxford: Hart Publishing (forthcoming).
——and Wasik, M. (1997) 'Civil Disqualifications attending Convictions: a Suggested Conceptual Framework', *Cambridge Law Journal*, 56: 599–626.
——, Knapp, K., and Tonry, M. (1987) *The Sentencing Commission and Its Guidelines*, Boston, MA: Northeastern University Press.
——, Bottoms, A.E., Burney, E., and Wikström, P.O. (1999) *Criminal Deterrence and Sentence Severity: An Analysis of Recent Research*, Oxford: Hart Publishing.
——, Roberts, J., Bottoms, A.E., *et al.* (eds) (2003) *Restorative Justice and Criminal Justice: Competing or Reconcilable Paradigms?* Oxford: Hart Publishing.
Walgrave, L. (2003) 'Imposing Restoration instead of Inflicting Pain', in A. von Hirsch, J. Roberts, A.E. Bottoms *et al.* (eds), *Restorative Justice and Criminal Justice: Competing or Reconcilable Paradigms?* Oxford: Hart Publishing.
Walker, N. (1991) *Why Punish?* Oxford: Oxford University Press.
——(1999) *Aggravation, Mitigation and Mercy in English Criminal Justice*, London: Blackstone.
Wasik, M. (1987) 'Guidelines, Guidance and Criminal Record', in M. Wasik and K. Pease (eds), *Sentencing Reform: Guidance or Guidelines?* Manchester: Manchester University Press.
——and von Hirsch, A. (1988) 'Non-Custodial Penalties and The Principles of Desert', *Criminal Law Review*, [1988]: 555–572.
——and von Hirsch, A. (1994) 'Section 29 Revised: Previous Convictions in Sentencing', *Criminal Law Review*, [1994]: 409–418.
Williams, B. (1973) 'A Critique of Utilitarianism', in J.J.C. Smart (ed), *Utilitarianism: For and Against*, Cambridge: Cambridge University Press.
——(1993) *Shame and Necessity*, Berkeley, CA: University of California Press.
Wilson, J.Q. (1975) *Thinking about Crime*, New York: Basic Books.
——(1983) *Thinking about Crime* (rev. edn), New York: Basic Books.
——and Kelling, G. (1982) 'Broken Windows: Police and Neighbourhood Safety', *Atlantic Monthly*, 249(3): 29–38.
Wood, D. (1988) 'Dangerous Offenders and the Morality of Protective Sentencing', *Criminal Law Review*, [1988]: 424–433.
Zedner, L. (1994) 'Reparation and Retribution: Are they Reconcilable?' *Modern Law Review*, 57: 228–50.
——(1998) 'Sentencing Young Offenders', in A. Ashworth and M. Wasik (eds), *Fundamentals of Sentencing Theory: Essays in Honour of Andrew von Hirsch*, Oxford: Clarendon Press.

Zehr, H. (1990) *Changing Lenses: A New Focus for Criminal Justice*, Scottsdale, PA: Herald Press.

Zimring, F.E. (1982) *The Changing Legal World of Adolescence*, New York: Free Press.

——(1998a) *American Youth Violence*, New York: Oxford University Press.

——(1998b) 'Toward a Jurisprudence of Youth Violence' in M. Tonry and M. Moore (eds), *Youth Violence. Crime and Justice: A Review of Research*, 24: 447–501, Chicago: University of Chicago Press.

Zimring, F.E. and Hawkins, G. (1995) *Incapacitation: Penal Confinement and the Restraint of Crime*, Oxford: Oxford University Press.

——and—— (1997) *Crime Is Not The Problem: Lethal Violence in America*, New York: Oxford University Press.

——, Hawkins, G., and Kamin, S. (2001) *Punishment and Democracy: Three Strikes and You're Out in California*, New York: Oxford University Press.

Index